FAMILIES
OF THE VINE

HARPER PERENNIAL

A hardcover edition of this book was published in 2005 by HarperCollins Publishers.

P.S.™ is a trademark of HarperCollins Publishers.

FIRST HARPER PERENNIAL EDITION PUBLISHED 2006.

Designed by Nancy Singer Olaguera

Library of Congress Cataloging-in-Publication Data is available upon request.

ISBN 0-06-055964-0
ISBN-10: 0-06-055965-9 (pbk.)
ISBN-13: 978-0-06-055965-6 (pbk.)

06 07 08 09 10 ❖/RRD 10 9 8 7 6 5 4 3 2 1

ALSO BY MICHAEL S. SANDERS

The Yard: Building a Destroyer at the Bath Iron Works

From Here, You Can't See Paris:
Seasons of a French Village and Its Restaurant

FAMILIES OF THE VINE

Seasons

Among the

Winemakers of

Southwest France

Michael S. Sanders

HARPER  PERENNIAL

NEW YORK ● LONDON ● TORONTO ● SYDN

For my mother,

who first showed me the world,

and taught me that it was not a place to fear

ACKNOWLEDGMENTS

I would like to thank the winemakers of Cahors, who, against considerable odds, are fighting the good fight to keep their vineyards healthy and their wine authentic. *Bon courage!*

To the whole Jouffreau-Hermann clan, particularly Martine, Yves, and Marise at Clos de Gamot: well, you have the results of your years of tutorials in front of you, and I hope you see my head was not nearly so hard as it first appeared. I appreciate all you did for me, showed me, your great passion. If I have captured one-tenth of it here, I'll consider that a good job. For Jean-Luc, Sabine, and Juliette Baldès: you made your home and vineyard, Clos Triguedina, a place of unending surprise and revelation to me, as well as a place of great warmth. To Philippe, last glimpsed running through the vines of Coutale in training for yet another marathon, faithful Pétrus at your side: you showed me a wholly different approach to the winemaking life, and for that I thank you.

It was in two very fine restaurants and with the help of two lovely restaurant families that the idea for this book was born. Jacques and Noëlle Ratier at La Récréation in Les Arques first got me curious about vin de Cahors, Noëlle especially sharing her interest and wide knowledge and steering me to the three vineyards represented here. On most of my research trips, your home became mine, your table my own. Your insights on the work as it progressed, often in leaps and bounds at that little table by the bar, pushed me when I needed pushing most. Laurent and Gilles Marre, and their wives, Corinne and Jacqueline, at Le Restaurant Le Balandre in Cahors, provided a further, and more pointed, education. Laurent, consummate sommelier, challenged me to learn as chef Gilles challenged me to taste; together, the two brothers provided me with a doubly rich immersion in the subtleties of southwestern French cuisine and the place of the region's wine in that cuisine.

Finally, I would like to thank the following for all their efforts on my behalf: Olivier Tesseire, winemaker at Château du Cèdre; the Springs of Domaine du Garinet in Le Boulvé; Alain Dominique Perrin at Château Lagrézette; Laurent Gatou and Cristal Dubuis at Les Caves d'Olt in Parnac; Jean-Luc Sylvain of the Sylvain Tonnellerie in Limogne, Bordeaux; Patrick Cantagrel, mayor of Les Arques; Martine Cousin, administrative director of Les Ateliers des Arques; Lionel Gramon; Jeanette and Tim Branwhite; Marcel Vialatte; Pierre Lagache and Martine Bouchet at the Departmental Tourism Committee of the Lot; Christophe Bordes; Bruce Neyers of Kermit Lynch Wines and Neyers Vineyards; Linus Kessler and Amy Louise Pommier of the Prospect Wine Shop in Park Slope, Brooklyn; the Mansengs of RP Imports; Ann Tessier of Tess's Market and Loyd Bowerman of Provisions, both my local wineshops in Brunswick, Maine; Michael Terrien of Acacia Winery for his close reading; and Jeff Rowe for his company on so many gastronomic adventures.

Contents

INTRODUCTION

I freely confess that, before I began traveling with my family to France for extended visits seven years ago, I knew very little about wine and even less about its making. The only *nose* I have is, sadly, the rather large one on my face, and I am told that the discrimination of a true connoisseur begins with innate gifts I apparently lack and necessarily requires training from an age far younger than my present years. I don't have a vaulted, thermo-controlled wine cellar but rather a basement, and it contains not thousands of bottles but fewer than a hundred, in a battered cabinet in one corner that was once used to store paint, to judge by the stains.

These are not recherché wines of great vintage. The allure of Margaux and Yquem and Cheval Blanc and Haut Brion is beyond my comprehension at the sums they fetch even in mediocre years, and I rarely participate, except in the most modest way, in the disorganized, over-sold Wild West lottery that is Californian wine. That market is, by the way, currently undergoing what a Wall Streeter would call "a long over-due correction," after almost two decades of rampant speculation, overplanting, and the consequent inflation of the price of land, grapes, and wine to ridiculous and unsustainable levels.

I first drank wine in the south of France when I was fourteen, the occasional half glass at dinner that my mother, bless her, allowed me to take as part of my maiden voyage of European discovery. I can remember one evening in particular, sitting on the garden terrace of a restaurant called Le Prieuré in Villeneuve-lès-Avignon, where we drank a bottle of Vieux-Télégraphe Châteauneuf-du-Pape—my mother, my grandmother, and I. A truffle omelette appeared in front of me, and I asked my mother where the truffles were. She laughed, pointing to two half-moons of deepest black, each the size of a dime, marooned in a sea of yellow egg. I don't remember what the wine tasted like, but I do remember the smell, impossible to explain except that it shared with the truffle a whiff of the earth and of heady caramel, and that it was a faded red, tinged brown at the edge, a sign, the waiter told us, of its age.

I have other vinous memories of that summer: an apprentice waiter at a cooking school restaurant fumbling with a corkscrew, increasingly red of face, until he finally succeeded in breaking the cork; the first sip of Calvados near Mont-Saint-Michel, in Normandy, that smooth, fiery apple brandy that had nothing to do with the throat-scorching applejack we sipped clandestinely at home as wannabe dissolute teens, skating at night on the frozen ponds of southeastern Pennsylvania. In Blois, after a visit to one Loire Valley château or another, it was a bracing white wine, a Sancerre I'm almost sure, whose acid cut the richness of the butter and garlic in the dish of snails I was consuming as fast as I could pop them out of their shells. We passed through Ain and Lyon, Rocamadour and Avignon, Saint-Malô and Chartres, a big circle which somehow did not include a stop in Bordeaux, a happy accident, as otherwise I might have later become one of those ever chasing after that which is beyond my purse! Having in these last years tasted my share of Bordeaux—old and young; renowned and not; out of bottles, carafes, and even the barrel—I am happy to report that, while Bordeaux can be a very good wine *of* France, it is not *the* wine of France, a country so rich in varieties of grape and variations of climate and geography and soil that it produces thousands of wines, all distinct in their own way.

When I began to be able to afford the decent bottle or two in my late twenties, it was to the reds of the Rhône, the only wines of which I had any experience, that I turned. What I buy and keep today, aside from a growing trove of the best Cahors, are thus Châteauneuf-du-Pape, Hermitage, Côte Rôtie, and Cornas, none of which, bought when they first come on the market, cost more than $50. Their lesser cousins, generally less than half that price—Crozes-Hermitage, Côtes-du-Rhône, Vacqueyras, and Saint Joseph—to name a few, come and go among a rotating series of lesser Chilean, Spanish, Italian, and French bottles as the table calls them. The oldest wine in my basement was a birthday gift from a Cahors winemaker, a 1961 Clos de Gamot presented to me to mark the year of my birth. Another Cahors, and another gift, a 1966 Clos la Coutale, also awaits an apt occasion. Both are lovely bottles that I haven't dared to open until I am a more practiced hand at decanting—and go out and buy a decanter.

I mention my own experience of wine not because it is so significant, but because this fundamental ignorance, coupled with a large measure of curiosity and the desire to learn more, is something I share with many Americans who have not grown up in a country where the culture of wine goes hand in hand with a highly developed culture of food and eating. On our side of the Atlantic, today, this situation is starting to change, but not necessarily always in a very positive way. By this I mean that, if you look at the way wine is marketed here—the advertising, the personalities, the foodies, the cult winemakers, the hoopla (and here I would point my finger at the Californians in particular)—the chosen image is still largely an exclusive, expensive, elite drink for thin, tan young people with very good teeth and nicer clothes. It doesn't have to be this way; in most of the rest of the wine-drinking world it is not.

Nowhere is this other attitude more evident than in the backcountry winegrowing corners of France, where the host's first question is usually, "Will you take water or wine?" It is understood, of course, that after a single glass of water to slake the thirst, you'll be ready for a little wine. In the lives and minds of the winemakers themselves, too, there is little of the exotic or romantic in what they do, or even in the way they think. Seen through their eyes, wine is not a mystery or an elixir reserved for members of the inner temple, but a product wrung from the earth by honest labor. "To be a winemaker," the winemaker Martine Jouffreau reminded me, "is to be a grower of vines first. If you don't have a close relationship with your land, its soil, the weather, the rootstocks and vines themselves, you cannot have good grapes. And without good grapes, well, you will always make a mediocre wine."

To them, wine is thus a living, certainly, but a living thing, too, the result of the elemental collision of two natural substances, yeast and grape juice, "and thus should the product of their union be natural as well," adds Martine's husband, Yves, "which means keeping your hands off it once it's begun to work." This way of thinking captures exactly what this book is about: wine shorn of pretense, more as part of a way of life than merely a simple commodity to be bought and sold.

One of the marvels of almost any part of rural France, except the north and Normandy where local ciders and beers prevail, is the abundance of what the French call *petits vins,* little wines: the local wine at a modest price (less than $10 a bottle, and usually far less, a liter pitcher accompanying a modest auberge meal at $2 or $3), appropriate to the regional food, and lacking even the most modest of pretensions. This necessarily reflects how most wine is drunk in France, not decanted after long consultation with a wine steward in black leather apron and then poured delicately into crystal stemware in a tony restaurant, but as a usual, healthful complement to lunch and dinner, consumed in moderation from a carafe or plain bottle and without any of the folderol many of us imagine from our image of the French at table. (The world's first microbiologist, Louis Pasteur, said, "Wine is the healthiest thing for man to drink." Every Frenchman knows this quotation, although, as French doctors are wont to point out, everyone leaves off the first three words: "Good water aside, . . .") Still today, a good portion of wine consumed in France, including veritable lakes of Bordeaux, sees the inside of a bottle only in passing from the plastic five- or ten-liter bulk container filled at the vineyard or local wineshop for a buck a liter to the dining room table. At the grocery, one notices, too, that many table wines are sold in returnable, refillable bottles!

The intellectual approach of the ordinary Frenchman to wine is thus more sensible than anything else, for he has grown up in a place where a knowledge of the grape begins to seep into his blood with his first glasses of watered wine consumed around the dinner table in adolescence. This knowledge broadens and deepens as a matter of course when, for example, the family goes together to this vineyard or that in the annual summer and fall wine-buying trips when many French families seek to fill the cellar for the coming holidays at the same time the winemakers must empty theirs to make way for the new harvest. In the early spring, many vineyards begin to invite their loyal customers to come for weekend tastings of the new wine, which, often still rough-edged and undistinguished, is nevertheless the occasion for all to argue, through purple-stained lips and black teeth, its future merits.

For the uninitiated, there is nothing more bizarre than wandering into such a tasting, a usually dark, usually cool room filled with people swooshing wine around in their mouths, odd gargling sounds emanating therefrom, then spitting and smacking lips, the whole performance followed by streams of adjectives filling the air like so much confetti—stewed fruit, leather, apricot, truffle, leaf mold, cherry, gunflint, tobacco, acacia, honey—seemingly apropos of nothing at all. Pick up a glass and join the game, however, armed with even the least bit of knowledge and encouragement, and you will soon understand the allure of the *dégustation*.

I went into my first tasting experiences with all the received knowledge I had absorbed from the columnists, wine pundits, and learned writers of guides and encyclopedias only to find that, well, in four words, from order comes chaos, and what lovely chaos it is, too. If your experience is anything like mine, the dirty little secret of wine experts the world over will be revealed to you in five seconds flat, or however long it takes for you to realize, after the first corks fly, that you all disagree! You and your six (or sixteen) friends may take up six (or sixteen) utterly different, diametrically opposed, irretrievably irreconcilable positions on the nature, good or bad, of the liquid in the glass. If you are tasting at a French vineyard, you should not be surprised to have the winemaker himself smile approvingly and say, *"Vive la différence!"*

And then there is Bordeaux. Stripling tippler of the grape, you take two steps into the wine world (or most wineshops), and you find yourself confronted straight away with the Minotaur, shelves upon shelves of imposing, grandiloquent, utterly intimidating labels, each of them screaming, "I may be expensive, but I'm a BORDEAUX!" If, like me, you find your ball of string pitifully small and inadequate given the monstrous task of mastering the Beast (someday, I will learn the classifications of 1855—premier cru, grand cru, enormous cru, and merely bourgeois cru—and someday, too, my basement might get organized, and my hair will grow back), it is only because that is what the marketers intend. Most

Bordeaux sold in wineshops is to Château Petrus what a $2 McDonald's hamburger is to a $150, beer-fed, hand-massaged Kobe steak. Yes, they are both beef, but exactly there the comparison ends.

Late one night during the very hot summer of 2003, I sat outside the Hôtel Bon Accueil in the small village of Cazals in the southwestern department of the Lot. I had been talking with Papi (Grandpa), a retired cloth merchant who helped Francette, the hotel's owner, doing odd jobs and serving drinks. Though he ate and drank there free, his real motivation was, I gathered, an occasional respite from the tedium of retirement, for the social contact such work afforded with all and sundry. That night, smack in the middle of nearly a month of 95-degree days, the clientele was those like me made restless from the heat and seeking the air before retiring. When the talk turned to wine, he remarked that he had the simplest of tastes, that he needed no expert to guide him. "An expert," he said, "he will put the glass to his lips and say, 'This wine is good or this wine is bad, and I'll tell you why.' Me, I say, I like this wine, or I don't like this wine. Everyone has his own taste buds, and no expert is going to change that."

Although Papi's truism seems impossibly simple, to me it makes all the sense in the world. Regarding the food and drink we put in our mouths, as in so many other things, the modern world seems to have lost its way, mistaking complexity for goodness, costliness for quality, modernity and technology for progress. In the world of wine, as I discovered, things are often not nearly as complicated as they seem. Nor do they have to be.

Hence my desire to demystify, to place wine in a more ordinary, unthreatening, everyday context. This is one reason I have chosen to build this book around one of France's secondary wine regions, and why I chose, in particular, the three winemakers—the Jouffreau-Hermann family, Philippe Bernède, and Jean-Luc Baldès—who color these pages. Their vines are scattered in plots throughout the valley and the low hillsides of the Lot River in southwest France south of Bordeaux and north of Toulouse. This is how I describe the location to Americans, but, as one French friend pointed out, this is about as precise as saying that Baltimore is north of Atlanta and south of Boston.

The wine here, called *vin de Cahors* after the region's ancient capital, is not Bordeaux or Burgundy, not even the lesser Rhône or up-and-coming Languedoc; this wine is made not from merlot, or cabernet sauvignon, zinfandel, or chardonnay grapes—those most familiar to an American wine-drinking public—but primarily from the malbec grape. Like the local people who grow it, this grape is small, thick-skinned, and sometimes hard to cultivate, resistant to easy companionship on first meeting but yielding a rich reward to those with the time and inclination to let the relationship mature.

Invited to lunch one day at Philippe Bernède's house, where the vines grow right up almost to the edge of the swimming pool, I found myself sitting across from Christophe Bordes. Philippe introduced his friend only a tad mockingly as "the king of *vin de Cahors*." Short and stocky, dressed head to toe in black, and with something of the bearing of a bantam in conversation as well as stature, he is one of the largest wholesalers of Cahors in the region and owner of three of its most important commercial wineshops.

When I asked him if it wasn't difficult to sell this wine elsewhere in France, given the competition, his chest puffed out and he gave me a withering look. "We are not Bordeaux, of course. But if you say 'Cahors' to any Frenchmen," he told me, "They'll say, 'wine,' and that's already a good thing. Cahors is one of the oldest wine regions of France, and they all know it. This is a tourist region, too, not just for foreigners, and the French drink the wine here, go home, and look for it there. And I am happy to help them be able to find it!"

Vin de Cahors is thus a difficult wine, a shy wine with a large potential, a wine seen even by many who grow it as one whose charms are not as immediately evident as those of its easy-drinking neighbors to the north, south, east, and west. The wines of Bergerac, Frontonnais, Madiran and Jurançon, Gaillac, and Buzet, for the most part, are less expensive, don't need much if any aging, and may accompany a wider range of foods. In the industry jargon, they are more "quaffable," softer and less tannic (true Madiran being the exception), both because of their grape varieties and of the way they are made. And yet the Lotois, winemakers and wine drinkers, believe in their *vin de Cahors* with a faith that any priest would envy in his parishioners.

All this makes it more interesting to me, especially because *vin de Cahors* has almost completely escaped Parkerization—that is, has escaped being ranked by number in Robert Parker's magazine *Wine Advocate,* and all that such ranking symbolizes. The Parker phenomenon is an insidious one. Once he assigns a high rating to a previously unknown wine, its price zooms up, and it becomes instantly unavailable to the ordinary consumer. More nefariously, the winemaker is tempted to try to re-create this wine year after year and in quantity, even when that is not what the grapes want.

(Many French people who work in the world of wine appreciate Parker's ratings, particularly the makers of the great Bordeaux of which he is so fond. But I have also heard French winemakers refer to Parker, with great venom, as "the American lawyer," "the fat one," and "that sonofabitch Par-khair." Partly this is the rancor of those who come up short in his estimation; but also, like any wine drinker, he apparently has his biases. The one thing that astonishes them all is his audacity, as an American who confesses to having discovered wine at the late age of twenty, no less, to put himself right up there, above their own critics, as the authority. Parker's stock has been in decline of late, ever since he neglected, in 2003, to bring his famous nose to VinExpo, the world's most important wine trade show, held every other year in Bordeaux. He didn't feel safe traveling, apparently, although the British press speculated that he wanted to avoid talking to the police about the activities of one of his French associates, who was being investigated for purported conflicts of interest. In the wake of his nonappearance, he left a posse of pissed-off Bordeaux chateau owners feeling doubly betrayed, bereft of his market-moving benisons at a time when sales of French wine were down generally, and sales in America off by as much a quarter in the first three months of that year.)

Though Parker may have only a tangential influence on the world of Cahors wine, he is important nevertheless as a harbinger of that ever-encroaching trend called globalization, a trend whose merest ripples can be just ascertained today on the fringes of that bastion of traditional winemaking, the family-owned, family-run vineyard. Cahors, so far only lightly touched, represents to me almost a "before" snapshot, an out-of-the-way river valley where, today, subscribers to *Wine Advocate* (Parker's magazine) and *Wine and Beverage News* (the trade monthly) are still few and far between and the winemakers are more tuned to the weather than to the stock market or any worldwide economic trend of the moment.

The family vineyards in this book, those of the Jouffreaus, the Bernèdes, and the Baldès, are all well established, intensely local operations. I have chosen these winemakers because they are genuine, both in their enthusiasm for their work and in their blood, and quite modest and matter-of-fact about what they do into the bargain. Their operations are not vast by American standards, yet they represent three axes of thinking, three coherent responses to the difficult times French winemakers are facing as trade barriers fall both within the European Union and around the world.

The small world of Cahors wine is also a place filled with surprises. Alain-Dominique Perrin, former CEO of the Cartier companies; and Prince Henrik of Denmark, the queen's consort, own quite extensive vineyards here. There are even a few English and Dutch people who have come, bought vineyards, and become just another piece of the landscape.

The Jouffreaus have been established here for 400 years; the Baldès and Bernède families (who happen to be related) trace their winemaking roots back more than a century and a half, always on the same land. The members of the current generation of the Jouffreau and Baldès families also share a more macabre tie in that they lost their fathers within months of each other to sudden deadly cancers, something that binds them to this day. A half hour's conversation with any of them reveals the importance—and sometimes the weight—of all that tradition and history, certainly in the large events which shaped them all, but what comes through as strongly as the sense of a living past is a certain uncomplicated passion, a down-to-earth enthusiasm they want to share. This is very much a part of the fundamental associations the French have with wine: quencher of thirst, yes, but also conviviality, welcome, celebration, relaxation at the end of the workday, a symbol of the simple pleasure in finding oneself in the company of friends and family, no matter how modest the occasion. It is this esprit that first drew me to this place and these people, and it is what made the years I spent at their side, following the grape from vine to barrel to glass, so consistently rewarding. Happily, you can share some of these discoveries, and much more than vicariously; they are only as far away as your glass.

FAMILIES
OF THE VINE

1

Yves and Martine Jouffreau at Clos de Gamot

When you drive up to Clos de Gamot, a vineyard owned by Yves and Martine Jouffreau-Hermann (referred to from here on as the Jouffreaus) in the Lot River valley in southwest France, there is no allée of hundred-year-old plane trees, no expanse of coiffed lawn rolling up to an old stone château whose leaded glass windows and lichened roof slates whisper of great age and past nobility. The only thing that runs up to the vast, unpretentious collection of buildings is row upon row of vines. As far as the eye can see in every direction, the vines run away from you, a sea of ordered green stretching across the broad valley to the rising limestone escarpment beyond the Lot River on the north and to another range of low hills several miles to the south. Thirty-two acres of this sea make up Clos de Gamot. It is one of the oldest and most reputable of the 500-odd players in the appellation called *vin de Cahors,* maker of wines served both at the White House and at the Elysées Palace, and I had expected something much more impressive. I had heard so much about this family and its wine, had read so much about the role that Martine's father, Jean Jouffreau, had played over his more than sixty-year career in resurrecting Cahors from a mediocre table wine to appellation status, that my mind had conjured up a grand château, or at least a large manor house.

Instead, a low hedge of neatly trimmed greenery marks the driveway leading back to a large parking lot, also surrounded by vines, with staked rosebushes blooming profusely red at the end of each row. Although they are here to add a touch of beauty, a welcome splash of color to relieve the unbroken green and brown of the vines, the roses have a purpose. Susceptible to the same plant and insect ravages as grapevines, such plantings are the vineyard equivalent of the canary in the coal mine, though today much more sophisticated methods exist to detect trouble. Still, while Clos de Gamot is neat and orderly, the roses are about the only bow to aesthetics in a place otherwise presenting a more sober, workmanlike demeanor to the world.

On the right long, low stuccoed buildings house offices; farther back, you see the first of several *chais,* the cavernous barns where the grapes are fermented into wine before being aged in huge wooden tuns. These buildings are also of putty-tinted stucco under putty-colored sheet-metal roofs, well maintained and simple in appearance. To the left a large, traditional two-story farmhouse rises, Martine's childhood home, its stone walls painted a dull gray, the dressed stones of doorways and windows marked out in a red once the color of the local wine, now faded to a mellow ochre. *"Dégustation,"* wine tasting, reads a sign affixed to the corner of the building, pointing the way to a small outbuilding tucked behind the house.

While the materials may be more utilitarian than luxurious, the entire place is clean and tidy, with bright pots of flowers here and there and not a scrap of trash or a single weed in evidence. Still, it is a far cry from the imposing châteaux of other wineries in the top ranks hereabouts, and thus the last place I would have expected to find a subterranean picture gallery, a museum in miniature enshrining the history and tradition of a single family.

It was the last week of July in the year 2002, a very hot, cloudless day, and I was looking forward to finally spending an uninterrupted couple of hours with the Jouffreaus when we could at last talk at length about their wine and their lives. My family and I had spent thirteen months in 2000–2001 in this region, living just over the ridge, where I had written a book (*From Here, You Can't See Paris*) about a very small village, Les Arques, and its restaurant. I had met Yves and Martine in passing, at tastings and once during the harvest at their second property, Château de Cayrou. When I had expressed interest in perhaps writing about their vineyard and winery some day, they had suggested I start with a visit. That had been almost a year ago.

It was Martine who met me, with a big smile and a hearty handshake, at the door of the office. Martine Jouffreau is, like her husband, short and stocky—and she is like him, too, in the way she stands, firmly rooted and upright, coming across very much as someone of the earth. There the resemblance ends. After her dazzling white smile, which crosses her wide features often, you notice her long raven-black hair and very smooth, pale skin. She speaks softly, too, and with a gentle formality that to me, at that early point in our acquaintance, signaled a distance, a sense of caution, the reasons for which it would take me some time to learn. All together she reminded me, at first, of a doe, so quiet and watchful, those almond-shaped brown eyes wide open and alert to any danger to her own.

After a bit of small talk, she suggested we begin with a visit to the "picture gallery" as she called it, and then finish with a wine tasting. I sighed inwardly, fully expecting a ghastly collection of artifacts, dioramas, and amateur hour at the easel, all contributing to that quaint and picturesque vision of nineteenth-century bucolic vineyard life that I already knew had almost nothing to do with reality. In other words, I feared it was the first step on the package tour.

We walked past the offices and entered the first barn. Martine stopped and inserted a key the size of her hand into an ancient lock. On the other side of the door was a staircase winding down. It was noticeably cooler at the bottom, where she opened another door, stepped into a room, and turned on the lights. As the overhead neons flickered on, I found myself in a room perhaps a hundred feet on a side, with a lovely, empty expanse of wooden floor and four walls hung with more than a score of oil paintings done in a style that seemed to be a cross between Grandma Moses and the potent allegorical illustrations in the *Child's Treasury of Bible Stories* my grandmother had given me when I was seven years old. Martine hadn't been exaggerating, for it was indeed a picture gallery, and quite imposing in its own way.

Martine let me take it all in for a few moments: the gold-leaf frames, each bearing the date of the given scene, from 1290 through 1993, each captioned with a laconic phrase or two on the order of "The Era of Prosperity" (eighteenth century) and "The Regrafting Succeeds! Guillaume and the Returning Lucien Replant the Vineyards" (1885). She led me to one corner, the start of the tale, and over the next hour recounted the entire history of her family and its wine.

"The first mention of the Jouffreau name is found in 1290," she began, "in Prayssac, and in 1450 we have the first citation of the place-name La Combe de Bélaye, the larger property from which, by 1610, Clos de Gamot emerged as a separate entity." The phrases, their edges well rounded from repetition and memory, fell from her lips in a soothing and artful cadence as we moved from tableau to tableau, and I had the impression I was listening to someone else entirely.

Nearly two years later, writing this, I realized with a smile that it was probably the voice of her father I had heard, the father at whose side as a young woman she would undoubtedly have listened so many times as he lectured visitors on the family history. This was his room; it was he who had commissioned the paintings from a well-known local artist, he who had wanted to leave behind more than a few bottles of evanescent wine as a legacy for his children and grandchildren. The voice, the phrases, even, I imagine, many of the gestures were her father's, as if the great Jean Jouffreau, who died suddenly in 1996, were still very much with us, however distant and imperfect the echo.

A few of the paintings struck me particularly, not because of their great artistic merit, but because they capture so simply the bones of 400 years of winemaking by one family in a single place. To put this in an American perspective, this family has been making wine here since ten years before the landing of the *Mayflower* at Plymouth Rock. After the earliest, perhaps less historically sure-footed paintings, the seventeenth- and eighteenth-century works portray a growing prosperity, with a cooperage at Gamot, and the big barges loaded from ox wagons delivering the wine for river travel to Bordeaux and beyond, particularly to England and the Antilles. Here, we began to touch memories passed on orally to the living. "There have always been coopers in the family, too," Martine remarked. "You had a cooper because that's how wine was shipped, all wine, in barrels. By the eighteenth century, Gamot is also the name of a little port on the river below where the *gabarres,* the barges, shipped the wine to Bordeaux. My great-grandmother was the daughter of a bargeman. Papa's grandmother, Angèle, told him stories of her parents, who made a living feeding the rivermen upriver."

Apparently, 1870 was a good year for the vineyard, because Jules Roy, a French historical novelist of that period, has a French garrison in Algeria commenting in one of his books on the Clos de Gamot the characters are drinking: "They touched glasses," Roy wrote, "and Denef smacked his lips. This wine, from Prayssac in the Lot and produced by Jouffreau father and son, was the fruit of noble grapes aged in oak barrels. It had an aftertaste of raspberry that the sea voyage had not diminished. To admire its clear ruby tint, he raised his glass." The occasion of a television series based on this writer's work, Martine related, led the film company to call up one day asking for a facsimile of an 1870 label for this scene.

There was 1883, the era of the phylloxera epidemic that devastated the vines in France. "Ruin, Desolation, and Exodus: Lucien Jouffreau Leaves to Enlist in the Army," reads the caption. Sack in hand, a pathetic figure whose back is bent in defeat—Lucien, Martine's great-grandfather—treads a dirt road through bleak fields of dying vines. This is followed shortly (1885) by the triumphant return of Lucien, this time in uniform, his father, Guillaume, welcoming him among young vines green with vigor.

"We never stopped living here; there has always been a Jouffreau who stayed and continued to grow grapes." From 1939 to 1945, Martine told me, "Marcel Jouffreau, my grandfather, was a prisoner, my father off in the resistance. My grandmother was a pianist, but she ran things even though she had no experience in the business. Her father-in-law helped, as did the village women. Always there have been sons, too, to carry on the name," Martine continued, speaking of the continuity in her family, "until this generation. Papa had no sons, only my sister and I, though I know he took me for his son, taught me as if I were his son." She was smiling slightly, remembering as she said this. I waited, hoping for more, but that would come another day.

"Today we are fighting to keep the name connected to the family and to the wine for the next sons, our son, Franck." A quirk of French law prevents Franck, who carries his father's surname of Hermann, from keeping "Jouffreau" as part of his official, legal identity. A vintage of Clos de Gamot without the Jouffreau name on the label would be, to this family, anathema. (Yves jokes that he and Martine could simply not have gotten married and could have had "illegitimate" children, in which case, in the eyes of the law, Franck would have taken his mother's name.)

As we proceeded slowly from wall to wall, the pace of Martine's exposition gradually overwhelmed my shorthand note-taking. I translate the French to English in my head (except for particularly juicy tidbits or things I don't understand) and then make notes, with the result that my notebooks are often incomprehensible to anyone but me. I stopped writing and began to look and to listen. Out of the great fog of details, it suddenly struck me that, of all the events, triumphs, trials, tribulations, and disasters—historical and other—that had overtaken this family, Jean Jouffreau had picked these as most important for others to remember. Who was he, this Jean Jouffreau of whom everyone spoke? I would have to find out. Looking around, I realized that he was in fact pictured very rarely; and when he appeared in a scene, it was always with the older generation, or his wife, represented at his side. What was so important about these particular moments?

Martine had moved to the early nineteenth century, and she was explaining a particular distinction of Clos de Gamot, one that sets it apart from the wines of all the other growers in the region. "Great-great-grandfather kept aside some vines [after phylloxera killed all the rest], kept regrafting them to uninfected rootstock, trying different rootstocks until one called Herbemont was discovered. It was resistant to phylloxera, and the vines flourished." Guillaume Jouffreau planted these last, pre-phylloxera malbec vines on ground which had been disinfected—burned over, left fallow, then turned over many times and burned again. "The year 1885 saw the first real replantings with shoots of the oldest malbec vines regrafted to resistant rootstock, which is why Gamot has the oldest vines in the Lot." Herbemont, imperfectly resistant to phylloxera, was a transitional rootstock that would permit the family later to regraft their vines to even more resistant varieties, thus saving the "family" grape.

Today, this "Old Vines" wine, the 2,000 to 3,000 bottles made in most years from the meager yield of vines more than 100 years old, is the most expensive the Jouffreaus sell ($20 a bottle for the 2000!), and with good reason. It is also financially unjustifiable, as new vines on the same ground would produce wine, even at a lower price, far in excess of the value of the old. Such bean-counter logic doesn't occur to Yves and Martine, however, who are proud to offer what is an old-style, rustic, and very special wine—a wine, moreover, that demands a commitment from the buyer to leave it untouched for up to ten years and sometimes longer in the bottle. And there is the promise Yves made to his father-in-law, that he will not rip out the old vines until their production becomes truly marginal.

The paintings of the modern era highlight more viticultural matters, stressing the hand-harvesting of the Clos de Gamot vines and the enormous amount of manual labor—turning over the soil around the roots and pruning, as well as the purchase of Château de Cayrou in 1971 and the Christie's auction in London of old vintages of Clos de Gamot (1893, 1904, 1914, 1918, 1927), which financed it. "Papa was very smart," Martine continued. "He saw that the appellation status was coming, and that it would make good vineyards more valuable." She went on to explain that Jean had also recognized that the era was gone when the thirty-two acres of Gamot could support three families, never mind the two who would be relying on it. Cayrou's nearly sixty-eight acres became, then, both an insurance policy and the canvas on which the next generation—Yves, Martine, and her sister, Marise—then coming into their own as winemakers, could leave their own mark.

The final two tableaux, both dated 1993, are stark signposts pointing to the future, all the while embracing the past. The first, "A Family Wine Tasting" is of a gathering where each—father, mother, daughters, son-in-law—holds a glass in contemplation. Pen and paper lie on the table in front of them, and Jean looks as if he's about to speak.

While you or I might see such a scene as a bunch of serious folks about to drink some wine, we would be far from the truth. This *dégustation en famille* is a moment both intimate and very important that comes each year in the late winter or early spring when the new wines are ready for their final blending. To simplify grossly, the wines yielded by grapes grown on chalky soil or on a hillside are different from those from the flatlands where the ground and the weather may be different. And yet the lover of Clos de Gamot will want, each year, to open that bottle and find a wine that, though naturally differing from year to year according to conditions, always displays some attributes he recognizes. The decisions that make a glass of Clos de Gamot ever a glass of Clos de Gamot, Martine observed pointedly, arise from the discussions and opinions of a family steeped in winemaking know-how, each member with something to offer, rather than the protocols of a white-coated enologist.

The last picture is of another vineyard, a young vineyard, this one planted in the old-fashioned way, on a hillside so steep that machines are largely useless there. The place is called "Clos St. Jean," and it is five acres out of the past, planted by Yves partly with cuttings from Clos de Gamot's oldest vines, and worked almost completely by hand. Jean died before he could taste the fruit of his labor, but it has become for Yves and Martine much more than an experiment in winemaking, more than a mere tribute to her father's name.

"The famous experiment!" Martine said, drawing in her breath sharply and then expelling it in a laugh. "It started rather unusually. Papa and my husband used to drive by that hillside on their way to and from Cahors, and they thought it a likely place to once have been planted in vines. They did some research and found, indeed, that a big part of it had belonged to the same family that owned Cayrou before we bought it, and had been in vines. First we had to uproot all the scrub, but otherwise we didn't touch the natural landscape. We left the big trees, the gullies unfilled, the stone walls, the little stone hollows where rainwater once collected, the stone walls to avoid erosion. We began with a respect for the shape of the land, its natural state. The grapes are very different, tiny. The wine is 'toasted,' very rich with spice, the flavors of *la garrigue* [brushland], wild herbs, thyme, like a Côte Rôtie. It gives you an idea of what our wine may have tasted like in the Middle Ages. But you do have to do everything by hand up there, which is why five acres are enough!" As Martine doused the lights and closed the door on the family's history ancient and modern, I wondered at this high premium put on the past. At that point, drowning in detail of what had been, I was curious to go out and see with Yves what the modern reality was.

We went into a room next to the office, this one quite different from the much quainter showpiece tasting room across the yard. In contrast to the atmospherics of framed press clippings and photos, the old cork pulls and dark wood up there, here it was all white Formica and stainless steel, a sink at one end, plain office furniture pushed against the other, in the middle of the room a big table clear of anything but a dozen clean wineglasses waiting to be filled. It is a sterile place, quiet and free of distraction to the eye or the ear, where something more serious and having nothing to do with passing tourists takes place.

We sat, and Martine alternately poured and discoursed on the wine in the glasses, listening to my feeble observations, guiding me gently to seek out and identify the great distinguishing characteristics of *vin de Cahors* and of their red wine in particular. Cahors wine, made of at least 70 percent malbec grapes, has a telltale very dark ruby-garnet tint and, to a nose in a glass, might suggest the smells of ripe red fruits in summer, plums, currants, raspberries, and blackberries, say, rather than the florals of a white or the heavy spice and smoke of a Rhône.

In older Cahors, I was told, the fruit takes a backseat to more dominant dark earth, truffle, and leather aromas. Young Cahors can be very tannic, one reason why it is often served cool and in a carafe. However, those tannins, together with the actual winemaking techniques that traditional Cahors winemakers like Yves and Martine employ, allow the more rustic wines of this area to live to a great age, mellowing into very complex, flavorful wines that in the best years can compete with good Bordeaux. All the Cahors winemakers with whom I've spent any time, *except* the Jouffreaus and the Baldès family, have dragged out the story of how one of their older bottles bested a Bordeaux in a blind tasting.

When I asked Martine to compare Cahors wine with that of

Bordeaux, its near northern neighbor, whose wine has historically flattened the rest of the southwest and especially Cahors both in the market and by reputation, she looked puzzled. It was a very un-French question, because, she responded, of course the answer lies in the mouth and nose, not in words. Then she went on to give the following portrait, as intriguing to me in the way she seemed to think of this wine—almost as a shy but alluring lover—as in its poetry.

"Our Cahors is perhaps more discreet, quiet, less well known. It is less easy to appreciate in a first tasting, more discreet in the nose, a very particular taste which you can't compare to others. One discovers it in a second time, but for people who appreciate Cahors, it is very *attachant,*" very engaging. "After, you fall in love with it. It is not a fashionable wine, not for someone superficial, shallow, but for someone who wants to discover, to learn. It is . . . *un vin d'intérieur, de recherche, de passion,* and after there is more a sentimental relationship with the wine. Especially it is a wine not for quaffing, but for appreciating. The wine is like the region itself, a hidden region, a little lost, the Lot. But once you've known it, you want to come back. It hides its charms, but once glimpsed, you want to discover more of it. So it is a wine for a public perhaps more refined, discriminating, not an easy wine to sell, but a wine which people become very faithful to."

Thirty minutes later I found myself bumping along a poorly maintained back road beside Yves, who alternately cursed and laughed, talking a mile a minute about everything from the weather to what mischief the local wine functionaries had gotten up to recently. His vines ran on either side of the road, and, responding to a question, he launched into an explanation of the morphology and climatology and geology of the region and his little bit of it, our speed decreasing in direct proportion to his verbal energy. Soon we were creeping along, Yves enthusiastically pointing out this aspect and that of the passing landscape as the engine grumbled and I imagined I could smell his gearbox smoking in protest.

Now, Yves is a small mountain of a man, and an emphatic character whose conversational style takes some getting used to. He loves to talk, but "talk" is a pale, sickly word to define what is, from his mouth, much more than mere syllables. His speech is positively rococo, the stream of words emerging amid a flurry of tics, flourishes, gestures, the whole embellished with dramatic pauses, heartrending sighs, sudden knee-slaps, and fingers held dramatically in the air as you wait, pinned like an insect, for the torrent to resume . . . and the point, sometimes several hours hence, to be reached.

That day he wore a black Patriots Super Bowl XXXVI cap, what was left of his dark hair escaping all around the back. He had evidently shaved both in haste and without the aid of a mirror, a dime-sized patch of beard on one side of his chin (which I would be staring at for the next six hours) having escaped the razor. His face, dark and much abused by the elements, is raven-like, with deep-set eyes of smoky amber under eyebrows also dark, and of such Einsteinian vigor that they appear to have been stuck on with spirit gum. The small beak of a nose is, like his mouth, surprisingly delicate. His most characteristic gesture employs all these elements when, in full conversational gallop, he stops abruptly, looks away off into the distance, sweeps off his hat, wipes his brow with the sleeve of his shirt, sighs deeply, harrumphs, puts his hat back on, then turns to you, his head to one side, eyes flashing, his mouth curled up into a knowing smile as he delivers the coup de grâce.

When, in the midst of this first of many perorations I would enjoy at his side, he finally noticed that the car was about to stall, he pulled to the verge, shut it off, and continued his lecture. My kind of man, I thought, one who considers the conversation more important than the destination. My original question had been about the idea of terraces, that the higher in elevation the vines grew, the higher the quality of the wine, other things being equal. When I first posed it, he had begun quite simply by shaking his head. "*Non*, Maiii-kul," he said, subjecting my name to the usual French torture and eyeing me with the look that the teacher gives a good-hearted but not particularly bright child. "*Non, non, non, non, non*. We will go see, on the ground, out there," he had added, gesturing across the valley, just before we'd gotten in the car. Since then, I'd listened to a rant covering the ignorance of the university-trained winemakers who thought a computer could tell them when to harvest their grapes; the perfidy of the local *négociants*, the big wholesalers, in league with the big supermarket wine buyers to depress wine prices; the lamentable lack of cohesiveness between independent growers in the face of today's market; the laziness of the young; and the failings of French socialism, which seemingly underlay all of these, and this in about half a mile of road!

We walked into the rows, and Yves stopped at a place not discernibly different from any other to my eyes. "Here, we are on the third terrace, the highest," Yves began. "These vines are sitting on a limestone base in soil that varies in depth but is never very deep. Happily, we planted our vines on a mesa, like above the Grand Canyon but on the European scale. Here, the Lot River dug the canyon. The heights eroded, and that action made our landscape, the Lot River forging the countryside. As the river descended, its bed moved back and forth, depositing matter in layers. It made islands. And it left banks of pebbles, flint, *les graves* or *les galets*." He pointed at our feet, then knelt to pick up several of the darker stones, some the size of a tennis ball but most smaller. "These we like because, well, two things. They store heat during the day and so warm the vines at night. Also, they reflect heat and light up at the grapes and help them ripen. Where do most of the grape clusters hang off the vine? Down low, closest to the soil. Understand?"

We walked through acres of vines planted on this gently sloping terrace and around a stand of trees that thrust itself starkly up like an island, completely surrounded by the vines. On the far side, Yves stopped again. "Here, we are at maybe a hundred feet above the river, which is at about three hundred feet above sea level. This is the second terrace, with the plateau of the third at our back. Now look, and tell me what you see." I looked and saw the undulating slopes flowing down, lower and lower, to what I took to be the river, although I could not see its waters. And that is all I saw.

"There is more wind here, and eventually these flat bits of limestone break through the soil. Also, the richness of the soil is always at the head of the slope, but it descends over time. Gravity, rainfall, eventually it will all end up at the bottom, which it mostly has done here.

You can create a transverse ridge at intervals down your slope and that will catch it, but not forever." He points to the trees at our back. "So, closer to the trees in this parcel, we want less production to tax the vines less. They have less vigor because the trees compete for water, nutrients, and other resources. So we will prune more severely; we will leave fewer eyes and thus get fewer grapes."

"Why not cut the trees down?" I asked. He shook his head wearily.

"The question is, *why* cut the trees down?" Proceeding Socratically, he asked me to observe the position of the trees. I saw that they were at the crown of the slope. He asked me to look at the ground under the trees, which I saw to be jumbled limestone broken up by time and the elements. Light dawned.

"You can't plant where there is no soil, only rocks, and there is less soil at the top of the slope, anyway," I remarked.

"And," Yves added, "those trees have been there awhile. Someone let them grow there for a reason, perhaps *knowing from experience that vines wouldn't do well there*."

He pointed to the steep wooded ridge that climbed up from the opposite bank of the distant river. "My father-in-law was like all the families here, each one owned a strip of woods over there. Every fall, you would go to cut wood, even in the 1940s and 1950s. This world around us has changed very quickly. It used to be the polyculture of the peasant world, where he had his vines, his horses, cows for milk, grew oats and corn to feed his animals. Everything he did, he did for the purpose of survival. That has changed. The peasant life, that was a fundamental way of life here in France. Today industrial society has abandoned rural society. Here, if you had wood, it was to heat your house in the winter. Everything had a place, a reason. I try to think of those things, keep them in mind."

Back in the car, bouncing seemingly without direction through the endless plots of vines, Yves sat back heavily in his seat. A house appeared around the corner, and he pulled up next to it, pointing once again, this time at a plaque covered with verdigris and set into the wall. It was a Geographic Survey altitude plaque and told us that we were at about 100 feet above the river. Yves knows where every single survey mark in the whole valley is, partly because this interests him, partly because it is necessary information. We continued, descending gently, until we were almost at the river.

"So, first terrace, the lowest. What makes the difference between this low-lying parcel here and the vines up top? Well, about one week of maturity in the grapes. They ripen here later because they get less sun." This seemingly obvious notion made sense to me only later, when I read that objects at a greater height, given the right orientation, get hit by the sun earlier in the day and stay in the sun until later in the day—hence all those classic landscape shots contrasting the dark of the valley with the sun kissing the tops of mountains, hills, or ridges in the distance.

"We don't work with a computer; we work with nature. We know that in a hot year, the upper terrace wine will lack tannins and fruit, and so we will add more of this first-terrace wine. When we get bad weather, cool and wet, that first-terrace wine will be too green, and so we'll add much less or none in the blending."

As we drove back up to the higher ground around the winery, I observed that, given what he had just shown me, the difference in elevation from lowest to highest parcels in the Lot was only something like 30 meters, or 100 feet. "There are more than thirty-five to forty meters between the heights of the terraces," he corrected me, "and we make the most of every meter! The differences are subtle, yes, but they are present." More important for his vineyard in particular, he pointed out, was "the microclimate of this tiny part of the river valley, with the surrounding hills that protect the vines from frost and high wind. They make a bowl and keep more of the heat in at night, and as a result our grapes have more of red fruit aromas, more fruit in the mouth, too."

On the road back to the winery, we passed two of his employees, Bernard and Jean-Marie, obviously leaving for the day a bit early. Yves looked at his watch, frowned, and shook his head. "You have to have a fist of iron in a velvet glove, that's what my father-in-law used to say. Baaf! You let them have a bit of slack now because you know, come September and the harvest, you're going to need their help." He fell uncharacteristically silent, and I imagined he was already worrying about that year's wine. When I asked as much, he chuckled, and waved a hand in the air. "It's not that, no. The wine will be what it will be, and no amount of worry changes that. No, I worry about getting there, the weather, enough sun and rain in particular. We've had a passable July but so far a terrible August, no sun when we need it and rain when we don't. The grapes are behind where they should be, and I wouldn't be surprised if we didn't start to harvest two weeks late this year."

I would make my travel plans around this widely shared prediction—and miss the harvest completely, arriving at the start of the winemaking after all the grapes were in.

Those who grow grapes for wine, the *viticulteurs* or *vignerons,* are like most farmers—never happy with the weather. (*Viticulteur* used to mean just a grower of grapes, *vigneron* one who grew the grapes and made the wine. The meanings are now so muddied that you have to read a wine label closely in order to figure out if the person whose name is on it did either.) Growers are obsessed by sun, rain, wind, humidity, and barometric pressure. Yves is a farmer of grapes as much as he is a winemaker, and so he has rain gauges in strategic locations in his vineyards; thermometers here and there, too; and various insect traps that alert him to periodic threats from this or that bug. He and Martine are out in the vines every day, peering, poking, prodding, tasting the grapes. They refuse to leave their vines almost from May through the end of fall winemaking, superstitious that disaster might strike in their absence. "Constant vigilance, Miih-kul! Constant vigilance!" Yves told me over and over.

Calling to talk with Yves between visits to France, I would ask how he was. "Well," he'd reply, "here at Gamot we had twenty millimeters of rain in the last few days and some good sun and heat. The ripening advances and I am not discontent with the progress of the grapes. We shall see. . . ." From there he would pass to the general state of the wine market and only then add, almost in passing, a few words about his wife; how Isabelle, his expectant daughter, was feeling; and his son Franck's progress at the university.

Back at Clos de Gamot later that afternoon, Yves pulled the old Citroën into a shed and heaved himself out, complaining all the while about his hip, which was quite simply, he said, wearing out after years of hard labor in the vines. "To the *chai*," Yves said, and we walked over to the largest wine barn, Yves unlocking the smaller door set into one of the huge sliding panels large enough for a tractor to pass through. He crossed to a panel of circuit breakers, and, as the lights flickered on, rows of shining stainless steel tanks, the *cuves,* rose out of the gloom nearly fifteen feet to the ceiling. There were eight of them, four running along each long wall of the barn, with stairs of steel grating at one end leading up to a walkway of the same material that gave access to the hatches at the top. Each round tank sits about four feet off the ground on massive steel legs, and each holds 150 hectoliters of wine. (In Europe, the hectoliter, 100 liters, or a little over 25 gallons, is the measure of bulk wine. It is also the measure of yield per hectare of finished wine.) Each tank thus holds a little more than 3,750 gallons of wine, or about twenty thousand 750-milliter bottles.

"This *chai,*" Yves told me, "was redone in 1992. My father-in-law and I planned it all out. Today, you have tanks like this but with bands of piping encircling them. You run cold water through the pipes and so control the heat of fermenting, slow it down. Ours have nozzles on top that can spray water down the sides. We use more water, and it's not so precise, but it does the same thing."

He pointed to three slightly smaller iron-banded wooden casks, their wide wooden staves darkened from years of use. "*Les foudres,*" the casks, "these are not for fermenting but for storing smaller batches of overflow temporarily. In winemaking you always have to have a container appropriate to the volume you're dealing with. Otherwise you get too much air on top, and the wine can get sick."

In French, this structure is called the *chai de vinification* (or, more rarely, the *cuverie,* the tank room), vinification being all those steps toward a finished wine from arrival of the grapes at the door through the initial fermentation when, with the tanks partially filled with destemmed, lightly crushed grapes, the natural yeast on their skins turns their sugar into alcohol over a period of days or weeks. There are many other things going on in the tank, of course, which we'll come to later. The wine barn (a curt and rather unromantic translation) is the domain of the cellarmaster, *le maître du chai,* who oversees the physical work of manipulating grapes and wine in tank and barrel.

The work of the cellarmaster begins where the work of the *chef de culture,* the vineyard manager responsible for the health of the vines and the growing and harvesting of the grapes, leaves off. Occupying an often more exalted middle ground and representing Athena's reason to Bacchus's chaos, is the enologist, a scientist whose background includes studies in chemistry, microbiology, geology, meteorology, and soil science, all in relation to grapes, wine, and especially fermentation and vinification. To this team we might, in a certain kind of winery, add a *caviste* or cellarman responsible for overseeing stocked wine, some of it probably quite old.

That, of course, is how the Baron Rothschilds and Château Margauxs of the world do it. Here at Clos de Gamot, as in thousands of vineyards across France, however, Yves and Martine divide up all these roles between them, except that of the enologist, who is employed in season on contract to do the technical analyses to verify that the wine is passing the various way points of fermentation and its aftermath through the fall and early winter.

"I do everything! Well, I have done everything," Martine told me once, "except drive a tractor. I don't know why; I just never learned." Yves is the vineyard manager, directing, in consultation with his wife, the various labors of the five or six full-time field workers in the spraying, pruning, fertilizing, and machine-harvesting at Clos de Gamot and Château de Cayrou. Their daughter, Isabelle, has become an emergency room nurse; their son, Franck, is finishing his studies in enology and agricultural engineering at the University of Toulouse. Franck returns home to help out for the holidays and during the long summer vacation, when he is not doing an apprenticeship in another vineyard somewhere in France.

Martine's younger sister, Marise Jouffreau, is largely responsible for marketing and distribution, shares the administrative work, and organizes the hand-harvesting at Clos de Gamot each fall. Her two sons, Hugo and Martin, are as yet too young to choose a direction; for now, more interested in rugby, they know Clos de Gamot as the place where Mami, their grandmother, still lives in the big house, and where the barns, sheds, and fields of vines are exciting places to play, especially during the hustle and bustle of harvest.

At the end of that very long day—after Yves had shown me the rest of the barns, where wine was stored in more *foudres,* huge oak tanks, to rest as long as two years before bottling; and the vast subterranean wine cellar, with its hundreds of thousands of bottles put aside through the years to mellow before sale—we returned to the modest office where I'd first arrived.

It was getting dark, those spectacular pinks and oranges and violets of a summer sunset in the Lot creeping across the sky, and I commented that they must be tired, ready for dinner at least. *Non, non,* they insisted, as generous in this first encounter as I would find them over the next two years of visits; we could talk as long as I still had questions. I of course had fifteen thousand questions but realized, happily, that I would have plenty of time to find the answers. In the company of two people so genuinely interested in communicating their own passion, I also realized that this adventure was going to be fulfilling in all the best ways, not at all the package tour I had first suspected. We said good-bye, and I pulled away, stopping at the end of the long drive to look back. They were walking, heads close together, across the tarmac toward their house, their short, stout forms casting long shadows behind them.

2

YOUNG MAN IN A HURRY
Philippe Bernède at Clos la Coutale

If the Jouffreaus have put their eggs in the venerable (and some would say vulnerable) basket of the past, one has only to drive ten minutes from their vineyard in Prayssac, to Vire-sur-Lot, to find a winemaker of an entirely different stripe. Due west through the heart of the nearly flat alluvial plain that makes up the largest part of Cahors wine country and with its back up against the hills that shelter it sprawls Clos la Coutale, the vineyard of Bernède *père et fils*. Philippe, the *fils*, who mostly runs the place now and has run it since his father retired in 1994, is possessed of a vision focused firmly on the future. His wine is different from more traditional Cahors: lighter, softer, and less tannic; *un vin charpenté, mais bien rond et fait sur le fruit,* a Frenchman would say. It is thus a wine that very much reflects the tastes of today's younger buyers, who may not have a wine cellar or even want to cellar it for the suggested five to eight years recommended for most Cahors, and who particularly don't like the thicker, blacker, more powerfully tannic and rustic wine of their grandfathers.

What's more, Philippe seeks, with the winemaker's artifice, to make more or less an identical wine year to year whatever the vagaries of rain, sun, frost, or hail; to make it well and with the most modern of techniques and equipment; and to export as much as possible rather than selling mostly locally. All these approaches combine to make him an exception among the other Cahors winemakers, some of whom tend to regard him with a bit of suspicion. Though his taste for late-model Swedish and German cars might provoke a twinge of envy in others, it is more his willingness (downright unseemly, his hastiness seems to some people here) to try what is new—not so much out in the vines as in the winemaking techniques and technology, and in new ways to sell his wine—that makes his neighbors suspicious.

Many Cahors winemakers consider their biennial excursion to *the* French wine show, VinExpo in Bordeaux, about two hours northwest, to be a major voyage. Many may also make periodic trips to Paris, Strasbourg, and the other important shows throughout France. Philippe, though, has a positive mania for travel, almost exclusively in the service of selling his wine. He will go anywhere he sees a potential market, and in a typical year his feet might touch the earth in Toronto, Montréal, Vancouver, New York, Chicago, Boston, Los Angeles, Seattle, Washington, D.C., Singapore, Hong Kong, Moscow, London, Amsterdam, Brussels, Munich, and Beijing. This doesn't prevent him from taking advantage of such trips to indulge his penchant for motorcycle touring, backcountry ATV adventures, scuba diving (tropical, deep-sea, and other), skiing, and running marathons, those of Boston and New York City being just two of the notches in his Nikes. He likes to try new things, to push himself even, or especially, when there is a bit of danger involved—diving to a steamboat wreck lying 100 feet down on the bottom of Québec's St. Lawrence River in June, with the water temperature at forty degrees, for example.

When Philippe told me he was going to be pouring his wine at one of the largest wine trade shows in New York City, I signed on immediately, hoping to see the man in a different—and perhaps more provocative—environment. I wasn't imagining a peasant loose in the city, exactly, but people are known to reveal themselves more easily when home is 3,000 miles away.

The show, formally (and a little gassily) known as the Fall 2002 Winebow Vintner's Harvest Tasting, is a trade-only event (sort of) to which the sponsoring distributor-importer, Winebow, invites its suppliers—other importers, but especially winemakers and distillers from all over the world—to show off their wares to thousands of buyers from the region's bars, restaurants, hotels, and liquor and wine stores. Winebow, depending on laws that vary from state to state, functions as importer, wholesaler, and distributor. It is very large and very successful, a company which sells nationally, but whose major presence is in the New York–New Jersey–Connecticut area, where its power in the market stems largely from its success as the sole distributor of dozens of the popular Italian wines known as super-Tuscans.

Winebow also distributes, in its east coast territories, the wines of the reputed west coast importer Kermit Lynch, who for more than thirty years has been introducing wines from what were lesser-known areas of France to an appreciative American public. His excellent book on the subject, *Adventures on the Wine Road,* recounts many of his discoveries along the way. Among his winemakers Lynch also has a formidable reputation as one who demands quality, who seeks out authenticity, and who is not hesitant with his own suggestions for improvement. He has long encouraged his winemakers to produce more natural wines from grapes grown without chemical fertilizers and with less spraying and filtering, and he began long ago to insist on shipment exclusively by refrigerated container so that wine in transit isn't either baked or frozen by extremes of weather during the ocean shipping season. (And he was the first person who dared to sell a French rosé, a Bandol, for $35 a bottle at retail!) He is, to Philippe's great good fortune, also the exclusive American importer of Clos la Coutale.

Lynch represents more than two dozen French winemakers, and one of his informal conditions for taking them on is that they appear periodically at tasting events like this one. He seems to have understood long ago that, as there are thousands of excellent wines from the world over all competing for the same export dollar, the one thing that can make the difference to the wholesale buyer is having met the face behind the label and heard the story behind the wine. And wine beyond a certain minimum price threshhold is one of those products, like oriental rugs, fine paintings, and handcrafted furniture, that one buys as much for the story (or the image) as for the thing itself—in this case, the liquid in the bottle.

Bruce Neyers, a California winemaker who doubles as Lynch's national sales director, together with his regional manager, Matt Cain, had spent weeks preparing for this year's fall road show, of which New York was the second stop after Washington, D.C., and before a similar show in Boston to follow.

When I spoke to Bruce on the phone to arrange an invitation, he warned me that the event might be a little overwhelming—"a real mind-fuck" were his exact words. As he is not normally given to obscenity, I assumed I was in for a very interesting afternoon. Because my seven A.M. direct flight from Portland, Maine, to La Guardia had been magically transformed by the airline into an 8:30 flight via Boston, my cab pulled up at the Metropolitan Pavilion in Chelsea more than an hour and a half after I'd arranged to meet Bruce and his group at the front door for the opening. On the sidewalk, small groups of people were already gathered, smoking, talking business, and sipping from small white plastic cups of what could only have been espresso. They had, in effect, created an impromptu European café in less than an hour. To one side was a whole clan of men in sharply cut double-breasted silk suits and the kind of butter-soft leather dress shoes only Italians seem able to make, their handsome dark faces lively as streams of Italian flowed back and forth between huddles over the thick, glossy show catalog. I also heard snatches of French, Russian, German, Japanese, and Spanish, all in the three minutes it took to ready notebook, pen, and tape recorder.

Once through the doors and up the steps to the reception area at the front, I saw a single enormous rectangular room for which the word "gridiron" would be only a slight understatement. Underfoot, acres of warm oak floor glowed, the creaking of the boards competing with the buzz of excited conversation and the periodic popping of corks, a sound that was so regular that day that I soon stopped hearing it. Everything about the space had been designed to be pleasantly neutral, from the white-painted walls and regularly spaced columns to the muted fluorescents and occasional soft spotlights above.

What was most impressive, even though the doors had opened less than two hours earlier, was the pong of wine that rolled over me as I stood at one end of the room surveying the scene. That and the noise, a wall of sound which was merely intense at that point, like a huge dinner party with a few hundred people all on their third cocktail, but which would rise to a headache-inducing roar as the day advanced. After collecting the one indispensable tool at this event, a wineglass (no cheap plastic here!), from a table to one side that held a mere 500 or so in pretty pyramids, I waded into the crowd, looking for Philippe and the rest of Bruce's Kermit Lynch contingent, eavesdropping madly while observing the crowd.

The floor was broken by lines of tables whose logic of placement was something you'd find only at a wine and spirits show. This is Winebow, and Winebow is Leonardo LoCascio. LoCascio controls the best "book" in New York, a very high-quality selection of imported (particularly Italian) and American wines, exclusively. He could be glimpsed occasionally, immaculately coiffed and silk-suited, at the head of a phalanx of equally elegantly dressed young men dashing off at a pointed finger to do his bidding. The Californians were on the right wall, along with some Oregonians and a few marooned Australians. On the wall behind one stand, I saw a complicated multicolored map showing the various geological substrates under the fellow's vines. Another winemaker had brought an enormous clear plastic box filled with rocks and dirt, which must have cost a fortune in overweight baggage charges, showing the same strata in situ.

Of the middle aisles, the most central was taken up, naturally, by an army of Italians, fifty vineyards strong, the clots of tasters with outstretched glasses surrounding each table demonstrating the current popularity of these strong, dark, hot wines. The next aisle over was ruled by the lesser Europeans, among them two islands defended by Kermit Lynch's French battalions, out in force to represent a good chunk of France: the regions of Rhône, Provence, Languedoc-Roussillon, Alsace, and the Loire Valley among them. Some South Americans popped up here and there, notably Rothschild's Los Vascos vineyards; there were some higher-end Spanish and Portuguese wine, port, and sherry houses as well. On the left wall I saw the odd men out: very expensive single malts, armagnacs, and cognacs; the more exclusive sambucas, gins, and grappas (which means only that I did not recognize any of their names); and a few hopeful overnight sensations like Brazilian pitú caipirinha (whose taste I can only compare to fermented dirt) and Mexican "single village" mescals, whatever the hell they are (fermented dirt with a hint of wool sock).

At either end of this outpost of spirits on the far wall were two stands absolutely necessary to the functioning of the whole gathering. The front of the room roared with the noise of a bank of espresso machines hissing out a river of high-octane Danesi *caffè*. At the back, a buffet of high-absorbency foods—various breads, pasta salads, *crudités*— and tall displays of miniature bottles of mineral water were laid out beside a small area of tables and chairs where buyers and sellers could get together for taking orders and transacting other business. The organizers' hopes were, apparently, to counteract the effects of all that wine by, on the one hand, mopping up what had already been drunk; and, on the other, stimulating the system with a few shots of strong coffee taken standing up. Refreshed and re-armed, one found oneself, coincidentally I'm sure, once again at the head of the room and ready to sally forth once more.

In this restless sea of smart-looking men and women, at that hour mostly in business dress, cell phones, digital personal organizers, and order books seemed to be the accoutrements of the day. It was easy to tell the generals, for their first lieutenants would approach, holding out a glass for a swirl, a sniff, and a gargle, then a discreet spit into one of the ubiquitous towel-draped wine buckets poised delicately at the edge of each table, said spittoons emptied periodically by circulating squads of young men and women pushing what were, underneath more fancy draped toweling, large plastic trash cans on rolling dollies. If there was a look to the early crowd, it was cool rather than buttoned up. There was no air-kissing in front of the tables, but lots of very American handshaking and shoulder-slapping.

I found Philippe almost in the middle of the room, with Matt Cain, Bruce's regional manager, at his side. They were behind two tables set at a slight angle, a pillar at their backs, twelve different kinds of Lynch's

French imports, Philippe's bottles among them, in neat ranks, many open and awaiting their sad fate, to be tasted but never drunk.

Philippe shook my hand, cocked his head back to take in the throngs, and said, succinctly as always, "*Il y a du monde et il y a du vin!*" Lots of people and lots of wine! Philippe is tall and well built, with clear blue eyes, a fringe of graying hair and a somewhat austere visage until he smiles, at which point he looks as if he were about twelve years old. The long dome of his forehead and the roundness of his eyes can make him seem a little sleepy, a little Homer Simpsonish, until, that is, he opens his mouth, and one of his sharp, short sentences drops out, bringing you to attention. In a light blue Oxford shirt with the sleeves neatly rolled up and dark slacks, he was one of the more casually dressed persons on the floor that day.

We chatted about that year's wine. "It's eleven to twelve degrees now, so the harvest won't be late, maybe September twenty-fifth for us," Philippe told me, in winemaker's shorthand. "During the flowering, it wasn't good weather, so the grapes won't get to more than twelve to thirteen degrees. It's good weather now; we hope it will hold." Winemakers often use this shorthand: degrees as a measure of the likely eventual alcoholic content based on the sugar of the grapes, a figure which should always be climbing with the ripening of the grapes in the lead-up to the harvest. As people came up to taste, I reflected on his calmness, for all the other winemakers I knew would never dare to leave their vineyards at such a delicate moment, just two weeks before the harvest. But then Philippe, I was learning, was different, judging it just as important to be here, doing this.

A woman in a tight black dress approached with a smile and a glass, and Philippe went into his patter. I leaned closer, never having heard him speak English. "Do you know the Cahors wine?" he began. "It is seventy percent of the malbec grape, we call that auxerrois, and fifteen percent of the merlot and fifteen percent of the tannat."

"I've heard kudos about your syrah!" she replied, and Philippe looked down at the bottles on the table (he was pouring, as accepted wine tasting courtesy demands, for a score of Lynch's other French winemakers, all absent from the event), trying to remember which of the several Rhônes might be mostly syrah. She swirled, sipped, and spat, watching as Philippe smiled and nodded as a subsequent river of incomprehensible winespeak, a dialect imprecise and often fatuous in any language, washed over him. She left, without tasting his wine, wobbling off on heels that would prove an increasing challenge as the afternoon turned into evening.

A few minutes later a young man approached with a big smile, saying, "I know your wine. I love Cahors!" (I have often thought what a shame it is that "Cahors" is so hard to pronounce for English speakers. This fellow had made the common mistake of pronouncing the "h" and the final "s" and accenting the second syllable, Cah-HORZ. The actual pronunciation is more like CAH-or, with a little hiccup of a pause in the middle between syllables.)

He was, according to his name tag, Linus Kessler, of the Prospect Wine Shop in Park Slope, Brooklyn. I hauled him aside after he had finished telling a charmed Philippe how much he admired his wine. Linus was only twenty-two but had, he told me, been buying and tasting wine since long before his twenty-first birthday. "It's a lot of fun," he continued, with a slightly purple smile, "but I do take it seriously!" I asked him, with the glass still hot in his hand, what he liked about Cahors, and what he knew about Cahors in general.

"A lot of the new Cahors," he said, "it's aged completely in new oak, glossy, not like this." He swirled the wine, inhaled deeply, then sipped. "Things lose their soul, lose their feel. There are exceptions, and, hey, Philippe is trying. [I like his wine] because he is of the old school style, because everyone else has left it in the dust. Everyone else has gone for a more international style, glossy, muscular, spoffulated—versus these, which are earthier, more rustic. Malbec is misunderstood and in the old style. People don't understand the grape varieties. This is not glossy in its texture, doesn't have that new *barrique* [barrel], American oak edge to it. It is softer, accessible, with less of a heavy signature like so many wines today. I like the grape. At $11.99 it's a great deal, too, and food-friendly. You can't pair such big glossy wines with food—they destroy the food."

Another taster, a Brit named Finn who moonlighted as a part-time wine buyer for Crabtree's Kittle House in Chappaqua, New York, drifted over after eavesdropping on our conversation. "I think people get it in their mind," he said, "that Cahors is a wine you can never drink young. Which is too bad. There are some interesting things going on in France now, especially in the smaller appellations like Cahors, the Côtes de Duras, Frontonnais, Bergerac, Gaillac, Buzet. That's the problem with some people in France, in the bigger appellations that everyone has heard of. They have the ostrich mentality: 'We don't have to prove anything. The Americans, they don't know anything about wine. How could they?' People have been making wine in America for four hundred years!"

Over the next several hours, I watched the parade of name tags, many from well-known restaurants and bars (Knickerbocker Bar, Aqua Grill, Luna, Gramercy Tavern, Pascale's, La Caravelle, Tribeca Grill, the River Cafe), but also from garden-variety corner liquor stores where wine was a distinct second-place finisher, places with names like Buy-Rite Liquors, Patterson Wines, Wine King, and Mike's Liquors in the Bronx.

Paul, a squarely-built liquor store owner from Staten Island, who had a heavy Russian accent and wore the worst toupee I'd seen in many years, stood back from the Lynch tables after tasting a series of French reds. He had a sour look on face. I asked him in Russian what his name was, as it certainly wasn't "Paul," and he smiled a bit, confessing that it was Pavel; that he was originally from the Ukraine, near Odessa; and did I know it? I asked if he had tried the *Kagorskoye vino,* the Cahors wine, a wine many Russians know because of the long historical association of Cahors both as the sacramental wine of the Russian Orthodox church and the officers' mess wine of the Russian army from the time of Catherine the Great. He looked over at Philippe and smiled briefly.

"I run a liquor store, and Americans who buy wine by me want sweeter wines. Do I know the Cahors?" He smiled again. "When Peter the Great had his stomach problems, what did his doctors tell him? Drink Cahors, it's the only wine that won't ruin your stomach, destroy your liver." He looked around at the crowd. "You Americans, all the time worrying. It's not that wine is bad for you. It's that people *think* wine is bad for them, and that thinking hurts their stomachs!" Ah, that Russian logic.

As Philippe poured and recited the vital statistics of his wine and the others on the table, and as I listened to the comments of the tasters, I began to understand what he and many other Cahors winemakers meant when they complained about the misconceptions people had regarding their wine. Several times I watched tasters holding up the glass, observing with surprise that, though almost black in hue, it was smooth and soft in the mouth, with, in winespeak, "good fruit" and "ripe, round tannins." What they meant was that it didn't pucker your lips and dry your mouth as if you'd been sucking lemons. Philippe would smile, sometimes almost painfully, and explain, as best he could, that it was the way he made the wine, with very ripe grapes, slow cool fermentation, microoxygenation, and good oak barrels used in moderation.

Philippe's limited English and an environment that encouraged speed tasting rather than deep reflection prevented him from expressing himself fully and to best effect. I asked him later, in French, no, seriously, why should anyone bother with a Cahors? Wasn't it just another *petit vin* from a backwater appellation, probably of uncertain and variable quality and bound to disappoint? I let myself in for an elegant earful.

"The advantages of Cahors, well, first it is a wine that has character; it's practically the only wine in France made with the malbec grape, and that makes it distinct already. It's a wine that you can age ten or fifteen years, and yet all this and still it is a very good value. I find that people are sometimes surprised by the quality of a good Cahors given the price they paid. Why does my wine sell so well in America? Well, it's less expensive than American wine, particularly Californian wine, maybe $12 a bottle in a wineshop, maybe $20 in a restaurant. And I've put a lot of work into selling it here."

But what distinguished it from, say, your garden-variety red Bordeaux or Côtes-du-Rhône?

"When you taste it, it should have on the one hand a good measure of fruit. A young Cahors will have a nose of red fruits, black fruits, cassis, blackberry, raspberry. After aging, the aromas become more earthy, an aspect, we would say, of mushroom, a woodsy smell, black truffle . . . and in the mouth these are structured wines, by which I mean there is tannin, concentrated flavors, in a nice balance with the fruit. A Cahors should be rich, with a good depth of color, deep dark red, and in the mouth well-rounded tannins, and a long finish. In a blind tasting, a good, well-aged Cahors can hold its own with some of the big Bordeaux, I think. Still, Cahors in a way appeals most to a certain clientele who like fleshy, chewy red wines, more substantial red wines.

"Americans are used to drinking big Californian reds, hot [high-alcohol] wines, and I think that Cahors fits in with that. Some of the Californians are hard—very alcoholic, I mean—and thick, substantial. But then Americans also like the wines that are loaded with that oaky flavor, which, me, I like less. Those wines, too, tend to lack acidity, and that makes for a wine that can seem heavy, lacking that freshness, that hint of fruit that you find in so many French reds."

In my own tasting that afternoon, particularly on the Californian side of the room, I had noticed that he was certainly correct in one measurable respect: many of the reds were at 13.5, 13.7, 14 degrees alcohol, and some even higher. A French red above 13 degrees is a rarity in all but the most southerly appellations, as the perception is that more than this makes a wine so heavy, with the alcohol so dominant, as to interfere with, if not destroy, the subtler flavors of the food which it is supposed to complement and enhance. (Hence the obsession with pairings of food and wine, which we in our blessed simplicity have reduced to the level of "white with fish and chicken, red with everything else," violating even those rules with happy abandon.)

By four P.M., the noise level in the cavernous, echoing room was more like that in a nightclub; faces were red and running sweat; and the food section, reduced to a few battle-weary shreds of lettuce, looked like it had been attacked by the Mongol hordes and their horses. A very large man in a tweed jacket that had seen better days lurched carefully about, leaving drops of espresso in a trail from the cup he held out in front of him. I also noticed a distinct change in the dress code, as if someone had suddenly decreed it the hour of the short black dress for her and the Don Johnson $2,000 jacket over a black or white T-shirt for him. The people were younger and hipper and had obviously sped out of work early to partake of that ever-rarer but ever-welcome New York ritual: free booze.

A woman came up to Philippe bearing a glass. "Do you have the heavy rains where you are in France?" she asked breathily. Philippe looked left, then right, as if she might have been speaking to someone else. She repeated the question, slowly and enunciating every word. She was either drunk or a language teacher, I thought. "No," Philippe said, somewhat taken aback. "Good for you!" she said, tasting, then continued on her unsteady way.

"It's a little calmer this year on the buying end," Philippe told me when I asked how much business he thought was going on. This I had heard over and over again, talking to those who were here selling wine rather than buying—that there was a pervasive gloominess about the immediate future, particularly here in New York, given the events of September 2001. Economically, the tristate region was one place where the wholesale disruption, and subsequent very local economic downturn caused by the displacement of so many big spenders, was having a measurably huge effect.

One northern New England regional distributor allied with Lynch is Ed Manseng, of RP Imports in Portland, Maine. He was there to scout, to deal a bit on the side, but mostly to take the temperature of the market as we moved into the all-important holiday season. At the moment, he was a bit disgusted with the turn the crowd had taken, more into drinking the wine than tasting it, more into talking and flirting and hanging out than ready to order fifty cases for Christmas.

"Winebow's got a great Italian book that it imports directly," he was saying. "It's nice; you taste a lot of wine you're not familiar with. This show is taken very seriously. But business is slow here. Also, at about five o' clock, like right now, it becomes cocktail hour," he said dismissively. His wife approached, bringing him a glass. He tasted, grimaced. "Tight," he said, turning back to me. "A cooling in the buyers has appeared in the last year. People are tentative about how much they'll spend on wine. And it's got two parts. What they'll drink that night, they used to pay $20 for; now they'll pay ten or twelve bucks. For an occasion wine, more special, it was $30 to $40 a bottle, but now they'll look at the $20 to $25 bottle. They're not drinking less; they're buying smarter. If the restaurant business is down, the retail is up because they're taking it home, cooking and eating at home. But the margins are thinner . . .

"It's almost a knee-jerk business, a knee-jerk reaction to the economy, what's going on in politics. That can put a stop on how much people are spending. When the news isn't good, they drink more. Champagne sales have gone up for the first time in two years, up twenty-five percent over last year.

"Philippe's wine is at a tremendous advantage for that; it's a great value. The problem is that they're obscure, the Cahors. The retailer has to go out and find the buyers and say, try it, bring it back if you don't like it. They never do! Philippe's wine will do better now. People are cautious, and they'll search those wines out. They don't have to ask, 'Is this too much money?' The Cahors are great food wines. They scream out for food, food calms them down. They're too acidic. The food takes the acid levels down. And he's quite entrepreneurial for a Frenchman!"

Three hours later, with the wine show behind them as well as perhaps a shower and a call home from their hotels, the Lynch contingent gathered at Frank's, a high-end steak joint in the meatpacking district, to unwind and to fill their ravenous bellies. I arrived once again after the opening bell to find a good two dozen people sitting in the glassed-off back room, two waiters coming and going with huge plates holding mixed appetizers. Bruce Neyers held court at one end, and some attempt had been made to mix the French and English speakers to avoid the linguistics apartheid that can sometimes reign at such gatherings.

"Frank's is the kind of place," Bruce told me, "where you have to know to order the prime rib; it's not on the menu. He cuts and hangs it himself." I asked him how he had found this place, and he told me the story of his old friend, "Bud" Trillin and Bud's wife, Alice, who was forever reproaching her husband for his unhealthy appetites but who, apparently, allowed that the very occasional visit to Frank's was somehow within her understanding, particularly when one of Bud's midwestern friends was in town.

As Bruce was talking, all around me I saw the French—for most of the team were French—puzzling over the menus and looking around as if a little lost as to the order of things. In their country, the meal proceeds by precise increments, beginning with the palate-awakening *amuse-bouches* or appetizers; followed by the entrée, then the main course, salad, cheese, and dessert; and then the whole put to bed with a small digestif with the coffee. Bruce, good host that he is, took note and suggested that everyone choose a main course and he would order the sides à la carte for the whole group.

A very short, very stout man pulled up a chair, greeting Bruce with a joke about how hefty the corkage fee would be that evening (every winemaker had brought at least three bottles of his own wine, it seemed). His chef's apron was turned down, and what was left of his glossy black hair was slicked back. Funky square-framed black glasses framed the face of a good eater. He was a treat to listen to, stories of a youth spent at the side of his immigrant grandfather, in the garden, in the butchery, rolling out in a thick, New York accent, stories punctuated by Yogi Berra–like punch lines.

"I could teach you how to make prosciutto, salami, sausage in a half an hour," he said at one point, "but it would take you twenty years to learn!" Of his house-cured prime rib: "When it's all gone, there's no more!"

Soon great bloody hunks of rare meat and a steady stream of steakhouse sides—creamed spinach, three kinds of potatoes, cauliflower au gratin, the works, began appearing magically in front of us. The excellent prime rib began to arrive, and it was good, so rare and tender you could cut it with your fork. They had drunk Bruce's chardonnay, a Champelou Vouvray, and the lighter red Chinon with the appetizers, and soon after I arrived the big guns rolled out—fat, hearty reds from the southeast and southwest, Provence, Roussillon, Collioure. By the end of the meal, Philippe was making coins disappear behind female guests' ears and doing scarf tricks, and this is when I learned that he is a gifted amateur magician, much taken to entertaining the crowd on the road.

During the meal, the talk had turned from the show and its rather muted results (I could only imagine what the crowd was like in a good year), a downward trend in wine prices given that low demand, much gossip about the French wine industry, and stories from the road, for this was a group in which many had traveled together, in France and in America, quite a bit over the years.

The corollary to the French winemakers' presence at shows like this one was that Lynch also insisted that his buyers and distributors travel the wine roads yearly, visiting the vineyards of origin and sampling vintages new and old, the better to know the wine and its makers for their customers. What this meant in actuality was twice-yearly marathon tasting trips when two vans of American buyers would discover many rural corners of France, marching bravely onward against an onslaught of many hundreds of wines in fourteen days.

I had migrated to Philippe's corner of the table, where, magic tricks safely stowed, he was marveling at Bruce's energy. "You saw him today, he never stops!" Philippe said. *"Bruce, c'est un bosseur, lui."* Bruce is a workhorse. "He is always on the road, traveling, traveling. He does what he has to, what we have to. Man, you have to show your face all the time here, show people you're still here so they'll keep on buying your wine. But he works too hard. I sure hope he doesn't have a heart attack and fall over someday."

I retired that night somewhat woozy from all the good wine but happy in the experience of the day: Philippe among a motley throng of Americans, coming out of himself at least a little bit to do what he did best—sell his wine. At home, where he was surrounded by his patch-work of vines and the stately stone walls of his vineyard, the cares of the day seemed to turn him inward, provoking a peasant reticence. There was not a hint of surliness or unease, it was just that, like many people in this river valley, he preferred to listen rather than to talk, to observe from a slight distance before stepping up and into the game. As this is my preferred stance as a writer, it often took the presence of others to impel him to sustained speech, to action, to expression beyond the ordinary.

The first time I had met Philippe, he was standing in the gravel driveway of his vineyard, on a hot day in the early fall, flip-flops on his feet, in shorts and a sun-faded shirt, his legs lean and muscled, those of the marathon runner he is. We were in front of a long low building of white stone; cut into one end were imposing doors of chestnut under a legend, "Clos la Coutale, 1895," carved into the arching stone. Next door was a large, two-story farmhouse, its exterior nicely if modestly restored, its lower floor having become a cave-like tasting room with cool tile floors and lots of imposing beams and darkly gleaming woodwork. I had seen the upstairs, where the renovations seemed to have stopped fifty years ago. Inside, it is very simple: more warm wood; comfortable, uncomplicated furnishings; a cozy kitchen, reminding the visitor that this is still as much a home as a showplace, no matter the clack of the credit card machine downstairs, for Philippe's mother and father live there still.

As I stood outside in the courtyard, from the open doors of the tasting room came the sound of a ringing phone, a bottle clinking against a glass, German being spoken. Philippe's mobile phone rang, and a car pulled up, reversing so that its trunk faced the wooden doors. The driver and his wife, two sunburned, middle-aged foreigners, got out, popped open the trunk and began taking empty five-liter brown plastic demijohns up to the barn. Phillippe excused himself to serve them, urging me to look around. Across the courtyard, he opened one of the tall doors, revealing what looked like a gleaming metal water tower in miniature but which was actually a *cuve,* an enormous stainless steel tank containing about 1,000 gallons of the kind of table wine most every vineyard sells in bulk, generally a house blend that has never seen the inside of an oaken barrel and will never know a bottle. Unaged and unoaked, it brings between $1 and $2 a liter and is sold only at the vineyard, not to the wholesale market. He grabbed a hose that had a nozzle fitted to it, filled the containers one by one, and then sent the customers in to where his mother tended the till, to pay. There, they could also buy a very few recent vintages in bottles from $7 to $11, perhaps even splurge on Philippe's premium offering, Le Grand Coutale at $22, made from his best grapes, picked each year by hand and aged a year at least in new oak.

When he came back, we walked to another set of doors at the far end of the building. These he opened, and we stepped into a cool graveled expanse every inch of which was taken up by wooden barrels lying on their sides in special racks, each with a sealed bunghole in its top.

The air was thick with the tang of the evaporated wine leaching through the wood of the barrels, but also held that particular sharp reek of fresh oak familiar to anyone who has ever worked with this wood. "It's resting," he said simply, watching the barrels intently as if they might get up and walk off. "For next year."

He took me around the corner, through iron gates and into the less picturesque but still very tidy backyard where the wine-buying public never goes. Pallets of new green glass wine bottles rose in twenty-foot tiers in one corner: 80,000 bottles in all, by my quick calculation. The oddest-looking tractor I'd ever seen, its body eight feet off the ground on spindly legs ending in tires, hulked next to the bottles, a mechanic standing on a ladder muttering over its exposed innards. It was a New Holland/Braud mechanical grape harvester and cost as much as a small house here, about $125,000.

On the other side of the yard was a barn less rustic than the *chai*, this one of clay brick, inside which a clanking, rattling, hissing, whooshing bottling line presently came to halt simultaneously with the appearance of a blue-coated worker emerging into the sunlight to consult with Philippe about a problem. Philippe apologized at the interruption as we entered the building, explaining that, with the harvest less than six weeks away, the rush was on to make way for the new wine by bottling the previous year's, much of which had already been sold. That problem attended to, there was then the representative of the cork company, lurking with a salesman's grin just inside the door, to deal with, and I again withdrew discreetly.

I saw four workers posted at various points along the line, which snaked from one end of the 150-foot-long space to the other. The line started up with a clank and one worker began taking empty bottles and putting them on a moving conveyor, where they wended their way through a sterilizing station; then were filled, corked, and labeled; and, finally, were inspected and boxed by two more sets of human hands at the other end.

Having read that the whole appellation of Cahors, of which Philippe's Clos la Coutale is but one of more than 400 vineyards, exports in aggregate less than 10 percent of its wine yearly, I asked where all this wine was going. He gestured with his ringing cell phone to the thousands of sealed cases marked *Fragile*. "Some are going to Germany; some to Holland, Belgium, England, America, and even Japan. I do a huge business with the province of Québec; Ontario, too." I remarked that that was quite impressive, and must represent a significant marketing effort for him.

"Most winemakers here sell locally, or to tourists and those who have summer homes here, to restaurants and wineshops. Then there are those who sell to middlemen; the supermarket chains and many of the smaller ones belong to the cooperative, which makes a few wines from all the grapes of many, many growers. Me, I love my *métier*. No one tells me what to do. I earn a good living. I prefer to sell all my own wine myself, because I know it best. I made it! I export 60 percent. It's good business. I am a sixth-generation winemaker, but that doesn't mean I have to live and work like my father and his father. The world evolves, and you have to keep up with it."

Philippe pauses before every sentence, considering his words, and this was a long speech for him. He speaks softly, plainly, and slowly, in a French heavily freighted with the local accent. Together with his casual appearance, this might lead one to conclude that he was just another hired hand. In his late forties, owner of a vineyard stretching in every direction as far as we can see, more than 125 acres of vines in all, which produce about 400,000 bottles of wine annually and generate a turnover of more than a few million dollars in a good year, he is one of the most successful winemakers in the area. His operation is unique in many respects, from his approach to winemaking to a thoroughly modern marketing program that takes him all over the world.

Instead of offering a range of wines and vintages in the bottle, as do many of his neighbors, he makes only one wine in any quantity. (He makes a few thousand bottles of a dry white and the perhaps 10,000 of that special vintage Grand Coutale, neither for export.) He doesn't hold on to a percentage of each vintage to speculate down the road, as do some here. (In the summer of 2003, for example, there was no 1998 to be had, only a bit of the 1999, and less of the 2000, but lots of the just-released 2001.) His export wine—a lighter, less tannic and therefore more accessible wine—is very different in character from that of the majority of Lotois winemakers, some of whom will flat-out tell you that Philippe's Coutale is therefore "not a true Cahors," even though by law it is made of the same grape varieties grown on the same land.

Later, we walked the vines, the rows six feet tall, the leaves brilliantly green that summer of 2002, interspersed with bunches of ripening grapes half as long as your arm. Underfoot, the ground was pebbly, dry, and to all appearances very poor, except for the evidence of the eye, those swelling grapes. Philippe stopped at the end of a row, and we both stood quietly for a moment, taking in the view, an Escher-like perspective of geometric row-ends marching off in every direction at slight angles, distorting the eye's perception of what was straight. "The sun is good, no?" he asked, smiling broadly, raising his arms and holding out his hands, palms up, as if to gather in its fierce heat. "For the grapes, too, at this time of year." We shook hands, and he turned to go. His phone rang, and he hurried off to the bottling line, the phone pressed to his ear, busy, happy, a man rushing ahead confident of his way.

3

Man in the Middle
Jean-Luc Baldès at Clos Triguedina

"I gave up. I left." Jean-Luc Baldès shrugged his shoulders, his voice matter-of-fact. He shifted in his chair, his hazel eyes staring out at me intently from under his formidable dark eyebrows. "I abandoned Triguedina, and I went to work in Bordeaux for three years. My father couldn't seem to make up his mind what to do with the vineyard, and I couldn't wait forever." *And I was very upset!* An excruciatingly private person, Jean-Luc would never say this, would never speak ill of the dead (his father died quite suddenly in 1996), but the intensity of that gaze, the tense shoulders, and the bitter smile spoke volumes. This had obviously been a difficult moment, when it had seemed to him as if what he had striven for, the thing to which he had dedicated his entire adult working life, was going to slip out of his grasp at the last moment. As he spoke, his wine-stained fingers toyed with the spoon in his demitasse cup. His cell phone rang abruptly, bleating out an upbeat jazz riff that seemed out of place in the shadowy tasting room where we sat. He excused himself and answered it, walking across the room and through the connecting door to the offices beyond.

That brilliantly clear day in July of 2002, I had come to Clos Triguedina to see and to taste, but really more to peel away a few layers of glossy official history in the hope of learning more about who Jean-Luc was, how he had been formed. I knew from many previous visits that Jean-Luc was slow to relax, and that physical activity, absorbing his restless energy, seemed to encourage his words. First, we had walked through the vines, where he had shown me his latest experiment, young vines planted nearly on top of each other, twice the normal density per acre, the competition for resources naturally limiting the yield of grapes. Then we had tasted the various wines of the new vintage, too, as nothing puts a winemaker more at his ease than expounding on his passion. Finally, we had settled in with coffee, and he had begun to talk.

As Jean-Luc's telephone call seemed to be dragging on, I got up from my comfortable leather chair in one corner, and went out into the sunny courtyard. An old mutt stirred from his bit of shade and came to sniff my hand, and chickens clucked and scratched at the ground. A diminutive tractor just narrow enough to fit between the vine rows trundled by on the way to the parcels of vines that, except for a narrow band of grass, garden, and trees, surround the homestead on all sides.

Clos Triguedina is all the more beautiful for its simple adornments, its cut-from-one-piece charm all the more authentic because it does have the rough edges of a working farm, of a place where people live. With its large house and barns of weathered stone under ochre clay tile roofs, it is the essence of a traditional nineteenth-century Lotois farmstead but without the false notes of pretension or modernity (no tennis court or quaint stone pigeoncote of recent vintage) one finds so often in a land currently under invasion by a wave of restorers, preservationists, and second-homers with money. These people want to have their authenticity and their modern luxuries, too; and this desire can sometimes lead to jarring juxtapositions. Clos Triguedina, thoroughly imbued with the hurly-burly of the vineyard workday, is an island marked by a timelessness that I found immediately soothing.

The first time I had come here, I had followed the signs along the main road which climbed gently up from the river at Puy l'Evêque, one of the larger market towns along the Lot, through the endless vines, then turned off around the back of the property onto the gravel drive that passed between the wine barns on its way to an open court in front of the tasting room and offices. Being the nosy parker that I am, I then continued around the front, to the 1830 stone farmhouse just next door, where Jean-Luc's mother still lives, as seven generations of Baldès winemakers have lived before her.

There are beds and pots of flowers everywhere, trellised roses, neat hedges of box and yew bordering the far side of the drive, and tall trees—oaks and cedars—sheltering two sides of the house from the cold winds of winter. The buildings and vineyards sit on the top of another of the small hills that the river built long ago, 115 acres of vines on some of the highest and best land for grapes in the whole appellation, and with spectacular vistas over the miles of vineyards to the river some miles distant. (Jean-Luc also has twenty-seven acres at Floressas, up on the plateau on the southern side of the valley.) One can easily imagine some long-ago seigneur stepping from his carriage at dusk on a summer's night, pausing in the drive to survey his domain, his fields, smiling contentedly at the ordered vines thick with bunches of ripening grapes.

I stepped back inside the tasting room, my eyes taking a moment to adjust to the gloom. The large, uncluttered space, airy and cool with terra-cotta floor tiles underfoot and gleaming wood overhead, is precise and studied, and with a touch of both formality and austerity, much like Jean-Luc, its creator. It has, on first experience, the atmosphere of a library or a museum, each aspect of its design and décor, I would discern over repeated visits, symbolizing the various elements of the vision he has put into place, the investment he has made, in the preceding years.

There are the usual gold, silver, and bronze medals from competitions Triguedina's wines have won in France and around Europe, and to the left at the back a handsome bar of dark wood with stools, to one side a barrel into one of whose ends a zinc funnel has been set serving as a discreet receptacle for those who wish to spit after tasting. I had sat on those stools a few times as Jean-Luc filled our glasses from the other side, chatting happily about this wine or that.

Across from the bar is a plain wooden table with a collection of jars on top, each holding a specimen for the interested visitor to sniff; the collected aromas, Jean-Luc suggests, represent the range of so-called notes, the sometimes obvious, sometimes very subtle, tastes and smells one can find in his wines. These are divided into different realms: plant or herbaceous notes, florals, fresh and stewed fruit, and spices, among others. The jars hold truffles, star anise, caraway seeds, walnuts, prunes, cloves, loam, vanilla and coffee beans, and black pepper. On the wall above are charts illustrating and naming the different shades of color (called the *robe*) one can find in white and red wine. I looked over the chart for the reds, finding sometimes fanciful, sometimes evocative names running from amber through brick, claret, and cherry; then, for the darker reds, pigeon's eye and burnt topaz. Thus the visitor feels encouraged to explore, to ask questions; and right away he discovers Jean-Luc's mission to educate others and his passion to lead them, glass in hand, down the happy road to discovering *vin de Cahors*. Right away, the visitor discovers, too, if he has been tasting up and down the vineyards of the valley, that a few of the Triguedina wines depart, some quite dramatically, from the norm.

I had my nose deep in the coffee beans when Jean-Luc returned, and I hastened to replace the lid and take my seat. He apologized for the interruption and said, "So, where were we? Ah, yes, the difficult succession. Well, I left." He smiled a bit grimly, leaving me to imagine what that moment must have been like. We were both quiet for a bit, and then, because voids in conversation, like potholes, have to be filled lest they grow bigger, he began to speak, not whining in self-justification, but wanting me to understand what had led to that stark decision.

"I worked my first vinification with my father in 1975." In winemaking families—and I've spent time with a few of them by now—this is a rite of passage during which a father begins to pass down to his scion the wisdom of the inner temple, the wine barn. It is also an exciting time, when, as well as being caught up in the headlong nonstop rush to get the grapes in, the young man (usually) begins to have his voice heard, even as he learns the subtleties of working the wine as those crucial processes of fermentation and maceration occur, the latter the "stewing" process when juice, skins, and pulp all sit together, the alcohol from fermentation helping leach out the substances that will give color, tannin, and body to the finished wine.

"And then in 1976," Jean-Luc continued, "we built the new barn with stainless steel tanks, and Triguedina was the first in Cahors, in the whole appellation, to do that. Things were just taking off, and it was an exciting time to be making wine here. That was when I decided that I would invest myself in *le domaine*. My parents had always steered me toward the vineyard as a métier. I was the oldest son, and that is the tradition among winemakers, to transmit their knowledge to the next generation. But it wasn't as if I had a choice, either. My dream was to travel, and I had even found a place in a vineyard in Oregon. But my father encouraged me, gave me the chance to spread my wings, and I threw myself into it because that is my nature. Instead of traveling, I stayed ten years, always working with my father."

"With four children, my father couldn't quite make up his mind about who would take over." It must be trying to spend more than a decade at the side of a Papa who alternately warms and cools to the idea of turning the whole over to you. At the very least not comfortable, I thought.

"And, with a vineyard of this size," he continued, "you can't share control. You have to have one *chef*. I couldn't be running around asking the others every time I wanted to buy a new tractor or some oak barrels. When I left for Bordeaux in 1987, I think it made my father reflect on the future." Later, I would learn that, though Jean Luc's father hadn't withdrawn from running the vineyard until the onset of his illness, he had brought in Jean-Luc's younger brother and others to help run both the vineyard and winery. Things did not go well, however, and this apparently served as a wake-up call to Papa.

"They were not serious." *Ils n'étaient pas sérieux,* Jean-Luc told me laconically, using that simple but damning French phrase that implies a lack of commitment and know-how, and, in the extreme, a sort of slouching laziness.

Further complicating the situation, Jean-Luc and Philippe Bernède are cousins, their mothers being sisters, and so I imagine, nasty mind that I have, that one winemaking family's eyes may have been cast, however lightly, o'er the lands of another at some point. I would also learn that, at one time, Jean-Luc's father had wanted his son to marry Martine Jouffreau of Clos de Gamot, going so far as to approach her father with his proposal and pointing out that then the families, united, would have much of the best lands in the region. Martine's father, she told me, had told him gently but firmly, "The Jouffreau women choose for themselves!"

"It was good for me," Jean-Luc was saying about his years away. "I was off making discoveries and getting experience I wouldn't otherwise have gotten. I worked for a time in the commercial end of things, and in Bordeaux they're a bit ahead of us in marketing their wines. And I was working at Château La Cardonne, one of the Rothschild vineyards, so that was good. I was plunged into making other wines, too, in the Barsac region, the sweet wines at Château Coutet, very different and very challenging. One day my father came to see me. I had been gone three years by then, and that allowed him to reflect, to organize the succession. He asked me to come home, to run the vineyard.

"Today the family does not participate in the activity of the vineyard. They still own part of it, but I have the controlling share. We meet a few times a year; they ask questions. But I don't ask them about changes or even when I make a substantial investment of capital. They've distanced themselves from it, probably because they're not so invested in it. They're happy as long as all goes well." He gave me that small, bleak smile again, some pain behind those words.

When you ask Jean-Luc if things are going well, given the upheavals currently roiling the world of French wine, he'll respond that yes, they are, but with just enough hesitation and doubt in his voice to let you know that they could be going better. This is certainly partly the superstitious farmer speaking, one who never dares boast of his good fortune lest the Good Mother snatch back her bounty in a single hailstorm. It also reflects Jean-Luc's sometimes dark nature as well as the fact that he, unwilling to rest on his laurels like others in the region, has taken real risks, made significant investments and changes, and is now waiting to see the results.

The motto of Philippe Bernède at Clos la Coutale might roughly be, "Modernize, commercialize, and export." That of the Jouffreaus of Clos de Gamot might be recast as, "We will sell no wine before its time, and in a really bad year, sell none at all under our own label." Somewhere between the modern, matter-of-fact practicality of the former and the tradition-steeped severity of the latter, Jean-Luc takes up a lot of the middle ground. If his face seems more careworn than it should for a man in his late forties, it might be because that middle ground, pockmarked with hidden sinkholes and patches of quicksand, is perhaps not the most comfortable to occupy.

As I contemplated the man sitting in front of me, the fleeting image of a raptor, perhaps a hawk or an eagle, came into my head. He is tall, six feet on a thin frame, his carelessly cut brown hair generously sprinkled with gray. The eyes, of a fine hazel color, are deeply set under a heavy brow and hooded and ringed with fatigue and the fine lines of someone who spends much of his day under the sun. The nose and chin are angular, adding to his somewhat stern appearance. He speaks quickly and with intensity; the hands, that day deeply stained from the wine he had been bottling, are never still; his head swivels on a long neck to the office door on one side, or to the hall leading to the wine barn next door. Perhaps a worried hawk, with chicks to feed and prey thin on the ground?

Jean-Luc is quite simply a juggler with a lot of balls in the air. In a certain sense, he is less established in this place, having celebrated his first harvest from what had been his parents' vineyard little more than a decade ago, after those years of exile laboring in the vineyards of others in Burgundy and Bordeaux. "A difficult succession," he had said, a phrase that in French has all the resonance of "a little bomb" or "a small cancer." The twisted complexities of Napoleonic inheritance law, which often pit brother against sister and grown children against elderly parents, particularly when there is a family business or substantial property involved, are something we Americans find hard to understand.

In order for Jean-Luc to step in and to make the changes he envisioned for Clos Triguedina to prosper once again (and he envisioned—and subsequently made—a *lot* of changes), he had to first persuade his brothers and sisters and mother to accept a yearly share of the profits rather than the simple sale of the property and division of the resulting sum among them. And this would have been *after* draining the capital of the estate to pay off the inheritance tax and *after*, I surmise, he had gone to the bank to borrow enough money to buy a controlling interest from the other family members.

Though small farmers and small-business owners in America face the same situation when the reins must pass from generation to generation, in France inheritance taxes are much more burdensome and the rights of offspring to their parents' estate much more explicit. (In France, for example, you do not necessarily have the right to disinherit your direct descendants, who in turn have great power to tie up an estate for decades on the slightest of pretexts. Also, there is no tax exemption on the first $2 million, as in the United States.) As a result, in a land where the majority of working people are still employed in small family businesses, each generation faces a heartbreaking decision: whether or not to continue a family tradition that often goes back hundreds of years. Whereas in America prudent parents save money over the long term to educate their children and to pay for their own retirement, in France the first priority of the owners of a family business is often to put aside money to pay the inheritance taxes so their children can have the chance to continue in their footsteps.

Long before the succession was even an issue, Jean-Luc had come to a few realizations about his father's operation.

"I came home [from a university in Burgundy] just for the winemaking of the 1975 vintage. At that time, my father did not have a theoretical background in winemaking," Jean-Luc had told me earlier that day, as we tasted his wines. "He had the experience of his father and grandfather, and of his own years, but he did not necessarily have all the basics he should have. He had a good operation, a wine barn with cement tanks, everything was clean and well maintained. But it was pretty cool that fall, in 1975, and I remember thinking, 'Why doesn't he heat the wine barn?' The heat gets the fermentation going more quickly, and that helps extract the maximum from the grapes. I knew already that if you could heat the barn, the fermentation would be healthier, and he could even get a wine with a few more degrees of alcohol."

About the worst thing that can happen to a winemaker during vinification is a "stuck" fermentation, when, usually because the ambient temperature is too low or the grapes are too high in sugar, the activity of the yeast in changing sugar to alcohol falls off or even refuses altogether to start. The longer the grapes and their juice sit without fermenting, the more likely it is that unwanted microbes will contaminate the wine. Also, sufficient alcohol is very important to a finished wine: to give it body, to help it age, and because a minimum percentage is required by law. The initial fermentation is the only opportunity the winemaker has to realize the potential of the grapes in this respect.

Jean-Luc also had, of course, his own ideas for wines he wanted to make. Most of the larger Cahors vineyards produce three or four different wines. There is always a bar brand, so to speak, a reasonably priced, accessible red made using the grape varieties permitted by the appellation—malbec, merlot, and tannat, the issue of grapes from the vineyard's second-best vines. There is then the prestige brand, which is always distinguished in some way to justify the higher price. Usually it is 100 percent malbec, the winemaker restricting himself to that grape being the equivalent of the sculptor working in marble rather than clay and with the same logic: if a winemaker can master this difficult grape and express all its subtleties in a finished wine, then he is a true artist and worthy of recognition. Further, the wine may be made from the oldest of the vineyard's vines on the best land, the grapes may have been hand-harvested and selected, and the resulting wine may perhaps then be aged in small barrels of new oak.

Truly audacious winemakers then offer, in the best years, a super-premium wine called a *cuvée prestige* or a *grande cuvée* or even a *grande cuvée prestige*, a wine so special that it commands a hefty premium over the vineyard's usual offerings. (Winemakers call such wines "GCs.") This wine will have been treated like a pasha, the grapes handpicked from vines in their golden age and treated accordingly, selected bunches cut in July to intensify the juice in those left to ripen, and that ripening enhanced by the labor-intensive removal of the leaves that shade them. These days, the latest rage is that they may even have been *fermented* in oak barrels, a risky and expensive proposition in itself, then gently nursed through the winter before a two-year finishing school in small, new oak barrels and a careful blending to form a final, superlative bottle that usually requires a few years more in a cool dark place before it is truly at its peak.

(A GC is not to be confused with a *grand cru,* by the way. The term *grand cru* on a bottle implies that the wine comes from grapes grown on lands classed by the National Institute of Appellations of Origin, the French national wine authority, as being at a certain high level of quality in the appellation. Such classifications have not been done in many appellations, and the Cahors winemaking world is at present convulsed with controversy over the plan to impose just such a classification there. Exactly why this is so controversial is explored in chapter 9.)

In addition to this Rolls-Royce of wines, many winemakers then complete their lines with the fruit of their playtime—rosés and whites made in small quantities because, quite simply, it amuses them to turn their hand to something different.

Philippe Bernède, who is not much interested in either radical experimentation or changing a formula already quite successful, makes but two wines, in some years three: his very drinkable Clos la Coutale, a white marketed locally; and Le Grand Coutale, a *grande cuvée* available in good years and then only in very small quantities at three times the price. Yves and Martine at their three vineyards offer their gold standard 100 percent malbec Clos de Gamot as well as the same wine of grapes from vines planted in 1895, their "Old Vines" or *Vieilles Vignes*. At their second vineyard, Château de Cayrou, they produce a less expensive, softer alternative to Gamot, and one that is drinkable far earlier, from a blend of the three grape varieties. (All Cahors must have at least 70 percent malbec. To make a softer, easier wine, some makers then use as much as 25 percent merlot, including a minimal amount of the tannat.) The first wine of Clos St. Jean, their four-acre experimental hillside vineyard in the old style, the 1997 vintage, they would sell only in 2004, and that in a run perhaps of as few as 1,500 bottles. They also produce small quantities of rosé and white.

Philippe produces at most three wines in one vineyard; Yves and Martine six wines from three vineyards; and Jean-Luc—well, Jean-Luc produces, from his two properties (he owns a further thirty-four acres, some contiguous to but not part of Triguedina, and those acres up in

Floressas on the high plateau), *eight* wines, not including a small line sold just to supermarkets. It seems as if, starting in 1990, he began to innovate and couldn't stop himself. After introducing changes to improve the culture of the vines and thus of the grapes they yielded, he turned to refining his father's most prestigious offering, the Prince Probus, which was first released in 1976. Their second wine, called simply Clos Triguedina, benefited not only from the increasing quality of the grapes but from oak aging as well. "Triguedina is the classic of our *domaine*," Jean-Luc described it. "It's made of the traditional grapes of the appellation: malbec, merlot, and a tiny bit of tannat. It's a wine that is made for you to drink and a wine made so that you can cellar it. Even when the wine is young, your mouth won't be attacked by tannins that are too sharp or too dry. If you do cellar it, it ages well, and you'll find in its later years other, different flavors and aromas, an evolution in the good direction."

Domaine Labrande and Balmont de Cahors are the Triguedina house brands, vinified to drink at a year or two of age, thus lighter, with more fruit but perhaps more assertive tannins. For the other five wines of Triguedina, Jean-Luc had his own ideas, and very different indeed several of them turned out to be from the rosé and dry whites, usually of some blend of chardonnay and sémillon, that other Cahors winemakers have produced recently.

This innovation has its root in Jean-Luc's desire, as he put it, to make *un grand vin de Cahors,* a "great wine" that can hold its own over time with the Bordeaux and Burgundies.

"When I came [home] in 1990, I thought it would be better to make a more authentic Probus, from 100 percent auxerrois [his father blended merlot with the tannic auxerrois to soften it], but all while having a wine that was well balanced, softer, in a way. I would say, before, I knew how to make good wine, all the technical end of things, but I didn't know how to make a great wine. They were good, but concentrated, not balanced, perhaps too tannic or with too strong tannins. I knew what direction I had to go in and how to do it, but I also got advice from a consultant in Bordeaux. Also 1990 was a very good year to launch this change, with a small harvest but grapes of an excellent ripeness. The vinification I did very carefully; the barrel-aging I had begun to master, too; and after a judicious assemblage, it turned out to be a very good wine. It won a gold medal at VinExpo, in fact." He told me this with a genuine smile and a glance across the room to where the framed certificate held pride of place on the wall. VinExpo is held in April, its location alternating between Bordeaux and a foreign city every other year; it is the largest, most prestigious wine trade show in the world.

"That really motivated me," he continued, "because it was the proof that I could do it, that we could make *un grand vin* here. That was the Probus, which has become our marquee wine, our best. Not that it is a *micro-cuvée,* but that it shows off our best vines. It represents a reasonable number of bottles, around fifty thousand, not a thousand or fifteen hundred. It's no *cuvée de garage,*" he finished, almost sneering at this last phrase.

A what? I asked. "In Bordeaux," he explained, "these *micro-cuvées* or *cuvées de garage* are all the rage, one guy fermenting and aging with a couple of barrels in his garage, making a super-exclusive wine from the free-run juice of the best bought grapes." This disdain for those who dally in winemaking, buying grapes, barrels, and the expertise of an enologist to make a single wine in very small quantities, was something I had run across before. Philippe and Yves had both told me, in different ways, that anyone could just take the best, skimming the cream so to speak, and make of it a fantastic wine. Most winemakers don't have the luxury of letting 90 percent of their harvest rot; to make money they must make the best wines from *all* their grapes. And they certainly don't have the choice to make no wine in a year of appalling weather and poor-quality grapes.

"Probus is thus the best of the best here," Jean-Luc was saying, "and we won't be out there with higher offerings. You're not going to see a super-Probus. It's no *grande cuvée* made from three barrels."

When Jean-Luc took a look around his father's vineyard in the late 1980s, he was smart enough to see that he would need not only to improve the offerings but to broaden his range of products in future years to attract a wider audience. He reached back into the not-so-distant past for inspiration, taking two old ideas and turning them into "concept" wines. (The world's best-known concept wine is *Beaujolais nouveau*, a wonder of French marketing in that entire countries now compete to see who can be the first each November to drink what has always seemed to me to be an expensive acidic, raw, young wine. Two American equivalents, though they are more brands of one producer than a particular kind of wine made by many producers in a single region, would be, at one end of the market, Robert Mondavi's Opus One, and at the other, Two Buck Chuck. The former currently retails in limited quantities for about $100 a bottle; the latter, drinkable whites and reds from the Charles Shaw winery, retails at $2 a bottle in California. The wine goes for $3 a bottle elsewhere, but Three Buck Chuck doesn't quite have the same ring to it.)

Jean-Luc began with a strength and a weakness. His father's premier wines, Prince Probus and Clos Triguedina, products of his best vines, have long been recognized as among the premier expressions of the winemaker's art in Cahors. How to distinguish the more copious amounts of very good wine that came from all his other vines? At the same time, Jean-Luc's earlier experiences had been in the elaboration not just of red wines but also of rosé and white wines, and particularly the sweet white dessert wines called *vins moelleux*. As sons are wont to do, he desired to make his own mark, his own wines, which is what he has, subsequently, done.

Which brings us to the windows. One of the reasons the tasting room is kept dim, I suspect, is to focus the eye on the pair of three- by five-foot stained-glass windows set into the wall at the back of the room, and on the gloriously-hued light that pours through them at certain times of day, spilling itself onto the floor in gaudy pools. On a previous visit, I had watched his daughter, Juliette, then three years old and in a stroller parked at that end of the room, putting her hands into the light, closing her fingers as if to catch its colors in her tiny fist, chortling in delight.

While amusing small children is well and good, the true purpose of each window is to tell a story, a story about a wine. Every salesman knows that people buy the story as often as they buy the product, and

Jean-Luc is, after all, only following in his father's footsteps, as the names Prince Probus and Triguedina both seek to attach the power of history and legend to the mystique of the wines bearing those names. Prince Probus was a Roman emperor who, in A.D. 280, overturned Emperor Domitian's 200-year-old ban on planting vines in the region. The peasants, showing what seems to be a universal preference for drink over food, had favored vines over wheat to such an extent that periodic famines raged, precipitating the ban. The name of the second Baldès wine, Clos Triguedina, invokes the thousand-year-old tradition of the pilgrimage to Saint James of Compostela, the property having been one, apparently much anticipated, stop on the long road from France over the Pyrenees to Spain. *Me trigo de dina,* in the local Occitan dialect, means "I can't wait for dinner!"

The window on the left is an allegorical depiction of a medieval tableau: Breughel-like figures are pouring deep purple wine into a cauldron over a fire whose flames, bright yellow and orange, lick at its black sides. The scene is set out in the vines as a seigneur (who looks a bit like Jesus, actually, albeit with a falcon perched on his robed arm) looks on haughtily. The allegory here refers to Jean-Luc's first concept wine. It draws on the thirteenth-century reputation of Cahors among the English, who came to call it the "black wine." In times when most barreled wines might begin a precipitous descent into vinegar after but a year, Cahors was known to last, and to last with good color and "punch." Some of this wine, which had to endure a rough sea voyage (just about the worst thing you can do to a new wine is to agitate it violently for weeks), was prepared in a special way. A portion of the grape juice was boiled down in cauldrons and then added back to the fermenting wine. The result was a kind of fortified wine, the reduction of liquid in proportion to sugar and tannin producing a darker and more powerful brew. Today, Jean-Luc makes the New Black Wine, as he has named it (in English on the label, too) in a more refined fashion, very slightly drying a small portion of the grapes in an oven before they go into the fermenting tank, lending the wine both more body and hints in the nose and mouth of red and black fruits and stewed plums.

As well, his father had acquired vineyards just contiguous to but not officially part of Triguedina. They produced a lot of wine, but not wine that could be sold under the Triguedina name. How do you turn such wines into something unique and valuable in their own right—especially when the land yields reasonably good wines but not ones that will ever be *grands vins*?

The second stained-glass window illustrates Jean-Luc's clever solution to this problem. By the milky light of a distant moon, a Harlequin figure kneels in the vines, one hand placing a bunch of grapes in the traditional square wooden harvest basket. She looks over her shoulder furtively as, in the background, the château towers loom menacingly.

Over the centuries the peasants of rural France, like most agricultural societies in which the landed gentry enjoyed privileges allowing them to plunder their serfs at every opportunity, developed myriad ways to screw the seigneur. One of them was the poetically named *vin de lune,* the wine of the moon. While gentler souls might imagine that the wine made of grapes harvested by moonlight possessed romantic or magical qualities, this allegorical interpretation of the phrase has little to do with reality. The peasants harvested the grapes by moonlight because they were stealing them before the next day's harvest, when they would have to turn over a large measure to the lord. And, if the wine they made on the sly was good, well, which grapes would you steal if you knew every acre intimately and could fit only so many into your (capacious) sack?

Though it was Jean-Luc's father who first made a white Vin de Lune, Jean-Luc saw the real potential and how to exploit it. He remade the Vin de Lune line to include rosé, red, white, and sweet white, all made in limited quantities and sold in a much wider range of venues than his other Cahors wines. (He also changed all the white wine grapes, viognier and chardonnay for the dry and chenin blanc for the sweet, because his father's white never had been very good.) Because they do not meet the Appellation Contrôlée standards, being of the wrong color or grape, he sells them as Vins de Pays du Comté Tolosan, a rather romantic name for nonappellation wines whose origins are in this geographical region. Made from grapes harvested in the cool of the early morning, they are meant to re-create the Wines of the Moon of yesteryear, if perhaps more in spirit than anything else.

Harvesting at night or in the early morning does have a vinicultural rationale, by the way. Even the minute amounts of water that
condense on the grapes as morning dew can dilute the sugar, and thus
the resulting alcohol, of a wine. The Springs, an English couple who
have a small property, Domaine du Garinet, in Le Boulvé and who
make award-winning dry whites, told me that before harvest, they go
out and gently shake the wires to which the vines cling, ridding the
bunches of dew before the harvester passes.

"The full sun of the afternoon," Jean-Luc pointed out, "can also
begin to oxidize the juice inside the grapes. Harvesting in the cool of
the morning means the grapes are cool, and then in the tank you'll get
more fruit, more freshness in the wine."

If eight wines seem a lot for one man to be responsible for, in Jean-
Luc's mind at least there is faultless logic at work.

"The place of each wine in our line is clear," he told me. "We offer
the Balmont, which is more commercial in style, easy to drink, but also
a typical Cahors. There's the classic Triguedina, and then the Probus.
So there's the whole range. Then, on the side, we offer some wines that
are different, more tied to history in a way. The New Black Wine, it is a
wine which has notes of dried fruit, cooked fruit, it's got more body,
and thus it lends itself to a different style of cooking. [You could drink
it] with stews and duck *confit,* with *les salées* [dishes made with salted or
smoked meats like ham, bacon, charcuterie, or aged sausage]. In that
sense, it's not a super-Probus, or a super-Triguedina. It's a wine apart.
It's a wine associated with the history of Cahors, with the history of
wine here. It has a clientele who appreciate the history, and the wine—
Belgians, English, French traveling in the region, wineshops around
the country, all sorts of people. People come to taste, they learn the
history, they like it or they don't, they buy it or not.

"The Wines of the Moon, those are because it is more interesting for
me [than just making red], but also there is a commercial rationale. It's a
good thing for people to arrive here at our vineyard in the Lot to find a
whole range of wines of quality—whites, rosés, and sweet dessert wines
too. It's a bit of a surprise, a bit amusing for them. It's true that AOC
Cahors is never white, so to come and find a white wine, a truly good

white wine, it can seduce them. I mean, why not, if the *terroir* lends itself to some white wine grapes, which it does, why not make a good white wine here? Passersby respond to it, and restaurateurs like to have local dry whites, but also rosés, on their wine lists. And for me, if I didn't like to make it, I wouldn't. It's different. I use what I learned in Bordeaux, where I worked for a château that made *premier cru classé* Sauternes; that experience does leave its mark. And that experience is *my* experience. Sure, my father used to make a sweet white, but it was, shall we say, not a wine people went out of their way to seek out!"

Jean-Luc's whites, both dry and sweet, are in fact so popular, particularly at local restaurants, that they are most often unavailable even a few months after their release in the late spring each year.

Although Jean-Luc does not and cannot do all the work himself, I have often arrived at the wine barn, in all seasons but particularly in the fall, to find him laboring alone, or with one other worker. He does have six people in the vines under a vineyard manager, and he did recently hire a cellarmaster. Still, there is just too much to do in his very complicated operation making and aging so many wines. The actual elaboration of the wines is solely his responsibility, as is every decision concerning the planting and culture of the vines.

While Jean-Luc's efforts may yet make him a more handsome, more stable living, today he is struggling, and largely struggling alone. The Jouffreau-Hermann family has tradition and time behind it (and a few hundred thousand bottles of old vintages put by), as well as a son, Franck, about to graduate from an agricultural engineering institute and then join the family business. Philippe Bernède, with a well-established export business, has already placed himself above the fray of Cahors winemakers all trying to sell to the same domestic audience of locals and tourists.

Jean-Luc, one senses, has taken some risks, does not have much to fall back on, and is fiercely independent into the bargain. He has resigned from the two regional marketing trade groups: from one because he perceived that he was treated as the country cousin; from the other because it sought a certain broad uniformity in the members' wines, anathema to any dedicated winemaker. He is going it alone and continues to look ahead to the next challenge: the coming of the *grand cru* classification that, if and when it happens, will put those who have the best acres in the position to sell their wines at a significant premium over their neighbors not similarly blessed. What is Jean-Luc doing?

"I've just replanted three hectares [7.5 acres] at a density of 7,500 vines the hectare, which is an enormous number of vines, and far more than people here in the appellation usually plant. But I'm happy because that is what you have to do if you want to have a *grand cru*. It takes a huge amount of rigor and attention, and many people here just aren't ready, in my opinion. You don't get to a *grand cru* by taking the easy road. On the contrary, you have to seek out the difficult, and it *is* hard. I made the decision in the 1990s, and here we are ten years later and I'm still not there yet. You don't make a decision one day and realize it the next. Vines are so slow. I began with the idea that perhaps we would get there in ten, fifteen, maybe even twenty years. It's very slow, so slow, the vine.

"It took two or three years just to find the land, and then it was expensive! Then you look for the right variety of rootstock, and then the right varietal. You have to find the right density; you plant, fertilize, and you pay all the time. The vine has to put down roots; it grows slowly at first; and you wait, one year, two years, three years, four years, always paying. It starts to produce, but hey, it's not great wine either! It's a *bon vin,* and you have to wait really until the vine is ten years old. So, at ten years, and if you have a good year with the weather and the harvest, you might begin to make a great wine—but even then you won't be selling that *grand vin* for another two or three years, because that's how long it takes to make, to age in the barrel. I don't even calculate how much it costs to bring a vine to maturity. It would drive me crazy. If I did, and I found out that I was earning the minimum wage, I'm not sure I'd be able to go on!"

4

A Short History of
Vin de Cahors

A young Frenchman, even one from the southwest and with some knowledge of wine, might look at the history of Cahors wine and see it extending back no farther, really, than 1971, when the law elevating *vin de Cahors* to an *appellation contrôlée* was passed with considerable arm-twisting by a native son, Georges Pompidou, who was then president. The young man's father might correct him, pointing out that actually Cahors as we know it came into being after the "great freeze" of 1956, when inferior hybrid vines were ripped out and the grapes we think of today—the tannat, the merlot, and particularly the malbec—were replanted. *His* father would shake his head and say: You're both far too young to know what you're talking about, for it was only after phylloxera, back around 1870, when almost every single vine sickened, died, and was uprooted and burned, that the vineyards as we know them came into being.

At that, the historian in the room would shake his or her head vehemently; light up the first of a series of Gauloises; refill their glasses with the meaty, almost black Cahors they were drinking; and tell them all to settle in for a long tale. . . .

The First Thousand Years of Cahors

When people talk of the wine made in this region of southwest France, they don't say "Lot River valley wine" or "wine of the Lot" or "wine of the uplands," referring to the dominant geographical landmarks; or even "Quercy wine," making use of the historical name of the region. Rather, the French say, simply, *vin de Cahors,* "the wine of Cahors," associating this particular and unique red wine with the city established more than 2,000 years ago in an oxbow of the Lot River by a Celtic people, the Cadurcians, who gave it their name. The written history of the area doesn't begin until the arrival of the Romans under Julius Caesar, around 50 B.C. They brought with them all the trappings of a more advanced civilization—their roads, aqueducts, monuments, amphitheaters, bridges, and temples—ruins of which one can find throughout the Lot. More important, they brought a thirst for wine.

Although the dates are imprecise, historians assume that the slaves accompanying Caesar's Roman legions, which overran the southwest toward the end of a campaign to subdue all of what was then called Gaul, brought with them winemaking expertise gained elsewhere in the empire. This led in the next centuries to the rapid development of a local wine industry in and around Cahors. Pliny the Elder, writing in the first century after Christ, records vines growing around Narbonne, in Languedoc-Roussillon—what is generally recognized as France's first, and oldest, wine-growing region. "Moderation in all things" being apparently more a Greek ideal than a French (or Roman) one, it wasn't even 200 years before wine and the vine began to cause political and social problems.

The two Roman emperors whose names still resound today in the history of French wine are Domitian and Probus, one reviled and the other celebrated. Emperor Domitian, after a period of famine and grain shortages which had touched even Rome, ordered in A.D. 92 that the vines of the provinces be uprooted, including those around Cahors, or Quercy, "Little Oak," as the Romans called the region after the stubby oak trees growing there. To the provincials, wine was not only profitable as a durable local trade good but also something safe to drink in a time when water was as likely to make you sick as to slake your thirst. Of course, wine also made you feel good. Several early chroniclers have noted the prodigious thirst for wine the Gauls quickly developed on short acquaintance with it. For all these reasons, particularly the last one, land once planted in cereal crops providing a staple food in bread was given over to vines, reducing the harvest whose surplus had once been exported to feed the Romans.

Domitian's decree was hugely unpopular and largely ignored, particularly the farther one ventured away from Rome. "Go ahead and rip out all our vines!" went a Roman ditty of the time. "We'll still have enough wine to drink to your demise!" After having poisoned his brother, Titus, and usurped Titus's throne, Domitian himself was apparently murdered, stabbed by his own wife and her minions. There is a moral here somewhere, but I'm not sure it has much to do with wine.

Near the end of the third century after Christ, Emperor Probus gave back to the legions—who had already occupied much of western Europe for several hundred years—the right to plant vines; and vines have been cultivated, and wine has been made of their grapes, continuously to our time. The Baldès' vineyard, Clos Triguedina, honors Probus to this day: their best oak-aged wine, of grapes from the oldest vines on the choicest parcels, has been called Le Prince Probus for almost fifty years.

From Eleanor of Aquitaine to Louis XVI

The Quercynois, as the inhabitants of the region came to be called, would become all too familiar, throughout the Middle Ages and into the modern era, with the unhappy experience of being ruled by others from afar and consequently suffering the effects of political and economic decisions having little or nothing to do with them and certainly not in their interests—an experience that began with the Romans. Today, the winemakers of Cahors are also suffering directly and indirectly at the hands of their oldest competitors, the winemakers of Bordeaux, who, in turn, owe the precedence of their wine and their region to two accidents, one historical and one geographic.

During the many centuries in which the absence of road and rail meant shipping any trade good by river barge and ship, those who controlled the rivers, and ultimately the coastal ports to which they flowed, controlled commerce. If you look at a map of France, you will see that all the rivers of southwestern France—the Dordogne, Lot, Garonne, and Tarn and their minor tributaries—feed eventually into the Gironde estuary at Bordeaux, which leads to the Atlantic and shipping routes to England, Holland, and the then very important markets of Scandinavia and Russia, all significant consumers of one vastly profitable export of the regions of the southwest, wine. The other components of this trade, what these ships carried to France, were English cloth, smoked or salted fish, and tin, and Baltic wheat to feed the Bordelais, the inhabitants of Bordeaux, whose vineyards had largely supplanted cereals.

And so the Bordelais, for about 600 years from about the middle of the twelfth century through the French Revolution in 1789, controlled this crucial choke point through which all goods had to pass. With that control came the ability to manipulate trade both through the levy of punitive export taxes and the regulation of rights to ship and warehouse at the port, to name just the two most important ways among many by which Bordeaux enriched itself, becoming the region's most important trading city.

Of course, France as we know it did not exist in the Middle Ages, nor did England. The great complicating factor, the historical accident, was the marriage of Eleanor of Aquitaine to Henry II, in 1152, after she had divorced her French husband, Louis VII. To Henry's titles—he was already duke of Normandy and count of Anjou, Maine, and Touraine—Eleanor added her own, bringing to the British crown as part of her dowry all of Gascony, which extended in a narrow strip along the Atlantic coast from around Bordeaux south to Bayonne and what is today nearly the Spanish border; and a huge scattering of lands bordering Gascony collectively known as Aquitaine (today, most of southwest France) and Guyenne, more to the north, with important cities like La Rochelle, on the Atlantic coast, and Poitiers, Eleanor's home capital. With this marriage, and on Henry's accession to the throne two years later, the English ruled more French territory than the king of France, who directly controlled little more than the northern provinces and Flanders.

Aquitaine, which included the regions between the Dordogne and Lot rivers then known as Périgord, Agenais, and Quercy, was an amorphous, ill-defined duchy whose ever-shifting borders—particularly on the northeastern frontiers with the fiercely independent Burgundians—and fickle rulers would feed acquisitive appetites, both French and English, for the next 500 years. The members of the local nobility found themselves in the awkward position of being newly minted English subjects, but with a far stronger, traditional fealty to the French crown. As long as they were left alone—that is, in times of relative peace—these rather remote regions were stable, even prosperous. Enter a hungry army of either stripe, however, and one saw much changing of alliances and shifting of sides depending on who was offering the best terms.

To begin to understand this period, it is wise to remember that the English royal family was as much French as it was English. Henry II spoke English only poorly; and his son, the crusading Richard the Lion-Hearted, spoke none at all. Richard spoke French and Occitan, the low Latin lingua franca of the southwest. The British court didn't just speak French; it drank French—and, particularly after the loss of the more northerly port of La Rochelle early in the thirteenth century, it drank with a marked preference for wines from the southwest provinces that were, after all, nominally English territories, wines over time shipped increasingly through Bordeaux. Much later its allegiance would shift once again, after the loss of Bordeaux, to port and sherry from Portugal and Spain.

During the thirteenth and fourteenth centuries, Quercy came into its own, particularly the Lot River valley dominated at its eastern end by the fortified cathedral city of Cahors, home to a series of influential bishops; a leading medieval university; and the rich trading and noble families, some from as far away as Venice, who had been steadily drawn to the region because of its potential. One monument to its prominence, begun in 1308, is the Pont Valentré, a magnificent stone bridge whose six arches and three towers still rise over the Lot River on the city's eastern edge. Designated a World Heritage Site by UNESCO, it stands as a rare, intact testament to the apogee of medieval defensive architecture, massively intimidating until you are actually crossing it on foot, when you down in a convivial setting and lift a glass, perhaps accompanied by food, they needed a place to do that, too. Medieval records show that in villages of as few as 300 souls, there might have been as many as six *cabarets, estaminets,* or *tavernes*—small bars catering to the local population. The locals were not drinking the export wine, the best and most expensive, but usually the less alcoholic second-quality wine sometimes called *clairette* or, the bottom of the barrel, *piquette:* thin, sour, wine for the poorest of purses, some of it made by adding sugar to the leavings and leftovers of the already pressed skins and heating the mixture until it refermented.

The basic unit of civilization was the village, and villages survived where there were the resources to support them, for initially self-sufficiency was an absolute requirement. As your boat drifted beyond the town, you would have noticed a particular pattern to the agriculture. The bottomlands, regularly flooded and so naturally enriched by deposits of effluvium, would have been planted in market garden crops or cereals, with orchards of fruit and nut trees on the gentlest slopes. The headlands rise quite abruptly in places; some of the craggy limestone *causses,* as they are called, are 700 feet above the river. Here, up top, many of the trees, even in 1300, would have long ago given way to vast pastures for sheep, cows, and goats, and more fields, usually with poor soil and so used for grains like oats and barley.

Between river and *causse,* on rising slopes too dry, too vertiginous, too lacking in topsoil—this was where the best vines were planted, often in narrow, terraced ribbons kept from plunging down the hill by low dry-stone walls of the plentiful local limestone. Even then, under the influence of erosion and gravity, the precious topsoil would have to be periodically carried up in reed baskets from the bottom of the hill.

This picture of prosperity endured until the outbreak of the Hundred Years' War in 1337, the beginning of more than a century of disruption during which France would lose almost half its population even as it more than doubled the territory under direct rule of the French crown. When Charles VII defeated the English at Castillon in 1453, England lost Bordeaux and the southwest provinces once and for all. It had lost Burgundy, its strongest outpost, twenty years earlier, and the era of English dominance on French territory was waning.

realize that two oxcarts would have had trouble passing each other on its narrow roadway.

Though political stability was relative, and was ruptured finally by the beginning of the Hundred Years' War in 1337, it was in the interests of all to keep the river trade open, and hence accommodations and arrangements were generally made even in times of upheaval elsewhere. By the early fourteenth century, the English kings were already deriving significant tax revenues paid both by the exporting Bordelais shippers and by the English and Gascon merchant cartels that imported them into London, where the majority of all wine was landed. Although the exact numbers varied hugely from year to year owing to factors like war, weather, and plague, even a century earlier it had not been unusual for the equivalent of 20 million bottles of wine to leave Bordeaux. One quarter of this was destined for consumption in England, usually by the court and the nobility, as wine was very expensive. The tax rate on wines coming down the rivers from the so-called high country, which included those from the vineyards of Cahors, Bergerac, Frontonnais, and Agenais, was always higher than what the English required of the Bordelais, a reward for their loyalty and a recognition of their powerful geographic position.

One of the most visible accommodations was the English *bastide* or fortified market town, an attempt by the crown to begin to exert its authority in isolated regions without the expense or commitment of an outright occupation. There, the nobles' first loyalty was usually to the French king, directly or indirectly through old, tangled commitments dating from before the Magna Carta. The *bastides*—there are dozens of them throughout the valleys between the Lot and Dordogne rivers—were primarily defensive outposts, many fortified with high, thick encircling walls which have since disappeared. One *bastide* in something like its original condition is Monpazier, about thirty miles northeast of Cahors in the Dordogne, authentic if a little cheesy in its touristy quaintness. Though they served as staging points in times of military action, their presence, their protection, drew peasant farmers and artisans whose surplus goods eventually found their way down the valleys to the rivers, where they were shipped out to larger market towns.

Wine was only part of a significant trade in all sorts of products from the southwest, whose economy was largely agricultural, as were its exports. This had been so for some time: when the divorce of Louis VII from Eleanor was decreed, sharp tongues quipped that while the king may have relieved himself of a troublesome wife, he had also relieved France of its storehouse. The Lot River valley between Fumel at its far eastern end and Cahors sprouted entire villages of warehouses, generally for wine. Today, if you walk through downtown Castelfranc, ten miles west of Cahors and built on the river's edge, you can still see that many of the imposingly solid stone houses were once entrepôts, distinguished by low archways at street level leading to cool cellars where barrels, filled with wine that had come by cart down out of the hills, were stored awaiting shipment downstream by barge. Another Lot village, Albas, has a spring wine festival whose most popular attraction is a long, bibulous walk up its main street, from river to central square. The price of entry is the purchase of a small wineglass at riverside, and all along the medieval street, the steeply rising stone houses open the massive wooden doors of their cellars, where, inside, any one of two dozen local wineries pours samples as musical groups of every description entertain the ever-changing crowd.

One of the few moments of my life when I have been tempted to believe in time travel came at this festival, listening to an a cappella trio, burly men in period costume weaving folk melodies in Occitan, the vaguely Latinate words flickering maddeningly just beyond my comprehension. Stubby glasses of almost black Cahors in their hands, they swayed to a troubadour's love song, their voices echoing in the vast *cave* with its slit windows high up, overlooking the Lot River far below. Peering through the gloom of the fading day, surrounded by their glorious sound, I had no difficulty at all seeing the *cave* filled with wine barrels, the riverbank thick with barges, the cobbled streets thronging with oxcarts.

All along the river, the layout and architecture of other villages— such as Luzech, Prayssac, Parnac, Puy l'Evêque, and Douelle—speak of a past largely tied to the river trade, as do the barge paths dug out of sometimes sheer limestone walls that form the riverbank in some places and on which muleteers once led their teams from village to village pulling flat-bottomed boats loaded with goods.

During this era, if you floated down the Lot River from Cahors, following the river's lazy meanders through the deep valleys and past numerous villages big and small, you would probably glimpse scenes of a rough but thriving agrarian and trade economy. By the middle of the twelfth century, there would already have been differences between river towns and the poorer villages tucked away in the surrounding hills. As early as 1219 the river way had been managed under an agreement between the bishop of Cahors and the local crown representative, and so it quickly became the major avenue for products—wool, wine, saffron, and iron among them—flowing out of the whole interior east and north to the major market city of Bordeaux. Around 1305, the peak before the Hundred Years' War, Bordeaux would ship the equivalent of more than 90 million bottles of wine abroad, approximately a third of that from Cahors and the southwest, and nearly half of it for consumption in England. Thirty million bottles was, by the way, approximately the amount of wine produced by all of Cahors in 1999, which should give some idea of how economically important this trade was 700 years ago.

A wine economy is labor-intensive. Not only does it require large families to do the vineyard work; it necessitates a whole series of allied trades. The only available movable container was the barrel, requiring a gifted barrel maker, who in turn needed good wood, necessitating a forester to grow and fell it and a sawyer to cut it, and strong iron hoops from the local blacksmith to bind the staves. Wine is heavy to transport, requiring oxen and oxcarts, wheelwrights and teamsters, and another whole layer of bargemen and their craft (which have to be built and maintained) to get it to its destination. All along the route, the *gabarriers,* the bargemen, and their animals, have to be housed and fed at night and during floods and bad weather.

The place-name "Gamot," from which Yves and Martine's Clos de Gamot takes its name, was originally one such bargemen's halt, and one that endured up into the recent past, when Martine's great-great-grandmother contributed to the family coffers by preparing meals for the hungry *gabarriers* who had come to tie up for the night right at the edge of the family's vines.

And when the locals wanted, at the end of their day of labor, to sit

Vineyards usually suffer in wartime, and the vineyards of *vin de Cahors* were no exception. They suffer in general because, unlike a burned-over field of barley or wheat that can be plowed, replanted, and yield a harvest the very next season, a vine requires ten years before it gives good grapes. Propagating new vines from cuttings also assumes long periods of stability, as does the attentive care young vines need in their first years. Politically, uprooting vines is an effective and very visible way to punish a lord or church authority (the churches often had extensive vineyards) for misplaced loyalties.

The unique situation of the vines in Cahors—the best up on the hillsides—also made them more vulnerable. Vines have to be cared for—fertilized, trained, pruned—to produce; and hillside vines, where animals cannot be used, require even more manpower, particularly to keep the terraces in good order. Men absent at war or casualties of the frequent conflicts large and small, rising brigandry along road and river, export markets cut off by rival armies, ports closed by blockade, the destruction and pillaging of villages and towns, famine, disease—all these sent Cahors wine into a steep decline from which it was never to recover. The fourteenth century truly was its apogee.

The Hundred Years' War, though it may have provided the most obvious reasons for the decline of Cahors' supremacy and popularity as a wine, is but one cause among many. Bordeaux's power as a trading capital during the Middle Ages was based originally on its geographic good luck and the political savvy of its burgesses and merchants, both manifest in its development as a collection and shipping point for trade—initially a large trade in the wine of others. Britain, for its part, long preferred what its inhabitants called the "black wine of Cahors," thick, alcoholic, deep-hued, and long-lasting, to Bordeaux's weaker, lighter "claret," a word sharing a root with the French word *claire*, meaning light.

Though some Burgundies can be more expensive, today we accept the primacy of Bordeaux wine as a given and assume it always was supreme. Actually, the vines of this province were planted late relative to the rest of the southwest and, unlike those of Cahors and other farming regions, planted not because the ground they grew on was good for nothing else. The traders, shippers, bankers, and ecclesiastical landowners, who were relieved of their vast stretches of farm and field by the revolution of 1789, had seen the money to be made with this commodity. The vineyards, planted on land previously given over to food crops, provided, over time, an ever larger proportion of the wine exported to the English, who in turn developed a taste for "claret," or Bordeaux, which eventually evolved into the various blends of cabernet sauvignon, merlot, and cabernet franc that define every "classic" red Bordeaux today.

The vineyards of Bordeaux were among the first true wine estates, land consecrated to vines and only to vines, supported by fermenting barns and coopers, with the goal being to make the finest wine possible, much of it for export. Unlike the polycultural Lot and most other regions, where other, necessary crops competed for the time and attention of the peasants, the Bordeaux region could concentrate on quality, on selective breeding of vinestock, on the kinds of improvements that led to wine clean and "healthy" enough to age. And maturing dry wine (versus sweet wine or wine doctored with brandy or other spirits) in an oak barrel and then aging it in a corked bottle, while certainly not innovations unique to Bordeaux, were carried to a high art there, establishing for the wines an early reputation that continues to this day.

Today, people still argue over the claim that the British "invented" Bordeaux wine. Though there is little question that the British did invent port and, to a lesser extent, sherry, that they were also responsible for France's most renowned wines would certainly be news to most French people. What you cannot deny, however, is that the British market, together with the still powerful merchants, shippers, and brokers, had an important role in shaping Bordeaux into the kind of wine it is today, as it was their tastes that guided the market for so long. Mercantile ties between Bordeaux and England, particularly London wine houses like Berry Brothers, were such that up until the end of the twentieth century, one could still find Bordeaux wines, or what they were calling Bordeaux, being shipped in bulk to London, where they were blended, bottled, and sold under the proprietary labels of those houses. You can still find today, to take one example, bottles of Château Palmer from the 1970s and 1980s, on whose labels the Berry Brothers name appears just under that of the château.

The major advantages Bordeaux had over other "high country" wines were quite simply price, exclusivity, and availability. The Bordelais, without onerous taxes, could sell the same quality of wine for less, relatively, and their wines were the first available abroad every season, so that they could ask a premium, particularly for the better wines. Since the glass bottle and the cork wouldn't come into regular use for some centuries, the freshness of the wine was very important. What had originally begun, after Eleanor brought Aquitaine and Gascony into the English fold, as an expedient political backhander from a distant British crown in the person of her grandson, Henry II, to its new French vassals—letting the burgesses and clergy of Bordeaux export relatively modest quantities of their own wine with little if any tax—over time became enshrined in onerous laws known as the Bordeaux privileges. Quite early on, the authorities began to distinguish between wine grown for export in the province of Bordeaux and wine for export from the so-called high countries, *les haut-pays,* among them today's appellations of Bergerac, Buzet, Frontonnais, Gaillac, Monbazillac, and of course Cahors.

Aside from less favorable taxes, these privileges dictated, for example, that wines other than those from Bordeaux had to wait for shipment, sometimes until after Christmas, when winter storms on the rough seas were more likely and shippers thus more hesitant to leave port, or at least until after all the Bordeaux wine had been sold and departed. The facilities provided for storing and loading this highly taxed high-country wine were distant from the port and awkward for handling large quantities, and the longer wait made the wines more likely to spoil after the jostling voyage.

While the fifteenth century was a time of slow rebuilding and recovery for the southwest, and of great improvements in winemaking and particularly in the quality and variety of vines, it was not a happy time for Cahors. Not only had the winemakers lost their strongest export market, but the Bordeaux privileges, after a short hiatus, were reconfirmed under the new French administration of Louis XI, again in the name of political accommodation. The Bordelais also won the unique right to use what had been the standard-size wine barrel and made all others use a different, slightly smaller one. Its descendant, still known today as the Bordeaux barrel, is the gold standard in barrels and holds 225 liters of wine. Aside from adding cost to the competition, this was a powerful form of early branding, making Bordeaux instantly recognizable abroad, and also making it easier for the Bordelais to quarantine "foreign" wine passing through their port.

For the French winemaker, one of the most positive changes in French society that began slowly following the Hundred Years' War, and continued until the watershed of the revolution 300 years later, was the rise of an affluent middle class who loved to show off by drinking good wine. These were the bourgeois, and they soon became an important force in French winemaking after winning the right to own vines, a privilege up until then restricted to nobles and the church. Eager to show themselves the equal of the debt-ridden nobility and dispossessed clergy, whose best lands they purchased with money made in trading, the bourgeois began to plant vines and make wine in quantity. The term *cru bourgeois*—which particularly in Bordeaux has denoted since 1855 wines of a quality just below the best, the *cru classés,* or classed growths—has its origins in this era. Once it was made, of course, the wine had to be sold. Here, too, the bourgeois had an advantage in that they also had the right to run *cabarets* and *tavernes* to dispose of the surplus.

This explosion of new harvests led, as it has done quite regularly throughout French history, to overproduction, lowering the prices vintners could get for their wine and punishing particularly those wines of second and third rank. It also led to periodic famines. By the end of the sixteenth century, there was a foreshadowing of modern events when the crown, ruling with a much more centralized, and effective, authority, first attempted to limit how much land under vines any one landowner could possess to one-third of the total. Further, the authorities forbade that any newly cleared, arable land be planted in grapes. (The next planting prohibition would come about 1750, under Louis XV.)

It wasn't until the nineteenth century that Cahors would experience another period of prosperity equal to that of the fourteenth. In the intervening years it had some notable successes, the excellence of its vines being recognized in their planting in the royal vineyards of

François I at Fontainebleau and later in the papal vineyards at Avignon. *Vin de Cahors* was adopted by the Russian Orthodox church as its holy wine and served in the Russian Army at the officers' mess. Cahors was the single wine recommended to Peter the Great by his doctors to treat his stomach ulcer, and even today one finds a wine still sold in Russia called Kagorskoye Vino, though the purely Russian version, made in the Crimea, is thick, sweet, and very alcoholic.

For every step forward, however, Cahors always seems to have paid with two steps backward. François I brought peace and encouraged a flowering of the arts, but with the subsequent reign of Henri III came the Wars of Religion, in which Catholic Cahors was besieged and pillaged by marauding Protestants. Henri IV reestablished order and peace in the kingdom, but at about the time of his death bubonic plague reappeared, bringing anarchy and desperate times once again. If Colbert, Louis XIV's powerful, repressive finance minister, restored the navigability of the Lot River and encouraged trade and industry, it was to reap more taxes, sinking the peasants and bourgeoisie ever deeper into the misery that would lead, not so many years later, to the revolution.

All the while, Bordeaux prospered from its monopoly of the river trade, heaping restriction upon restriction on the wines of others. There was a tax on every barrel; there were tolls on roads and rivers, and taxes on warehouses and on wine stored. The port was still closed to the export of high-country wines until Christmas. In a particularly nefarious twist, those wines had to be out of the port by the first of May; thus as the date approached there was a steady downward pressure on the price the Bordelais *négociants,* the wholesalers and shippers, would pay for the wine of others that would otherwise have to be shipped back to its point of origin.

During the sixteenth and seventeenth centuries, however, as the French navy was resurrected and France expanded its colonies, Cahors established its reputation, not as a fine wine for the connoisseur, but as a sturdy wine capable of surviving long sea voyages and assuaging sailors' homesickness. It was one of the few wines that didn't spoil in the heat of France's tropical possessions; garrisons in the Caribbean were an important market, and if the wine cheered soldiers with a taste of home, so much the better. Grown on the well-exposed slopes of the Lot River, the auxerrois, or malbec, grape gave very dark-colored, tannic, and long-lasting wines of high alcohol content. The cabernet and merlot of Bordeaux were more likely, in bad years, to yield a wine too light in color and substance for what the market demanded, leading to the widespread use of Cahors as *un vin docteur,* the wine of choice to blend with it, bringing it up to the right color and alcoholic strength.

Historical records tell us that this best-quality trade wine, even much longer than 400 years ago, was made largely if not wholly from malbec grapes. Though no one knows how it first arrived in the southwest, that it survived to become the most important grape was no accident. And it is unique to this region, Cahors being the only appellation in France today in which malbec is by long tradition the dominant varietal. Its characteristics—tolerance of heat and drought and an ability to thrive in poor but calcium-heavy soils—are ideal for the area even if it is, in other ways, a difficult grape. The peasants who worked the hillside vines learned early on that malbec grew well there while other varieties did not, the sunny slopes yielding good wine for which there existed a ready market, locally and abroad. Generation after generation, they propagated the best vines and determined which were the best parcels for them.

However, they were not all growing a single kind of grape to produce a single kind of wine. This was still an era when most of what you consumed was produced locally, generally by you or your neighbor. If you wanted white wine, rosé, or table wine, you planted the vines and made it yourself for your own consumption, perhaps with the surplus sold to neighbors, merchants, and other locals who came with their own small barrels or, later, bottles, to pick it up in the late winter or early spring.

Clos de Gamot, Clos Triguedina, and Clos la Coutale today all carry on this tradition, selling small quantities of white, or rosé, or both in the local market, often to regional restaurateurs who like to offer their customers a full range of local wine. This tradition of producing very local *petits vins,* pleasant little wines drunk young and meant for the everyday table, as a sideline to the more important vintages, is alive all over France; and the discovery of such *petit vins* is one of the pleasures of traveling there still.

One fall day, as I was walking amid the lower vines of Clos de Gamot with Yves and Martine, Yves pointed out, to my surprise, a whole parcel of vines neither malbec, merlot, nor tannat, the three red wine grapes that go into AOC Cahors wine. Below us were a few rows of cabernet franc and then white wine grapes: sauvignon blanc and chardonnay. "We make the white and the rosé for our own amusement, because it makes a change, a little something different," Martine told me. "And," added Yves, "people seem to like it. We never have enough."

Many farm families who did not sell wine nevertheless made their own in the same spirit of self-sufficiency that involved keeping a pig or two, a few cows for milk, and chickens for eggs and the pot, and growing sufficient corn to feed them. The family would cultivate an acre or two of vines near the house, often planted underneath or between rows of chestnut or walnut trees, next to fields of barley and oats. They didn't plant malbec exclusively but included hardier, higher-yielding vines that produced rough but adequate wine for the table.

Though the tradition is fading, in the Lot one still sees these *vignobles de famille,* family vineyards—small patches of vines, usually with a fig tree at one end to shade the weary at noontime, often surrounded by stone walls and near the homestead. Far up into the hills and off the roads, sometimes on horseback, I have come across more isolated homesteads, now abandoned, their clay tile roofs fallen in and walls descending slowly into piles and heaps of stone, beside them a plot of vines long abandoned, mostly dead brown stalks in rows growing up between the weeds, with, in summer, the few still alive sending out their runners in a green riot over the ground. There are few sights more evocative of the passing of a way of life than this, a family's abandoned vineyard.

Many, many times, talking with older city dwellers whose roots are in the country, I have heard happy memories of returning home for the grape harvest, the meals, the dances, the atmosphere of celebration. *Les vendanges,* the harvest, bringing in the grapes and making the wine, that and killing and dressing a pig for winter, these were the bookends of the season. This history survives in the food, with a big family meal on All Saints' Day, October 31, after a visit to bless and dress the family graves. Fresh blood sausage from a neighbor or the butcher; sweet, creamy new walnuts; duck, *confit* or rich bloodred breasts from birds slaughtered for their fattened livers—this is the food of the season. In rural France, there are never more than two degrees of separation between any individual and a source of good local wine, and so, to wash down the feast, Oncle Georges or Papi Henri or Cousine Marie will arrive, setting unlabeled bottles of the new wine on the table. Still rough edged and staining lips and teeth purple, it has fierce tannins that cut the richness of the food; and what better way to celebrate the dead than with young wine, that potent symbol of life, prosperity, and all good things.

That all the ingredients for this meal are still today locally produced and widely available demonstrates to what extent the region has kept its agricultural roots.

THE MODERN ERA: CAHORS LOSES ITS WAY

From the French Revolution through the middle of the 1800s, the new department of the Lot, created in 1789 with Cahors as its capital, seemed stuck in time. The great industries then just beginning to establish themselves in France sprang up everywhere but in the southwest, which, lacking a developed infrastructure and having few easily available natural resources, was consciously passed over by the central government when investments were considered.

The most important export was still wine, and in this regard not much would change at all. Although the Bordeaux privileges went the way of the monarchy, the Bordelais had by then become an overpowering and ubiquitous presence, exerting commercial influence as *courtiers* and *négociants*, entrenched cartels of brokers and buyers, the only ones with the financial sophistication to support what is by its nature a capital-dependent trade. Wine had already become a commodity, and one subject to wide swings in price and supply from which the producers and consumers relied on the *négociants* to protect them, paying handsomely in the process. This is a situation that continues to this day, with the *négociants* exerting the greatest influence, and fixing prices, in many appellations.

The innovations of the 1800s—particularly Louis Pasteur's ground-breaking discovery of the microbes that made wine spoil and how to combat them with new sanitary methods of winemaking and storage; and Dr. Jules Guyot's studies of the best pruning and planting methods—coincided with a huge upsurge in the production of Cahors. At a time when people were leaving for jobs in cities burgeoning with new industry, regional and national markets seemed as if they could swallow every drop. Also, a virulent vine disease, oïdium, or powdery mildew, attacked most of the rest of the significant vineyards in the country, leaving the southwest in a position to sell its wine at very high prices.

Today, when you walk through the countryside of the region, you'll see that many of the dates carved into the lintels of the most imposing farmhouses and grandest wine barns are from that period between 1850 and the coming of phylloxera toward the end of the century. From 1850 to 1880, after which the grip of phylloxera became truly deadly, the region throve as it had not done for more than 500 years, with new vineyards planted farther and farther away from the river, up on the *causses,* in fields formerly of oats, rye, and barley. That fleeting prosperity is responsible for the region's rich trove of buildings in stone, which today continue to feed the appetite of the French and foreigners for traditional houses to restore as second homes.

The first great upheaval in the modern history of Cahors came with the invasion of that vine pest, phylloxera, originally brought in on imported American rootstocks being used for grafting experiments. Whereas American vines have a natural resistance to it, European vines do not. This lesson took some time to sink in, apparently, as the nascent California wine industry was all but destroyed just after this by the same pest growing on the same kinds of vines, French vinestocks imported to America! Phylloxera continues to appear periodically there.

All over Europe, the vines sickened and died, leaving appalling scars on the landscape as entire regions watched their lifeblood seep away. From one decade to the next, the rural economy collapsed, the young moved off the farms to look for work in the cities, and those left behind tried every method they knew to bring back the vines.

Even before the turn of the twentieth century, government agricultural researchers had found one answer, to graft French vinestock, the plant producing the grapes, onto resistant American rootstock. The initial graftings, though successful in that the hybrids were healthy and productive, did not make very good wine, and it would take many decades of further experimentation before more appropriate vines yielding authentic wines were developed.

In the meantime, the Lot was a disaster area. When the vines died, many farmers were plunged into penury. They watched their capital, their vines, disappear. While the farmers didn't starve, polyculture still being the rule rather than the exception, the terraces fell into ruin, leading to massive erosion on the hillsides. The growers up on the *causses,* planted most recently, were particularly hard hit. These growers had invested heavily preparing land never before planted in vines, and had spent money on wine barns and all the cooperage necessary to ferment and store wine; their vines had had less time to pay them back with yearly harvests.

About twenty miles north of the Lot River, in just such a region of escarpments and tablelands called Sud-Bouriane, lies a hilltop village, Les Arques, which is a good example of what happened to many upland villages in this era. (The life of this village and its restaurant is the subject of my second book, *From Here, You Can't See Paris.*) This was an area where the vines had come late but quickly became very important as a cash crop. Today, as you drive on the narrow winding roads that crisscross the steeply undulating land, your eye catches, on many of the well-exposed hillsides, the faint contours of what were once terraces for vines. Today, the farmers of the commune grow fields of sunflowers, corn, barley, oats, rapeseed, and silage crops for their milk cows. There are some walnut orchards, and stands of ramrod-straight poplars rise in neat squares in marshy bottomlands that are not good for anything else. But there are almost no vines; the few remaining patches in surrounding communes are not commercially important.

"Before 1900," Raymond Laval, the former mayor of Les Arques, told me, "we exported wine. My house was a wine depot, and the wagons would come down out of the hills with their barrels, waiting for further transport to Castelfranc," where they would be shipped by a new (in 1850) rail link to Cahors for export as far away as the Antilles. Lionel Gramon, an avid local amateur historian, showed me a photograph of L'Adoux, the largest estate in Les Arques, taken about 1900, hundreds of acres of prime land, its slate-roofed manor house in brick and stone rising above an army of vines. There are only vines, with no trees or bushes even as ornamentation. You can't tell the season because the vines are all dead or dying, and the image that comes to mind, the orderly rows of stark black stalks marching across the hillsides, is that of a graveyard. In fact, the year 1866 marks the commune's peak population, 813 inhabitants, just before the outbreak of phylloxera. One-third of those would leave in the next forty years; by the 1960s the population would fall to 230. L'Adoux, which the mayor told me once employed more than twenty people, as a place where young men went to pick up work as day laborers, particularly during the harvests of grain, grapes, or nuts, sank into abandon. Today its fields are covered with brush and scrub forest and its barns are in ruins. The proud house hunkers down in the gloom of the overgrown woods, its shutters closed, on them sprayed in red paint the words: Keep Out! There's nothing to steal here anyway!

Down in the river valley, though times would still be extraordinarily tough with the end of the hillside vines, things would take a different turn. The tunnel proved longer than most expected while the light at its end was often a faint glimmer indeed. By the time the research institutes had discovered and propagated the new, resistant grafted vines, the manpower to replant the slopes had gone. Over the next thirty years, the first and second world wars would, between them, take the life of one out of every three young Frenchmen, and the sheer amount of labor required to reestablish the hillside vineyards was too much for those who stayed on the land, even had the capital been available.

After the war, the circumstances of even the most established Cahors winemakers were much reduced. Because the presence of the German army in the region had been relatively light, they had come home to find their homes and vineyards—and their cellars—intact, which was not the case in Bordeaux and Champagne. In the long years of conflict, however, when wives, children, and the older generation made up the entire workforce, the vines had suffered, and the harvests with them. At Clos de Gamot, for example, Martine's grandmother, Lucienne, whose training was as a pianist, took over, with much help from the village women and from her father-in-law. With so little wine to sell, and the peasants' reluctance to spend "capital"—older, stocked wines—many turned to market-garden crops until their stocks returned to normal. At Clos de Gamot, this meant raising strawberries for the English market; at Clos Triguedina, the Baldès family grew peaches. Others grew plums and nuts, and even planted acres of truffle oaks, the association between old vineyards and that valuable mushroom, the truffle, having been long established.

While the most dedicated winemakers worked patiently to reestablish the health and productivity of their traditional grapes, many others, for whom grapes were but one crop among many, and one that had to yield a little something each year, had long ago ripped out their old malbec vines and planted higher-yielding, disease- and frost-resistant vines. This trend became particularly prevalent after the spring freeze of 1956 that killed so many young vines. In 1958, the appellation produced just under 200,000 bottles of wine sold as "Cahors"; the rest, a thin red low in alcohol and destined never to see the inside of a bottle, was sold in bulk at a few pennies a liter to middlemen.

Even then, almost fifty years ago, the conflicting forces within the appellation were evident. One smaller group made up mostly of winemakers who had always made the best wine on the best land (also joined by a *négociant* or two)—a group whose identity, way of life, and family traditions, not to mention their living, became bound up with their vines long ago—has pushed constantly for improvement. Its members have experimented both in the vineyard and in the wine barn and have organized to promote their wine. They have long sought to recapture some of the romance and reputation of the *vin de Cahors* of old by making and selling a consistently excellent, unique, and reasonably priced wine, a wine having much to do with its origins and traditions.

On the other side are two groups whose interests are not necessarily so much allied as identical for different reasons, the *viticulteurs* and the *négociants*. There are still hundreds of *viticulteurs* in the Lot, farmers who grow grapes, usually on small plots, and who sell their harvest either to the local cooperative of which they are members or to others, usually *négociants,* to make wine. These farmers, as long as they receive a reasonable minimum price each year, have little incentive to raise their quality with expensive investments such as replanting with better vines on better land.

The *négociants,* who can be all at once brokers, regional and national wholesalers, and winemakers in their own right (with both their own grapes and those bought from others), are very powerful regionally, since it is they who set the benchmark price for bulk wine from month to month. Nationally and internationally, however, they are at the mercy of what is happening in venues as different as Bordeaux, California, South Africa, the Far East, and Australia. Should fine weather everywhere produce huge yields of good wine all over the world, these *négociants* still have to dispose of all the wine they have contracted to buy, some of it months and years in advance.

In the long term, their situation is a complicated one. Should they aim high, expending the enormous effort and cost to establish Cahors as a premium or very good wine in the hope of selling each bottle for a little more money? Or should they emphasize quantity over quality, hoping to position Cahors as, for example, an "airline wine," the kind that comes in tiny bottles in tourist class and that is sold by the tens of millions of gallons a year in just this one market alone?

Although I didn't realize it when I first set foot in the vineyards of Cahors in 1999, the battle over how to answer this question, which is not a trivial one for those involved, was in at least its fifth decade and heading for a climax. I would learn that reputations had been won and lost; businesses had prospered or been destroyed; and heart attacks, cancers, and even an untimely death or two had been attributed by some to anguish and stress over the fight. In Cahors, the winemakers take their wine very seriously—as they should. It is the ultimate expression of their land; it is their living; and it is the embodiment of centuries of personal history.

5

IT'S THE *TERROIR,* STUPID!

The appellation of *vin de Cahors,* one thirtieth the size of Bordeaux, runs from a bit south and east of Cahors, then west along the Lot River for about thirty miles, and is less than eight miles wide at its broadest. In the Lot valley, where the hills rise steeply up on either side of the alluvial plains on which are planted most of the appellation's 10,000 acres, the vines make of the land a lush Eden in spring and summer, and even in winter lend it a sere, rather stark, beauty. The scrub pines and plots of trees still used as woodlots give the merest brush of green against the white limestone and gray schist; the river loops sinuously back and forth in enormous meanders, each oxbow of which might be five miles deep. Relieving the eye are the villages and hamlets scattered throughout the valley, and the occasional fields, in early spring and after the fall harvest, of newly turned red clay waiting for the sowing of corn, barley, sunflowers, or oats. On land too poor or wet for vines rise plantations of poplar, particularly at the river's edge. Driving along the tracks that crisscross the valley, you find yourself continually surprised by the broad, placid river, appearing out of nowhere when you thought it was behind you, on the left when you thought it was to the right. Just in the sixteen miles between the major river towns of Cahors and Puy l'Evêque, the river is said to flow almost fifty miles.

Today, the vineyards in the appellation are either in the valley (more than two-thirds) or in much smaller areas on the plateaus on top of the surrounding hills, with the very rare exception being vines planted on the steep slopes in between—Yves and Martine's Clos St. Jean is an example of these.

When French winemakers talk about what makes their wine unique, different from all others, they will all invoke, as surely as night follows day, the *terroir*, a maddeningly imprecise word that defies a simple black-and-white definition.

Look it up in the dictionary, and you'll find the meager entry of "earth" and "soil," both helpful only if we imagine a farmer, feet planted firmly in the dirt, surveying his fields and proclaiming to the young man next to him, "It's the *land*, son, it's the *land*." In other words, yes, there is the land—the actual dirt, the stones, the roll of the fields, the rock underneath, and the stand of trees beyond—but *terroir* embraces much more, including a particular approach to the land, to its working, and to the elaboration of its fruits. There is even—and here I'm going to be accused of sentimentality—an emotional connotation which comes, I think, from the fact that so many of these families have been working the same patch of land for so many generations. Also, the grapevine is a very long-lived being, with a single parcel planted by one man enduring to be worked through successive generations, sometimes down to his great-great-grandson or -granddaughter.

Below are some of the more concrete components of *terroir*:

· The sun hits higher elevations first and shines on them longer; thus the altitude of a field of vines and its orientation toward the sun are important for the grapes to ripen properly and fully.
· Local topography, the shape of the land, in combination with general climatic trends—winds from a certain direction in particular seasons; the presence of sheltering hills, foothills, and even the lowest rises of land; and how vines are laid out on such rises—can be very important, particularly in the sensitive seasons: from spring, when the vines bud, up to the fall harvest.
· Geology can be both macro and micro. Grapevines need topsoil, but not too much or too rich. Layers of clay hold water. Roots can't penetrate bedrock. Small rocks of the right size and color can

collect the day's heat and warm the grapes at night. Rivers generate fog and also raise the local humidity.

· Water flows downhill, and so does soil; better wine seems to come from vines in certain kinds of poor soils and vines grown on slopes and plateaus rather than in a low valley or along a river where the ground would be wetter.

· Ecology: respecting what was on the land before the vines also has an effect. Trees bring birds; birds eat insects that can damage vines and grapes themselves and also carry diseases.

If we define *terroir* most narrowly, in terms of geology and soil type, Cahors has only two distinct types: the valley lands at elevations from 350 to 500 feet; and the chalk plateaus in places like Floressas, where Jean-Luc has several parcels, at about 1,000 feet. The best land for wine, and the land which used to hold most of the vines before phylloxera, is in between on the slopes, the *coteaux*. Today, it is simply too expensive and too arduous, and requires too much hand labor, to justify replanting—all reasons why others think Yves and Martine crazy to have stuck their Clos St. Jean up there.

There are also only a few kinds of soil in the region: thin, crumbly limestone mixed with some organic material over bedrock up on the more exposed plateaus; the clay-silt-gravel-sand of alluvial deposits along the river; and in between, if you're lucky, a mix of clay and limestone with some schist and flinty pebbles. In any one vineyard, however, depending on the course of the river as it dug out the valley and laid down layers of different composition over the eons (and subsequent erosion and other factors), you can find all kinds and all mixes of these soils, including some places where iron ores tinge the dirt red.

The state wine authorities, in an attempt to identify the best lands for vines in the valley (the first step toward taking the poorer parcels out of production), long ago defined three so-called terraces, or bands of cultivation, at steadily rising elevations. Every parcel of vines was classed, according to elevation, as being either on the first (lowest), second (middle), or third (highest and best) terrace—a yardstick with which not even the most stubborn winemaker could argue.

Talk to any Cahors winemaker, and about the second thing out of his mouth, after the excellence of his wine, will be that his parcels are on the second and third—the highest—terraces. This should give you some idea of the reputation of grapes grown anywhere near the river, on the first terrace. These claims to quality associated solely with the higher terraces turn up on the label on the bottle and in winemakers' brochures, and it isn't unusual to find that the quaint illustrations on those labels often depict vines climbing a steep hillside.

First-terrace parcels, which begin at about 350 feet above sea level (the river is at 300 feet), are generally wetter and have more clay and deeper alluvial soil, and their vines tend to overproduce grapes that ripen later, are of lower acidity, and are of lower quality than those higher up. The second terrace has poorer soils, and, because it is higher, gets slightly better exposure to the sun and less humidity from the river—both good things. The highest elevations in the valley, the third-terrace parcels, are only about 500 feet above sea level at their highest.

When you do the math, it turns out that each terrace represents only about a fifty-foot rise in elevation. Thus some very pointed claims are being made about purported differences found in wine from grapes grown at altitudes that differ by only 150 feet!

The chalky plateaus, the other *terroir,* are generally around 1,000 feet above sea level. Judging by the new plantings at these higher elevations, these lands are coming into their own solely on the basis of the higher quality of the wine they produce.

Climate is generally the element of *terroir* cited next most often. Here, Cahors finds itself blessed. It is equidistant from the Atlantic, the Pyrenees, and the Mediterranean, but most of its weather comes from the west, making it an Atlantic climate. In contrast, very hot, dry climates, as in Languedoc-Roussillon, have the reputation of producing unbalanced wines of high alcohol and low acidity. The exception in Cahors is a usually hotter, drier, sometimes very stiff wind from the southeast called *le vent d'autan,* coming in late summer and early fall and thus uniquely suited to help in the late ripening of the grapes. To this we add the microclimate, in this case the fact that the bowl-shaped valley protected by the surrounding hills holds heat and the oxbows of the Lot River distribute humidity—both good things that help protect against spring frost damage and help ripening over the sometimes cooler nights of early fall.

Geology and climate seem to be only the most obvious elements of *terroir*. In my own experience with this slippery concept, I have stood in the vines with a winemaker immersed in his musings and watched, smiling, as he pointed up to the sky, or down at the earth; as he knelt to crumble friable limestone soil between his fingers; as he kicked at the pebbles so prized for storing and reflecting up the day's heat to ripen the grapes; as he lifted his nose to sniff the fresh breeze from north, south, east, or west; or as he swept fog-deposited water from the leaves of his vines. He may have been squinting from the sun or bemoaning his pale skin, licking his dry lips or cursing the rain, complaining at the iron-tinged redness of his soil or smiling contentedly at the minute seashell fossils in a clump of dirt.

Far down this list, he might then get to mentioning the actual varieties of grapes he grows, and how everything that comes before figures into how he actually makes his wine. So to this soup of *terroir* we then add man himself—not only his manipulations as he works the ground, but also his ideas, his machines, and what he adds to the earth. All this we can think of as contributing to *terroir*.

Built into the concept of terroir—and this is where the newcomers to winemaking get into trouble—is also the simple acknowledgment that the French winemaker *knows* all this as a sailor knows from the way his boat moves through the water that his sails are trimmed as they should be. The winemaker knows the historical patterns, often over generations if not centuries, of rain, hail, sun, and drought; the least details of varying subsoils and changing geology from parcel to parcel; the nuances of microclimate that local topology and weather can produce; and what the real effect of it all might be on how he prunes or fertilizes and on how he will treat the grapes once they're in the tank, and later the barrel.

He (less often, she) knows it because he has lived it, because his father and mother and grandfather and grandmother passed it on in their own words to him, knows it from the historical record left in the wine itself, which, if he is any kind of winemaker, he has tasted with that same parentage, who, in their wisdom, kept enough of it back, much as a library keeps reference books for future generations, that he might have the great good fortune to be able to have his sons and daughters taste of it as well.

During the great drought of 2003, when so many in France watched as their grapes stopped ripening, then wrinkled and dried into raisins on the vine, Yves, possessed as always of a farmer's fatalism, paused in his day as we moved from dessicated parcel to dessicated parcel, to slip off to the cellar. He disappeared into a storehouse at Cayrou, emerging with a dust-covered bottle without a label, and the enigmatic words, delivered with his mischievous grin, "We will see, Michael, we will see."

Two hours later, over a lunch of lamb, roasted potatoes, and salad, he popped its cork, poured, swirled, and finally sniffed. Grinning at me over the lip of his glass, he tasted and sighed. I did, too, following as I had done so often in the past months with him, imbibing a lovely elixir imbued with a grace and subtlety found only in an old lady of a wine, but one still proud enough of her beauteous form to cloak it in fine raiment at the appearance of a proper gentleman.

"This," he said dramatically, "is the 1976. That was a drought year, too. You see what the vines can produce, even in such conditions?" he asked. I nodded sheepishly, having been tricked once again by my own gullibility. He and Martine had opened the bottle only for me, to prove to me that all was not lost even though the vines had, by that point, suffered through more than two months of drought and extreme heat. The larger point was also, I realized later, that they already knew the 1976; knew it as a good old friend come through a rough patch but doing all right, thank you; knew they didn't have to open that bottle but for the presence of a doubting stranger who had read too much in the newspaper, watched too much bad news from the evening pundits. The year 1976 was for Yves and Martine one reference among many, one book on the shelf, a volume unique like all the others to which they might refer, or to whose memory they might refer, when present circumstances necessitated. That day in 2003, the wine of 1976 was also a reference that might help actively guide them as they harvested and made the grapes into wine later that fall.

The *terroir* of their vineyards, Clos de Gamot and Château de Cayrou, is thus captured in the ensemble of that library: partly tangible in the ranks of bottles in their various cellars there for the consulting;

partly existing in their senses and their taste and olfactory memories preserved as others can recall a Shakespearean sonnet, the cut of a Chanel dress from between the wars, or the line of a Picasso drawing.

But it is also in what they do every day, in a thousand subtleties of vineyard savoir faire one would miss unless one were there, beside them, in all seasons. Here is Yves of Clos de Gamot, talking about a few of these very ordinary but quite important details.

"You notice we have lots of roses growing at the row ends," he told me once as we walked the vines in late spring. "All the tourists think they're pretty. Why do we have them there? Because, if there is oïdium [powdery mildew] in the roses, it is a good indicator of the same disease in the vines and you'd better treat them. They are a barometer.

"We put out our own butterfly traps baited with pheromones in the vines, too, to determine how many *cicadelles* there are. They lay their eggs on the leaves and grapes, and the tiny worms eat the grapes and make them rot. The butterflies, they eat the edges of the leaves, which in turn leads the vine to produce less sugar, which can mean less alcohol in the finished wine.

"At Cayrou, on the pebbles, there are always a few attacks of the worms, and we know it and we treat it. The regional authority puts out its own traps, but only here and there. They can't tell you which parts of your different *terroirs* are infested. . . ."

To me, the echoes of *terroir* are in all this—in Yves' many rain gauges and daily thermometer readings, in the butterfly traps and the dark tan of Yves and Martine's skin, in their son learning the intimacies of this parcel and that one at his parents' side, and even in observing the neighbors.

"It's just common sense," Yves was telling me one day as we talked about man's influence. "The more you screw with the land, the more likely you'll take it in the face. It's simple. I'll tell you a story.

"You know our little parcel in front along the road at Gamot, the one that's all plowed up? We had some centenary vines there, planted just after phylloxera, and they weren't producing anymore. So we ripped them out. To do that, you have a plow with blades this long." He held out his hand at waist level. "You go deep to get out the roots. And there were rocks, of course, that came up with the plow blades. Lots of rocks! So we lifted out all the rocks, set them aside.

"At the same time our neighbor is doing the same thing, clearing the field next to ours of old vines. Except that he brings in this 450-horsepower crusher and breaks all the stones into little pieces." Yves' son, Franck, studying vineyard management and winemaking at the university, was home for the summer holidays and had watched these developments along with his father. "Now Franck says to me, 'Dad, you did the right thing. Did you know that by breaking up the rocks, he's heading for a problem? He's going to put too much calcium back into the soil. He'll have to add iron to get a healthy vine.'" Yves looked at me, proud as only a father can be.

"We pull out all the rocks because that's what they've done forever. Look at all the stone walls around here. Where do you think the stone came from?" he finished. "When you don't pull out the rocks, because you're lazy or you have a machine handy, that's when you begin to have problems."

Finally, we come to the varietal, the specific kind of grape or grapes that the winemaker chooses to plant in his *terroir*. No one really knows precisely when the grape of Cahors, malbec (locally called *cot* or *auxerrois*), came to be the dominant varietal, but we do know that it has been grown here for at least 600 or 700 years. As to the "why," why malbec and not cabernet sauvignon or cabernet franc or any of the other Bordeaux varieties that grow so well not 150 miles to the northeast, that is easier to answer. Malbec is a difficult grape, and here it grows very well, yielding a unique wine, a characteristic wine, a wine that tastes and smells like no other in France. Indeed, Cahors is the only appellation in which malbec is the dominant grape—and often the only grape.

When I asked Jean-Luc about the importance of the actual varietal, he started off talking, not about malbec, but about the appellation of Cahors. "In France," he said, "we favor the *terroir* and the hand of man while the grape variety has less importance. It takes a very long time to create an appellation—a thousand years in some parts of France—to discover what vines do best. In other places like California, you can experiment. Here, you can't. Sure, people get permission to plant other kinds of vines here, and some of them are interesting wines. But they're not Cahors, and they never can be."

This is not to say that appellations can't and don't evolve. It was not until the 1970s, after Cahors was elevated to appellation status from a mid-level VDQS ("Delimited Wine of Superior Quality," just below AOC and above *vin de pays* in quality), that merlot and tannat became the only officially permitted blending grapes one could add to malbec. There were historical reasons to justify both of these, too. Merlot has long been used in this region and elsewhere as a softening wine of good alcohol; tannat, a dark, very tannic grape, is another traditional wine of the southwest known for the qualities it can impart to a blend over the long term.

This brings us to the notion that one can think of any specific appellation as an embodiment of a specific *terroir*. When you see "AOC Cahors" on the label, you know not only where it came from and what grapes might be in it, but also the maximum yield permitted in the vineyards; the minimum degree of alcohol of the wine; and a host of things about how the vine was grown, pruned, harvested, and even made. Though some French winemakers complain about the rigidities of the system, it is what has permitted each of France's more than 440 appellations to create and to retain over time a distinct identity, preventing the kind of market-driven creeping homogeneity one finds in the wines of so many other countries.

To vastly oversimplify, the difference between favoring appellation over grape variety is the difference between planting certain kinds of grapes in a particular place and watching what happens over many generations or centuries, instead of throwing in any old thing, particularly any old thing today's market is demanding (read: chardonnay and merlot), any old where and then trying to make a drinkable wine of the grapes afterward.

In this we find one of the more evident differences between the new world and old, between the twenty-first century and all that came before. California, whose recent winemaking history has been so much about throwing off an industrial tradition in favor of an artisanal one (or, more awkwardly, trying to marry the two), is still in the thrall of the varietal, pushing the extremes of the possibilities of any single grape variety much as Detroit pushed the size of its cars and their engines in the modern era.

This has led in our time to grotesqueries of the first order, wines at 14.5, 15, even 16 percent alcohol—called "hot" wines in the trade—which no one in his right mind would serve with food, even though, according to the labels, their makers would have you do so. Not only would the guests be incapable of tasting the food; they would risk keeling over into their plates after a few glasses. Fruit bombs, powerhouses, hothouse flowers, juice on steroids, whatever you want to call them, such wines can often seem mere curiosities than enduring works of art. Enologically speaking, such wines may be a pleasure, but an all too brief one. Overly ripe grapes and high alcohol generally imply low acidity and a lack of the right kind of tannins, both of which are needed for a wine to age beyond several years in any way that is interesting.

Creeping homogeneity is evident in the fact that it is impossible to find a decent—and decently priced—rosé for summer drinking from this country, Australia, or even South America. I am sure such rosés exist, but French, Italian, and less often Portuguese and Spanish rosés at premium prices tend to be what one can find in better wineshops. In Europe, these are easy, generally light-alcohol wines released in the year of their making or shortly thereafter and meant to be drunk cool, outside, under the sun with the foods of summer—grills, salads, and picnic food. Here, the Gallos of the world have convinced us that those overly sweet concoctions called "blush" or "white zinfandel" are really the same thing, so why go to the trouble to make a real rosé anyway?

This is not to say that California can't produce very sophisticated, finely balanced wines. Some of the more subtle varieties—pinot noir and viognier, to name just two—have found quite refreshing and sublime expression there (in Washington and Oregon, too); and there exist many restrained, long-lived, quite elegant Bordeaux blends where the cabernet and merlot work happily together rather than duking it out in the glass under a cloud of oak fumes.

I have, from time to time, taken select bottles of American wines to the French winemakers with whom I worked, and often heard the same comments. "Interesting." "Very hot." "I didn't know you could get merlot to taste like that." Yves and Martine, Philippe, and Jean-Luc have all traveled in American wine country; all have contacts there. They are curious to see what goes on there; they subscribe to American wine industry publications; and they always asked me questions, many of which I was ill prepared to answer. In America, we don't have appellations, we have AVAs, or American Viticultural Areas, which are very loosely defined geographical distinctions beginning and ending almost right at that. In America, winemakers are allowed to manipulate their wines in ways unheard of in France, particularly to make them "quaffable" or "easy" wines pleasing to the majority. The French perception is that American winemakers, with few constraints, tend to follow the market, planting zinfandel, chardonnay, merlot, malbec, or whatever else is the flavor of the month, rather than getting to know the land first. Either that or they grow what they think they can sell easily. The winemakers of Cahors, perhaps because they know no other way, approach things quite differently, with *terroir* at the very center of all they do.

"It is the natural world and the systems of nature that condition the life of winemaker, his character and sensibility," Yves told me once, as always with a bit of drama. "When the winemaker is there, planted in the earth, in his particular *terroir,* in his climate, he will assimilate it, stay in harmony with it, keep hold of his better human qualities and not those tied to the rigidities of science. Nature explains, makes us understand.

"With science, you can rationalize anything, and if there has been one big evolution in society, it is toward science. I don't deny that technology and genetic research in vine selection can be good. They can lead to more appropriate clones according to soil, rainfall, and other aspects of our *terroir.* But today, time is money; everything depends on, is judged by, time. I don't feel at home in that world.

"A winemaker is a man of adaptation. Every day you have to change according to what nature throws at you. I am against any method where they give you a calendar, a schedule, because what if you have a frost in April? You follow the behavior of the vines, the climate, the weather, the soil. And I know all these things; I am responsible for my wine. I know what is best. . . ."

What a Frenchman will take 250 words to say, often quite poetically, an American can often sum up more directly in a few. As I once heard a California winemaker say, "You can't buy *terroir.*"

6

❧

The Long, Hot Summer

PART ONE: JULY

"Hot and Dry, with Locally Unimportant Precipitation"

When I arrived to spend a morning with Jean-Luc at Clos Triguedina at the start of July 2003, the tasting room was locked up, the courtyard deserted. I followed the distant drone of a tractor, past the barns, the main house, across a patchy lawn, and through a small vegetable garden and finally headed out into the vines. Though not even nine A.M., it was already stifling, a hazy day with not a breath of wind stirring. Once over the crown of the slight rise that represents the highest and the best of Triguedina's parcels, I saw Jean-Luc atop a tractor pulling a tank of water, both straddling rows of young vines. Moving at a halting crawl, Jean-Luc was twisted around backward and leaning out of the seat, looking around the tank to a woman wielding a hose. "Make sure you give each one a good soak!" I heard him calling as I approached. The putt-putt of the tractor and the clang of metal against rock, another worker laboring a few rows over, were the only sounds in the still air.

Jean-Luc turned and saw me, a rare smile coming to his face and just as quickly going. He can often look like a bereft hound dog, his gaze intense, his impressive dark brows wrinkled, and that is how he looked then, a man with a thousand problems, the weight of the world on his shoulders. "*Salut*, Michael!" he called. "Not too hot?" He stopped at the end of the row, removed his faded orange cap, and wiped the sweat from his brow with a forearm. He hopped down nimbly from the tractor and came to join me at the edge of the newly planted vines. "We have to water the new vines in this heat." His gray T-shirt, ripped shorts, and worn sneakers were tinted orange by the dust of the vineyard. His bare legs and arms, lean but corded with the muscle of one used to the hard physical work of the vineyard, were deeply tanned by the sun; his wiry frame seemed thinner than usual. He looked altogether more like a dirt farmer than the head of a sophisticated million-dollar winery. His eyes were dark with fatigue, and I knew he'd risen at five that morning, as he had every morning for weeks, to steal a march on the oppressive heat of an unusually dry, hot summer.

He updated me on the state of the mature vines—"healthy, good vigor, good sun, but no real rain since May"—then gestured proudly at the two acres of even, closely spaced rows of young vines, half planted a year earlier and the other half just a few months ago. "These will make a future *grand cru*, I hope!" he said, referring to that elite classification, for Cahors still some way off, of the best vineyards in Bordeaux and Burgundy, which use vine densities like this. "I plant now because I won't be able to in ten years." Physically, psychologically, or legally? I wondered aloud. He laughed again.

"All of the above," he answered. "No, it's more the idea that I won't be of an age or inclination to bring them to fruition. This last bit took thirteen people five days to plant. There are thirty-three hundred vines to the acre, almost twice as many as normal, the eighteen hundred you can get away with to make a regular AOC Cahors wine." Vines planted more densely will, properly cultivated and pruned, produce far fewer grapes, but of a far higher quality, than those given more room to grow.

As we talked I watched the worker across the rows, a woman, straighten up and stretch, putting a hand to the small of her back. Under a white painter's cap, she looked to be forty-five or fifty years old. Her garb suggested a moonlighting housewife, though her flow-ered housedress was somewhat at odds with the pants and work boots below. She was preparing another row for watering, each new vine six to eight inches tall and with but a few leafy fronds gracing a thin, green stalk. With a short-handled mattock, she chopped a shallow circular depression around each vine, loosening the drought-hardened soil and removing debris, rocks, and the leftover roots of the scrub trees that had grown here until Jean-Luc had grubbed them up. She was efficient, smooth, using economical strokes, one and then another to break up the hard soil, two shallow scrapes to scoop out a bowl and on to the next plant, all the while careful not to hit the young vine or disturb its roots with the blade of her tool.

For their first year, the vines would be supported simply by individual wooden stakes. The more elaborate fence-like supports called vertical trellises, made up of posts and wires strung between them, would be unnecessary until the more mature plant began to bear in its fourth year. By 2008, Jean-Luc would begin to have some idea of what kind of wine their harvest would make someday; and perhaps by 2018, if all disaster had been avoided, he might even begin to profit from a hand well played. It was exactly times like this—no one chooses to plant new vines in a drought—that had put the silver in his hair and the lines around his eyes.

"We've already watered twice. I hope it rains soon," Jean-Luc was saying, a bit of concern in his voice. I would be back many times over the next two months, and he would still be watering. Even so, by the fall nearly a fifth of the young vines would die from the fierce heat and parching wind, their shallow roots unable to pull what little water there was from the ground.

A little later, he sent me down to one of the lower parcels, where a small group of mostly young people were doing the work of July, leaf thinning and bunch thinning. In French, the former is called *l'effeuillage,* the latter *les vendanges vertes,* literally, a green harvest. Leaf thinning better exposes the ripening grapes to the sun and air. Bunch thinning means leaving only some bunches from any one vine to mature and pruning away the rest. My guide to understanding this was Diamantine Marmier, a short, fit woman with a lovely, lived-in face who looked at home settled back on her heels, surveying the vines, and then attacking them with both hands and her secateur.

"It goes well—but hotly!" she said after I introduced myself, then went back to her work, explaining it between grunts of effort. "You pull off the leaves shading the grapes because the bunches will fill out, and the air has to pass between the individual grapes so they don't rot, get diseased. Then you let fall all but a few good bunches."

In the vineyards of Cahors, most vines are trained up into what is called a goblet or fan shape, technically known as a *Guyot simple*. Each dark, woody vine stalk rises vertically out of the ground and splits into two horizontal canes at about two feet off the ground, and then each of these arms climbs up another three or four feet: canes, vines, and leaves espaliered flat against the *palissage,* the supporting trellis, so that the pint-size tractors can pass between the rows to till, spray, and otherwise work the vines without damaging them. You also, though more rarely, find vineyards whose vines are pruned to have but a single major arm.

Along every row of grapevines, the *palissage* consists of horizontal posts of wood, metal, or concrete every ten or twelve feet and sturdy wires strung horizontally at three levels, the lowest being where the main cane splits into two, then two more wires above that at intervals of one to two feet. Grapevines bear fruit on only two-year-old wood. When you look at the vine closely after fruiting, you can see that the two branches are different: one thicker, with more wood than cane and with immature bunches hanging down; the other, without fruit, much leafier.

The vines are pruned so that the fruit emerges from spurs that sprout at intervals along that thicker horizontal cane (*la baguette* or *le pissevin,* in French) that has been fastened to the lowest wire. The wire supports the weight of the bunches, while the viny growth above firmly embraces the wires with its curly tendrils to provide further stability against wind and weather, sprouting an abundance of rich green foliage that changes sunlight into plant energy through photosynthesis.

Though what Diamantine had said sounded simple, it wasn't. With both hands she quickly ripped away all leaves above, below, and around the grapes, yanking at the vine with surprising violence; the leaves came away with a tearing sound and the whole trellis rattled. Then she took up her secateur and attacked the vine, snip, snip, snip, leaving just the best bunches, those fullest and best formed, to mature. A vine with twelve bunches might finish with eight after she had passed. She also pruned off those behind the wooden support posts, which a harvester couldn't reach and which would thus only rot.

"Before, we didn't do this here [in the vineyards of Cahors], and the wine was not as good. You cut out the bad grapes, the bunches that won't ripen, and then the ones that remain get more sun, more sugar. They're happier, healthier, and so they make better wine.

"And look at this." She cradled two bunches that had grown together. "One is rotten." She snipped it off at the stem and then gently shook the rotten grapes loose, leaving the healthy bunch to fill out unencumbered. She also cut the secondary smaller bunches which sometimes grow higher up on the vine and which, because they get less sap and grow more slowly, will never fill out and ripen as well as those below. Finally, she snipped off the occasional sucker growing from the base of the vine and suckers at the level of the grapes, as well as any deadwood. It looked as if a violent storm had passed in her wake—the ground was littered with leaves, stalks, and bunches of unripe grapes—but every vine was "groomed." That single word, by the way, is just about the highest compliment you'll hear from one winemaker commenting on the vines of another (*chez lui, la vigne est bien soignée!*), and it is very high praise indeed.

At the end of the row she stood up, surveying the teenagers who appeared to be doing more gossiping than pruning. "Not everyone pays as much attention as he should. I'm not the boss. It's Gerard's job—he's Monsieur Baldès' vineyard manager—not mine to urge them to apply themselves," she remarked, even though I would hear her upbraiding them later for their laxity. "I'll have to go behind them and clean up."

This is a problem common to all winemakers here and one I would see repeated over and over again, particularly during the harvest—a lack of dedicated, skilled personnel. Though growing grapes and making wine are only seasonal in their requirements for manpower, even this demand is complicated by France's employment laws, particularly by the "law of thirty-five," the thirty-five-hour workweek, which went into full effect beginning in January 2002. Higher seasonal demands at many vineyards, Jean-Luc's and Yves and Martine's among them, in the past had been filled by full-time employees working overtime and more part-time help than the vineyards can afford to employ today. The law abolished many kinds of temporary work contracts, required employers to reduce the hours of all full-time employees from thirty-nine to thirty-five per week without lowering their pay, and outlawed all but the most minimal overtime, with huge additional social insurance penalties to the employer when any employee did put in extra hours. Though the intent had been to create more jobs, the effect has been to make hiring any additional employee, even part-time, so burdensome as to discourage it.

Today, in the vineyards, the seasonal work may be done in part by mostly young, mostly unemployed people who put their names on a list at an agency. By law, they lose their benefits if they work more than a certain number of hours per month; thus they have no incentive to stay, to work any longer than their quota allows, or to work particularly hard or well in the hope of turning a small job into a larger one. Farmwork is also considered by many of the younger generation to be onerous, dirty, and unpleasant. As well, in France, the tax burden on the individual is so heavy that working two jobs is effectively unprofitable. What happens in practice, particularly now with the reduced workweek, is that some people have a second part-time job under the table. Even though owners often have their families to draw on and tend to work extremely long hours themselves, many French vineyards I have been in appear to be run with less than the optimum staff.

The vineyards of the Jouffreau clan employ, in addition to the owners—Yves, Martine, and her sister, Marise—only two full-time employees plus one part-timer to do the vineyard work; one more in shipping and administration, with the help of a part-timer; and several seasonal part-time workers during the spring, summer, and harvest, when the tasting and sales rooms need to be staffed. Jean-Luc has a vineyard manager, a cellarmaster (who helps with the making and aging of the wine), two full-time laborers, and an apprentice for the harvest and vinification. He has a larger sales and administrative staff, four all together; and Sabine, his wife, also works half-time, turning her hand to almost anything that needs doing. Philippe at Clos la Coutale runs his vineyard on an even leaner mix, with no managers at all for his five workers and two secretaries, but then he sells most of the single wine he produces in any quantity himself, abroad, a less complicated proposition than the arrangement at the other two vineyards.

These are not huge staffs for companies doing a few million dollars a year in business, but the burdens of unemployment and social insurance put on French employers, which can represent an additional 100 percent of the salary, make hiring more people an expensive gamble. And God forbid that you should have to let them go, for whatever reason—for then the employee has the right to collect up to three years of wages. (The power of the state over business in France would make most American businesspeople cry. When Marks & Spencer, the British retailer, announced in 2000 that it had to shut its stores in France immediately or risk bankruptcy, the French government howled. The stores closed in 2002.) So the vineyards rely either on itinerant North African guest workers, who serve the same purpose in France as undocumented agricultural workers in America, or, this particular year for reasons we'll get to, on the unemployed.

They end up out in the vines doing work that, while not as complicated as winter pruning, does require attention and some physical stamina. Diamantine is more of a permanent part-time worker, called in many times during the year whenever a reliable hand is needed. Still, she earns the same wage, about $9 an hour, as the slackers, though she's more efficient and competent.

Even while we were talking, for example, she moved steadily along, crouching or on her knees, relentlessly going at the vines, taking not more than thirty seconds to bully each one into a leaner, cleaner shape. "Now, we need rain," she was telling me, looking up at the cloudless sky. "Before it was sun and we had plenty, but now rain is necessary to water the roots to swell the grapes. This is the first time in three years we've had such beautiful grapes. I watch the vines develop beginning in March. I do anything Monsieur Baldès wants, replacing posts and training the vines to the wires, this work, labeling and bottling, and harvesting. I live out in the grapes, I watch them grow. It's beautiful in the vines, and Triguedina is a gorgeous vineyard. Of course, Monsieur Baldès is often out and about, seeing that everything is in order, as it should be. You have to. You have to put your heart into it to do what he does here, to make very good wine."

Jean-Luc had confirmed what I'd already heard from Yves and Martine at Clos de Gamot, and from Philippe at Clos la Coutale—that, while the valley could use rain, the grapes were in very good, very promising condition, with the heat and sun working their magic. The vines higher up, on the more arid plateau, were suffering, but not yet inordinately. The winemakers were cautiously hopeful that this might even be a very good year.

The first hint of even mild alarm I heard had come from Yves a few weeks before I arrived. He would call me at home in America from time to time, updating me on recent vinicultural, political, and familial events in the area. He was talking about the weather (this is how he begins every conversation when I haven't seen him for a while), when he delivered a single phrase that struck me. "Man does not control the faucet," he had said, speaking of the nascent drought; "and sometimes we forget that, in this technological world where they tell us we can control everything."

The day after I had seen Jean-Luc, I found myself bumping along the dirt road up to Yves and Martine's experimental hillside vineyard, Clos St. Jean, a few hectares of vines planted high up on a very steep slope in a vineyard whose every element recalls an authentic pre-phylloxera nineteenth-century Cahors *vignoble de côte*. If the vines were suffering, up there, I would surely see it. We came out of the trees to a view of the valley made more spectacular by the total absence of humidity from the air. As we walked down into the vines, Yves began to berate himself. "I haven't been here for two or three weeks! And I should have been—to cut the grass, to plow the rows, clip the tops of the vines. But I'm not going to stress out over it. Now, with all the constraints we work under, I'm trying to live with a new philosophy." He looked around, frowning.

If, when I had been up here last summer and fall, I had thought it was merely barren and sere, now it looked like a desert, the meager leaves of the vines the only color, and many of those mottled, some yellow, some brown or sickly green. Underfoot, the ground was cracked and dry, with no weeds except for an occasional thistle.

"The problem is, up here, with a dry summer and no grass, if we get a big storm, we'll have lots of erosion. And we have chlorosis, too." This disease causes a yellowing of the leaves from a lack of iron. In the Lot, there is plenty of iron in the soil, but it tends to bind chemically with the abundant lime from friable limestone and is thus unavailable to the roots of the vines.

"Look, tiny plants, tiny grapes, but that's how it is. We're always in extreme conditions here, so we have to be careful. We get phytotoxicity," a harmful interaction of sun and chemicals which can burn the leaf, "so I haven't sprayed in a month." He pointed to leaves with brown, curled edges and scars. "That's burned. And that!" he said. "Better to have left everything alone than to try to make guesses about this or that." I asked if they ever did leaf thinning and green harvest here. He almost burst out of his shorts with laughter. "Leaf thinning is a perversion, a grotesquerie! Why grow a vine with leaves only to rip off the leaves? And bunches of grapes only to leave half of them to rot in the dirt? [Those who do] are trying to re-create through artificial means what we would have naturally if we just followed a more responsible course—*la justesse,* an appropriate course."

We tramped downhill into the rows, and he seemed to be searching for something. He stopped between two rows and spread his arms. *"Voilà!"* he crowed, "there's our example." His left hand pointed to three spindly vines whose small leaves hadn't even covered the wires, and from which hung a handful of bunches, their fruit pea-size and green. At his right were three magnificent vines, lustrous green leaves hiding the wires they clung to, with long, full bunches of small but obviously healthy grapes, some of which had begun to color. "It's like one is the United States and the other Switzerland!" He fingered the poor ones. "Some of these have chlorosis *and* cariose [another vine disease]. The rich get richer, and the poor get poorer." He finished, "You see, I am managing a whole heterogeneous population. Sometimes I prefer nature to man. But don't get me wrong. I'm a winemaker, not an environmentalist." We passed into another parcel, where he had planted another malbec clone whose needs he hadn't yet mastered. "Next year, here, I'll put in manure. These vines clearly need it, and will benefit from it."

As we worked our way back up the hill, I watched as sweat bloomed in dark patches on his back. Yves was all in green that day, green Nitrophoska Elite gimme cap, light green T-shirt now dark with sweat, green khaki work pants amply dusted with the red, brown, and white soils of his vineyards. He looked like a soldier, if a slightly beaten about, overweight soldier.

I had noticed that, in fact, he'd lost a good bit of weight since the previous winter when I saw him last. "Homeopathic medicines," he said, "to bring my body back into balance. Either that or it's the stress, Michael, the stress!" Later, my ears popped as we descended in the battered panel van from the blasted hell of Clos St. Jean into the valley. We followed the twisting course of the Lot River through Castelfranc, then Prayssac before turning off into the vines once again toward Château de Cayrou, the largest of their three vineyards. "Making wine here is a lot like this river," he said at one point, one hand twisting and turning through the air. "You have to follow a torturous course!"

At Cayrou, Pierre, one of Yves' full-time workers, was driving a small tractor pulling a special machine through the vines. "*Décavaillon-nage,*" Yves told me, which is grubbing up the earth between each vine along the row to aerate and remove weeds. This requires much care in order not to damage the foot of the vine, particularly the more delicate part where the graft is. "A piece dropped off that machine yesterday and now he's using the old one. The new one must be thirty years old. You know how hard it is to find a replacement? It's a pain in the ass!"

Coming down from Clos St. Jean, the contrast was stark. Everything here was bigger: the vines were taller and bushier, the leaves and bunches larger and more numerous, the grapes themselves plumper and seemingly riper, although there was still not much vegetation between the rows. Even the roses marking the end of each row were vigorously healthy, their red blooms bright against the darker green of the vines. Always, in the valley and closer to the river, Yves had told me, there is more water, more humidity, and also more clay in the subsoil to hold previous rainfall.

"It will not be an excessive harvest," Yves said, a rare understatement quietly delivered. He palmed the bunches. "They're not enormous, the grapes, and the bunches aren't too numerous, are they?" He turned a bunch to me and pointed with a dirty finger to black spots. "See, these have taken a *coup de soleil*," a blow from the sun. "They usually get burned lower to the ground, because the woody vine is darker, concentrating the heat of the sun." He ran his fingers along the thinner canes emerging from the knobby stump to where the vine is pruned off every year. "The wood is ripening, too," he said. "It's green in the spring when it emerges. Now it's red, so you know the vine is not suffering. There is not an excess of leaves here, either. I mean, what are you going to thin here when there aren't exactly a huge number of leaves, eh?" he asked rhetorically, emphasizing his earlier point about the uselessness of thinning them.

The property of Cayrou is L-shaped, with the bottom leg a series of gently sloping parcels running down toward the river, and the other leg more vines in ranks up to the château, its slate-roofed towers and mature conical pines a conspicuous anomaly in what is everywhere else a low carpet of subtly marked greens. Every other row had been plowed, the grass turned under, and this made walking difficult, as anyone who has ever tried to cross the furrows of a newly plowed field knows. "We turned under every other row this year," Yves was telling me. Why?

Most winemakers used to keep the spaces between the rows clean of any vegetation at all in the belief that the grass and weeds stole nourishment from the vines. Looking out over the vineyards in that era only a generation ago, you would have seen gravel, pebbles, rock, and scant topsoil under the vines. Two problems led to a change in thinking. First, the hard rains, particularly in the winter, washed away the topsoil over time, particularly on any parcel with a slope; and second, the lack of ground cover drove away all the game, disturbing the natural balance of flora and fauna—and depriving hunters of a favorite fall delicacy, the vineyard hare.

Today, judicious "grassing in" of the rows (*enherbement*) has become the accepted practice. It is one more arrow in the winegrower's quiver, one more way to try to control the fecundity of the grapes all the while battling soil erosion and helping to create a more natural environment in the vines. The growers can plow under the grass in every row, every three rows, or no rows at all according to the fullness of what nature has given in other measures—sun, rain, heat, cool. Turning the grass under returns organic matter to the soil, adding to the nutrients available to the vine roots as well as removing a source of competition in the growing grass and weeds. The larger principle here is called "parasitism," and it is the notion that the winegrower can manipulate the competition for resources in order to control the fecundity of the vine more naturally than by pruning bunches or adding organic matter like composted manure. In a different way, this is just what Jean-Luc is doing by doubling the density of his vines per acre, stressing them through competition.

As we went back to the car, Yves was talking about when the harvest might be that fall. "It won't be later than the fifteenth of September. The only thing is, with this heat, if we have a good soaking and more sun behind that, it could be earlier. There is no way to know. We could have a drought that goes through October. Or through July and August and then a rainy September, which would push everything back. All these different elements make it so we can't predict. All we can do is compare with what has gone before."

For Yves and Martine, it had already been a difficult start to the summer. Their son, Franck, completing his second year of enological and agricultural engineering studies, was to have his knee ligaments repaired after a rugby injury, the operation to be followed by a long convalescence. This entailed the regular absence of one or both of his parents from the vineyard to drive him where he needed to go, and to spend time with him in the hospital and at the rehabilitation center on the other side of Toulouse, almost four hours distant. Aside from the time, there were of course a parent's natural worries for a child about to have a long and serious operation. Their daughter, Isabelle, had had a baby just a few months earlier—Juliette, whose first weeks had been complicated by stomach trouble, now resolved, but also a source of concern. As well, Martine had twisted her ankle and was currently hobbling around. Both she and her husband were on a diet, which, given that the evening meal seemed to be the single purely enjoyable, unstressed time of their long day, must have been annoying. Finally, their television had, for no good reason, apparently just popped and sizzled itself into oblivion when they had switched it on one night early in the month, and they had also taken this as a bad portent.

Back at Clos de Gamot several hours later, we met up with Martine, who immediately asked Yves how the vines were doing up top, at Clos St. Jean. She expressed the same slight worry over the lack of rain, but she was more concerned with their present crisis-mode schedule. "I don't even have time to do the food shopping!" she told me. "Summers are never calm for us. We have the summer visitors who come and want to taste, some of whom have been coming for years and years and who have houses here. We have to be open on the weekends; it's good to sell the wine! But we are so restricted when it comes to help that often we are the only ones here on the weekend. There is no time to rest, and, should we be called away, well, we just have to close. You can't ask an employee to work extra hours any longer. It's just not possible."

"Today," Yves added, "we have fewer employees who can work fewer hours, so we have to come up with new ways to save labor. And it is things like chasing after spare parts that are a pain in the ass. The métier of a winemaker, it's also things like that stupid part that fell off, this weather we're having, dealing with a shortage of workers, and what the hell all that has to do with making a bottle of wine. People don't look past appearances, the superficial; it's a problem of our society today." He paused to draw breath then went on ranting. "They just did a survey. Seventy percent of the French under the age of twenty-five want to be functionaries, to work for the government. That's pathetic! That's apathy for you! And those are the young people! It's going to be the other thirty percent who end up supporting them."

During the last weeks of July, nothing much changed. The weather broke only once, on July 14, Bastille Day, a brief evening rain shower followed by a cool morning the next day. "It was enough to barely wet the ground at Cayrou and Gamot," Martine related in a phone call, her voice strained, "but not enough to benefit the grapes." At Triguedina, Jean-Luc was equally blunt. "We're beginning to be concerned here," he told me. "I've never seen anything like it, and all we can do is wait."

Philippe at Clos la Coutale had been the most relaxed, the most laid-back and confident, when I had seen him shortly after our arrival, but that was his usual state. He had invited my wife and daughter and me to join a group of his old friends for a barbecue and a celebration. When we arrived at Philippe's luxurious house nestled into the vines just up the road from his vineyard, it was seven P.M., still blazingly hot, with not a cloud in the sky or a whisper of a breeze. Philippe's big news lay in a bassinet beside his longtime companion, Babette, mother of his three-month-old son, Mathis, who had been passed through a succession of arms before falling asleep. His two older sons by a previous marriage, eight and twelve, splashed in the pool with a coterie of visiting young girls, who had instantly sucked my daughter, Lily, into their vortex for the evening. Philippe's huge brown-spotted Dalmatian, Pétrus (leave it to a winemaker to name his dog after a famous Bordeaux vineyard), wandered through our legs, eyeing the food just out of his reach and giving us meaningful glances and bumps with his massive head.

As we sat around a big table under a stone portico beside the pool drinking cool rosé, Philippe recounted his latest adventures, in this case travel to various European and American cities to sell a recent invention. This is a new kind of corkscrew, the Coutale (sales: 450,000 and counting), whose most salient innovation is that it reverses the normal operation of pushing the handle down after inserting the screw, and that pulling up is handier and easier, particularly, he thinks, for women sitting down at a table during, say, a dinner party. He had also almost bought another vineyard, this one in Languedoc, until he learned that the château pedigree on the label, an established name, wasn't, somewhat mysteriously, included in the sale. Never one to sit still for very long, he was already looking for other properties, investigating other ventures.

As for his vines, he wasn't too worried. "We're at the back of the valley here," he remarked, his voice soft as always and marked with that soothing local lilt. "And yes, we need rain, too, but we usually harvest a little later than the others, so that gives us a bit more time. It is too early to worry about what has not yet happened." And that pretty much sums up Philippe's approach. I'll worry about it when I have to, and in the meantime I'll go about my business. And how was his business, especially in America, given the unfavorable political and trade climate? "Kermit Lynch," the exclusive American importer of Philippe's wine, "hasn't reduced his reservation this year," Philippe commented. "I hear that some restaurants are taking less, but we're not suffering. My wine is still a very good value in your country, and besides, I do much more business in Canada." He shrugged, and our conversation moved on to other things.

Now, the last week of July, when I had stopped by to see him, he was talking like the others. "It's beyond 1976, beyond my experience," he told me with just a bit of edge to his voice as we sat in his office. "It's beyond my father's experience, too. And these grapes, the state they're in . . ." He paused, gesturing with his head in the direction of the vines. "You've seen them, no? Go out front there, they're starting to get *crammé* [grilled]. . . .But we still have a month or more. It could rain next week!" Somehow, he didn't sound very confident.

PART TWO: DOG DAYS OF AUGUST

It was a terrible thing, but the more time I spent with the winemakers that summer, the more it felt like I was holding vigil over a slow death in the family. And, as with a death, I watched as they began to pass, slowly but inexorably, from denial of the disaster taking shape; through the stages of anguish, grief, and mourning; and finally on to a fatalistic acceptance of the losses they were facing and a resolve to make the best of what nature had given them.

All the newspapers could write of was the heat, the drought. The local sheet of the southwest, a rugby-obsessed sporting rag called *La Dépêche du Midi,* is the kind of paper whose writers can never simply say, "Madame X died." Instead, Madame has been transported to that better place, met her last reward, been welcomed into the arms of eternal slumber, departed this green earth, or gone on to greet those in the next life.

Their headline writers, perhaps stupefied by the heat, got off to a slow start ("HOT HOT HOT," "DROUGHT GRIPS COUNTRY," "FARMERS ANXIOUS OVER LACK OF RAIN, HEAT") and then moved into a sort of interrogative indignation ("WILL THE HEAT NEVER BREAK???" "HOW HOT CAN IT GET?" "WHY THE HEAT, DROUGHT?"). By the middle of August, however, they had clearly pulled out all the stops as they cataloged the country's growing ills: rising prices for fresh produce at the markets ("BLAST OF COLD FOR THE FOOD INDUSTRY"), suffering livestock ("SAVE THE CATTLE!"), threatened electricity shortages ("POWER CUTS: SUSPENSE DOWN THE LINE" and "HIGH TENSION OVER ELECTRIC SUPPLY"), the cancellation of fireworks displays ("HEAT WAVE EXTINGUISHES FIREWORKS"), and the growing cost to the government ("HEAT WAVE INFLAMES BUDGET") were just a few of the region's travails they reported in increasingly purple prose.

The first signs of real trouble were benign enough in their effect on daily life—bans on watering lawns or gardens and washing cars; warnings against open campfires at campgrounds; the cancellation of the fireworks displays which are so beloved of every flyspeck French village and which take place every Friday, Saturday, and Sunday night all over provincial France throughout the summer. Low flow and water levels in some rivers led to cases of bacterial disease in swimmers and left canoes and kayaks and their concessionaires dead in the water on the Lot and Dordogne.

There were daily incantations against heatstroke and dehydration, the big killer, at every turn, and each night the television news would show hospitals and emergency rooms filled with mostly the very old, oxygen masks to their faces, clutching bottles of mineral water. The statistics were followed by a personal story of the sort that began with a close-up of a middle-aged woman, in tears, saying "I found her on the floor in front of the stove, barely breathing and burning up! I *told* Maman to drink water, but she would forget . . ." while in the background, a whey-faced old woman on a stretcher was being wheeled out to a waiting ambulance by medics. The advisories of various state agencies involved, the police and firemen, the health and weather services, the local drought committees, at the start of the summer mild and vaguely cautionary, now became full-blown exhortations. Stay inside, drink water, don't overexert yourself, and call for help if you need it.

The village volunteer firemen had a terrible summer, continually rushing away from their jobs when the siren wailed, as it did sometimes a half dozen times a day. At the café, you could always tell who was on call because, as soon as the air horn sounded, the firemen jumped to their feet and then waited, counting the number of siren calls to see if the fire was local or in one of the neighboring towns. Most often, they were racing off to field fires. Many was the chagrined farmer who set his own crop alight with a stray spark from the harvester, and some farmers took to having the firemen stand by as they reaped, just in case. The firemen were also called out in their role as paramedics, particularly in the cities, and they began to talk about what they were seeing. Their stories, of delays from lack of manpower and finding elderly shut-ins dead for no good reason, were at first alarming, then became steadily grimmer until, by the middle of August, the country was in a state of outrage.

People had been dying, it seems, in huge numbers, and nobody, least of all the powers that be, had known it. The first estimates, at the end of July, were that 3,000 people had perished in the heat. By mid-August this number had risen to 5,000; then it rose to 10,000 in early September. In the big cities, particularly Paris, throughout the last half of July and the beginning of August, a time when doctors and medical personnel take a month's holiday (like everyone else in France), the hospitals and emergency rooms were overwhelmed while the paramedics, nurses, and firemen, the only available help, worked double and triple shifts. The morgues began to overflow, and ranks of refrigerated trucks to store the bodies became a common sight outside the big hospitals. A sick joke began to make the rounds: What do you have to do to get air-conditioning and medical attention in Paris? Well, first, you have to die. . . .

By the time it was all over, more than 12,000 Frenchmen and Frenchwomen, mostly the elderly and most living alone in the larger cities, would die of heat-related causes that July and August, a crisis that would lead to the resignation of the health minister and the condemnation of Prime Minister Raffarin's government as ineffectual, corrupt, and incapable of looking after even the most basic needs of the French people. While it is true that most homes, offices, and even public health facilities—clinics, hospitals, nursing homes—in France lack air-conditioning, that alone didn't explain why so many more people died in the cities than in rural France. Old people in the villages and towns out in the country fared much better, the authorities later concluded, because they were less isolated. They knew their neighbors, and their neighbors looked out for them, stopping by during the day to make sure they were not in trouble.

You didn't have to read the paper or watch the news to see that something was going seriously awry with the world. All you had to do was look out the window of your car as you drove through the countryside. By the beginning of August, more than three months of drought and five weeks of intense, unending heat had begun to have a deleterious effect on just about everything. In the Lot, already an arid place, the smaller streams dried up entirely, spring-fed ponds disappeared, and some villages that relied on wells for water found them dry, existing on water trucked in by tanker.

The rhythms of the natural world were out of whack, with strange and worrisome effects. The crowns of trees, mostly oak and chestnut, were dying, their yellow-brown patches dirtying the usually green view of the hillsides all around. The light wind of dusk, usually the harbinger of rain, brought only more heat and dust. We began to see odd behaviors among the fauna—a moth drinking out of a Perrier bottle at the café one afternoon and swallows dipping in and out of our neighbors' pool to catch a drink on the fly, oblivious of the people swimming.

Farmers who fed their beasts over the winter on a staple diet of hay and usually looked forward to two, sometimes even three, cuttings of their fields between May and October were looking at a deficit of more than half of their needs. Thieves, using the back roads and forest tracks late at night, took to stealing the big round bales of precious hay from the more isolated fields. In the afternoons, the roads would be filled with tractors pulling wagons filled with corn. This was not the autumn crop of bright yellow ears, for this year there would be no harvest—the ears were too few and their kernels were stunted and misshapen by the lack of water. No, this was the entire plant, ground into silage, a poor winter feed for the cows, and no substitute for grain.

French nuclear reactors, which generate the majority of the country's electric power, got permission to release water from their cooling towers into the rivers at higher temperatures, but two larger problems loomed. The rivers were very low, and the average temperature of the water was already very high, leading to massive fish kills. Also, the river water was less effective at the higher temperature for cooling the reactors, reducing the amount of electricity they could generate at the time the country needed it most.

The chitchat of daily life became rich with the vocabulary of heat, much of which I heard from winemakers bemoaning the fate of their grapes—*grillé, crammé, confit, cuit, braisé, passer au four,* and a dozen phrases invoking the *four, fourneau,* or *fournaise*—all taken from the imagery of the oven or kitchen and suggesting that everything in the world was being slowly cooked by the sun. (Respectively: grilled, burned up, stewed, cooked, braised, put in the oven, furnace, oven, stove.) The duration and intensity of the heat wave began to break all records. First 1976 fell, then 1949, and finally in mid-August, Lydia Bouysset, the lively greengrocer in Cazals, where we were living, told me that the meteorologists were back to 1893.

While some heat and the stress it brings are good for grapes, too much, coupled with drought, had begun to do strange things to the vines, too. A hot summer can be beneficial when sufficient rain has fallen in the spring and early summer because the lack of humidity discourages many vine diseases and concentrates the juice inside the grapes. With so little rain from April through August, however, the situation prevailing throughout the appellation was a deepening disequilibrium in both the health and the state of ripening of the grapes, depending on the vines' location. In the valley, where deeper clay soils store water and where the coils of the river provide some humidity through evaporation and the persistent morning fog, the vines on the higher terraces were not themselves suffering, though their grapes were being burned up by the heat. Higher up, on the plateaus in the thinnest soils, particularly those over shale or rock, the situation was graver, with the vines showing real effects of a long-term lack of water.

When I stopped by Triguedina on the first of August, it was to find a preoccupied Jean-Luc passing the hottest hours of the workday doing paperwork in his office. "About three-quarters of the grapes in the highest parcels have started to ripen; and farther down, on the second terrace, about half. With this drought, we can't know how the grapes will mature. Up top here, despite everything, they're ripening and not getting too fried by the sun and lack of water. Up at Floressas," the plateau at the back of the valley where he has reds and whites, too, "the ripening is blocked by the drought and the vines are stressed. You can see that with your eyes—the leaves wither, dry, and then fall. Happily, not all of our vines are up on the plateau, because otherwise we'd be very worried about having anything to harvest."

"Anything can happen," he continued when I pressed him about the effect of so much heat on the eventual wine. "It's too early. If we have another month and a half of drought . . . There's no water to the leaves, to the grapes, to the body of the vine. The grapes are smaller, to be sure, as are the bunches. *Au lieu de mûrir, ils vont confire!*" Instead of ripening, they'll just stew in their skins! I chuckled at his rhyme, and he smiled, but painfully.

"That's not a joke. If there is no rain, there won't be a lot of juice in the grape, the grapes in drier ground won't ripen well. We will lose volume, certainly, but, once the grape is in a mature state, it will lose moisture and stew rather than ripen. It presents us with a problem— are we going to harvest earlier or are we going to wait until the grapes are truly ripe and risk losing everything? Just because the grape seems ripe doesn't mean the tannins of skin and seed will be fine for a finished wine. If the juice inside the grape becomes concentrated before the grape is truly ripe, you're not going necessarily to be able to make good wine from it. In my opinion, this year, we're going to have some parcels that are very interesting, and those that are less so in terms of the wine they make. It's always like that, sure, but this year is one of extremes already. I know that I won't have the homogeneity of ripeness and quality that I have had the last years."

This was a long speech for Jean-Luc, with some subtle points. When a winemaker uses the word "interesting" or, sometimes, "original" to describe a wine from a parcel or even from a whole vineyard or an entire vintage, it is generally a clear signal that something is afoot. Earlier, I had asked him to explain the press coming out of Bordeaux, a few of the great names already pronouncing in the papers and on television that this was going to be a year of fantastic wine, even if the amount available would be reduced. At that, he had smiled his bitter smile.

"Michael, these are winemakers talking! A winemaker is going to tell you—every year—that this year's wine is the best he's made, ever, until the moment you have the glass lifted to your lips, at which point he may aver that there were perhaps a few problems with the weather at harvest or some such."

And so, "interesting"? What did that mean, exactly, I asked him.

"It used to be that the merlot always ripened first," he said, "but now, for the last four or five years, we've been starting with the auxerrois, and finished up with the merlot. We can do that, start the harvest, stop a couple of days, start again. It's not a problem. In fact, that's how it always goes, a couple of days here, then another parcel is ready a few days later. Also, normally, the merlot comes in at a degree *less* in sugar than the malbec, but this year it might be the other way around. If we have in the next time good weather, well, in some of our parcels of merlot all the grapes are already blue and very healthy. They could end up in the tank at 14 or 15 degrees!"

These are grapes very high in sugar, Jean-Luc went on to explain, which, after fermentation, would make a flabby wine, almost certainly too alcoholic and probably lacking the acid and tannins to make it balanced, or a wine that could age to any degree of complexity. These are in fact, exactly the problems of dry, hot country vineyards in more southerly latitudes: they make wines with too much alcohol and not enough acid or ripe tannins, the constituents that add complexity, balance, and character to a wine and that allow it to age in the bottle. A perfect example of this kind of flabby wine is the famous, or infamous, Two Buck Chuck, from Charles Shaw in California. The red, especially the merlot, tends to be particularly flat and boozy, but what do you expect for $2?

All the winemakers here use merlot as a blending grape, to add softness and roundness to the more astringent malbec. How could they find a balance with nothing to blend? "And you can't add water, either, you know." He laughed. "What you see now, usually you wouldn't see until the fifteenth of August, so we're two weeks ahead this year. We've got those beautiful days of September, too, which could really push up the sugar in the grapes."

I pressed him on what he would lose in yield. "I expect"—he looked around the room, not eager to put a figure to his losses—"I expect fifteen to twenty percent less. Even if the grape appears to be the same size, there will be more solid matter inside, and so the effect is a more concentrated juice.

"I think we've had something like thirty-three millimeters [1.2 inches] of rain at Triguedina since *April*," Jean-Luc said, shaking his head. Normal rainfall for just the month of August has been historically a little less than two inches. "We don't know what to expect. It reminds me of 1976, but then we had cloudbursts in July, and the wine was very good. This year, I can't tell you too much about it. Ask me on September fifteenth! Either the grapes won't ripen fully, the tannins won't develop as they should, or we'll have a precocious overripeness that we'll have to deal with. I just don't know!"

That was the first of August. By the end of the next week, everything had changed.

It got hotter.

The temperature in full sun, which had been generally at 100 degrees or just above in the afternoon, climbed to 105 degrees, and finally, on the fifth and sixth of August, the red column rose to 110 degrees, a torture made more unbearable by a blistering wind that blew through the valley. What I remember most from those days was the ubiquity of the heat; the breeze was so hot that it sucked the moisture from your eyes and nostrils. You could not escape it, not even in the lakes and ponds, whose temperatures were sometimes in the low nineties, unpleasantly warm.

After more than a month of almost continuous heat, I began to notice that a kind of drought ritual had imposed itself on us all. The villagers were out and about with the first light, doing their shopping, stopping by the Café de Paris for a social café, and then going back inside by nine or ten. The streets were otherwise completely deserted, particularly from noon to four or five, except for quick forays to the butcher or the baker for the essentials. Then, in the late afternoon, you would see people venturing out in the street, their eyes cast eastward,

toward the villages of Gindou and Mongesty, hoping to see the billow-
ing clouds of a thunderhead and, behind them, black sky. All were
hoping for a rising wind, too, hot at first, blowing with it a tide wrack
of grit and red dust, sand, trash, leaves, and, then, later, if we were
lucky, the first hints of coolness.

So many early evenings, the clouds gathered, the wind rose, and I
sat in the courtyard of our house, waiting. I found myself looking up
anxiously, consciously willing the rain to fall. My newspaper would tick
with one drop and then another, more and more so that I would put it
down, get up, and venture into the street, from where I could better
watch the approach of the storm. Then the drops would taper off, accel-
erate, slow maddeningly, and then stop altogether. The sun would
come from behind the clouds, not so fierce but still too much, and the
heat would set in once more.

And then, on the seventh of August, it rained.

My wife and I had arrived at La Fontaine, the stable where we've
been riding for four years now, at six o'clock that evening for a ride at
dusk. It had been only 103 degrees that afternoon, the same dry unre-
lenting heat we had more or less learned to live with since we had
arrived in the Lot. It hadn't rained since the fourteenth of July, and
that rain had only been a passing sprinkle, a storm that exhausted
itself in an impressive warm-up of lightning and thunder and hadn't,
in the end, even produced enough rain to fill the cellar cistern which
was the only thing permitting us to water our landlady's luxurious
bushes and flowers in the courtyard. The cistern and dishwater, which
we collected assiduously. Our neighbors, I noticed, could often be
found outside with a whispering hose after eleven at night, padding
about in their slippers from planter to planter, smiling only a bit
guiltily at you as you passed.

By the time we reached the upper fields to get the horses, the light
breeze, so welcome when we arrived, had blown up into something
more serious, a scorching, very dry, dust-filled windstorm. Iris, the
usually placid horse I rode, was stamping his feet and rolling his eyes,
jerking his head away as I tried to halter him. I looked up to see the
eastern sky filling with dark angry masses shot through with glassy

openings, the sun pouring down in shafts as in some seventeenth-century pastoral painting. In the west, the sky was like broken glass, shimmering in a jagged light, the sun an orange ball sitting on the horizon. Abandoning any thought of riding, we hurried down to the stables, where the now forty-miles-per-hour gusts were lifting horse blankets, pads, anything light and loose, into the air. After securing what could be secured, we hopped into the car, hoping to race the storm home before it could do any damage to our house.

A quarter mile down the road, we saw that a neighbor's field was on fire, the low flames racing this way and that through the parched grass. This field was just up the road from a sawmill, where piles of drying lumber lay just waiting for a spark. Driving far faster than was safe, I pulled up one minute later in front of the Hostellerie de Goujounac, the local hotel-restaurant, and my wife raced inside to call the firemen. While she was inside, I heard the sirens, and a fire truck rushed past, tires squealing. On the road out of town, still hurrying along, the storm arrived, huge gouts of rain staining the road, sending up puffs of dust, and we relaxed a bit, knowing that the fire must surely have been extinguished and that our friends and their horses were safe. The air was filled with the perfume of a storm, that smell of ozone and old paper that tickles the nostrils. All around us, the landscape was tinged with an eerie, rosy light, the greens and grays and violets intense and saturated, the leaves on the trees turning, bending, branches whipping as if in a storm at sea. Odd bits of leaves and debris, caught up in clouds of dust, rolled over the crowns of the hills around us, giving shape to the wind. Now we were driving through puddles thick with the scum of pollen, the road already breached in places by washes of mud and gravel. And what, I wondered, watching this amazing instantaneous natural violence, was happening in the vines?

As we drove the twenty miles home, I watched the temperature fall on the dashboard readout, from 100 degrees on our arrival at the stable, to ninety-five at our abrupt departure, down to eighty-eight five minutes later, then sinking below seventy-five. Driving past the last farms before Cazals and our rented house, we saw horses standing in the fields, heads down, enjoying the rain. The roads were already filled with fallen branches and flooded with muddy puddles, and rivulets ran across them. By the time we got home, it was fifty-eight degrees. I stood just under the roof's edge and felt the cold sting of the rain on my face. I could hear the cistern gurgling, already filled by the flow from the gutters. Everything, everyone was breathing. What was this thing in the air? Humidity! You could almost hear the earth drinking, and everything that was green breathing.

The next morning, after the first good night's sleep in a month, we awoke to find a brilliant green praying mantis on the kitchen table, and my wife would come back after a long walk to tell me she'd happened on a crayfish crossing the road, hundreds of yards from any water.

I would like to report that the rain fell throughout the night and into the next day, in twenty-four hours banishing the drought and putting to rest the deeper fears of all those farmers and orchard men and wine-growers. "What we need," Yves had told me, "is two or three days of light rain, a good few inches over a long enough period so that the ground can absorb it. If it rains too hard, the water will just run off."

The dog days returned after that single night of respite, that brief tantalizing interlude having done nothing more than taunt us. The winemakers told me that less than half an inch fell on the vines in most parts of the valley, not enough to make a difference one way or another, and that the heat and sun were now putting the whole vin-tage at risk. Not that it would make bad wine, but that it would make little or no wine, that there would be very few grapes healthy enough or ripe enough to be worth harvesting.

A few days later, having invited Yves and Martine out to dinner, my wife and I sat in the courtyard of Jacques Ratier's restaurant, La Récréation, up in the hills about twelve miles north of the river in the small village of Les Arques. They arrived, appearing weary after a diffi-cult few days (their son had moved from the hospital to the rehabilita-tion center after his successful operation) but ready, that night, to relax and to have a good meal. Yves was looking very sporty indeed, in shorts and a bright plaid short-sleeved shirt, his hair neatly cut and his tanned face (unusually) well shaven. Martine, her glossy black hair set-ting off the paleness of her face, looked almost cool in a short-sleeved, open-necked blue polka-dotted dress.

I ordered a bottle of a white Cahors, a Château du Cèdre, advertised as a sémillon-viognier blend perhaps to justify the slightly audacious price of $18. (Viognier is a low-yielding, hard-to-grow white wine grape from the Rhône, the grape of the well-known and very expensive Condrieu and Château-Grillet wines.) We all tasted it, and Yves and Martine, who know all the winemakers' tricks, exchanged glances. "A lot more sémillon than viognier," Yves grumbled. "Don't!" his wife scolded him, and, to me, "It is fine!" I was quite sure she shared his opinion but equally sure that any glass taken in the company of winemakers is an invitation to disputation.

In tasting as in all things connected with wine, Yves has taken on the role of my teacher. Later, to accompany our main dishes, I ordered a bottle of red Chinon wine because I knew it would be fresh, served cool or even chilled, something different and good in this heat. "And what is the red grape of the Loire?" Yves asked, looking at me challengingly over his bushy eyebrows. I took a breath and concentrated, quickly eliminating the cabernet sauvignon and merlot of Bordeaux; the malbec of Cahors, the syrah, and grenache of the Rhône; and the carignan of Bandol. Pinot noir? I guessed, the red-wine grape of Burgundy. "Cabernet franc," he said in mock reproach, "and that is why it is so graceful and light."

"This heat," Yves was saying, "It's worse than 1976, worse than 1949, and now we're into uncharted territory. You saw the vines last week?" We had been out together, walking and tasting grapes at Cayrou and Clos de Gamot. I remembered, at Cayrou, Yves chomping down on two or three, then deliberately crunching the seeds between his teeth. He had stuck his tongue out at me abruptly, and I laughed and stared, a bit puzzled. "See that color?" he had said, sticking his tongue out again and pointing to the blue-purple stain on it. "That means the skins are already ripening, and you can taste a bit of the sugar in the pulp, too. But they have some way to go. The seeds are still green and astringent, not ripe at all." I crunched a few myself, and indeed, they had the sharp, tannic bite of a sour apple. "They have to ripen, too, for the tannins to be good," he had told me.

"Well, everything has changed since then." Yves was saying, tucking into the lovely cold gazpacho we had all ordered to start. "We had that very hot wind that blew through. Until then, the vines were healthy. The grapes, in proportion to the lack of water, they were fine. Then this *coup de chaleur*, a hundred ten degrees, and now everything is deranged. First the fruit suffers, the grapes, then the plant itself, the leaves, and it risks dying. The harvest is going to be very, very small. . . ."

"*Une trie à la main*," Martine said, unsmiling. "Sorting them by hand as we harvest and after . . ."

"We don't know. If it rains now, the grapes will begin to ripen, and very quickly we'll have to harvest or else risk overripeness. We've been talking to people. We called a drought expert in Toulouse. He told us he hadn't seen anything like this since he consulted for a chardonnay grower in California. The grapes are being dessicated on the vine by the sun. And the sap doesn't rise as it should."

He went on, "We chose grafts that were more resistant to frost and disease first, and not so suited to drought, but we never thought to see such drought here, in the river valley. Up at Clos St. Jean, we knew it would be very dry and planted accordingly. Those vines are doing fine. But down below, no."

I had been by to see Jean-Luc and Philippe as well, and they, too, were talking about steep losses. And yet, I had noticed that, as the disaster loomed ever closer (and disaster it was—imagine for a moment your salary cut from one day to the next by half or more, and that for a year!) they seemed, after those first terrible days, to get calmer, more fatalistic.

Even at that point, ever the optimistic and ill-informed American, I found it very hard to accept that there was not something to be done. Were they just going to let the whole harvest turn to raisins before their eyes, let the vines, in the worst case, suffer perhaps irreparable damage? In Cahors, indeed in most appellations of France, no *appellation contrôlée* vines may be irrigated. This follows on the quite rational logic that any land that can't consistently support a vine and its fruit to maturity on what falls from the skies and comes up from the ground is not land well suited to vines at all.

As well, that summer, with the drought then entering its fourth month, water rationing was already a reality in some regions, and here irrigation was strictly illegal and punishable by stiff fines. Nevertheless, a few days earlier in the late afternoon Yves had walked me out behind his vines, up over the hill, and pointed to a neighbor's vineyard, where revolving sprinkler heads hooked up to high-pressure hoses filled the air with a shower of drops brilliant against the setting sun. When I had asked Yves why he didn't report the man, Yves just shook his head wearily. "It's not worth it," he had said. "It's not like he's going to improve his wine, and believe me, around here, what goes around, comes around." I was left to imagine the implications of that last remark.

Sitting at the restaurant table, he said simply, "It's not a question of what one can do, Michael, but of what *is*." Martine nodded in agreement. "In the time of our fathers and grandfathers, they knew that nothing was for certain. Some years, you would suffer. That's how it is. Almost without exception we've had nearly ten good years. So this year nature takes back what she has before given so freely."

The unusual conditions, perhaps the stress of the current situation, had, lately, brought out a different, more reflective side of Yves, I had noticed. "I was thirty-two years old in 1983 when my father died," he was saying. His family had had land and vines and made wine in Algeria before being forced to flee with nothing after de Gaulle's disengagement in 1956. "At times like this I miss him. I miss my father-in-law, too. Now, I feel I have things to talk about with them, advice to seek."

The meal was certainly not somber, as Yves' natural ebullience and humor boiled up throughout, but he and Martine were more quiet than usual, their thoughts constantly returning, I presumed, to worries over what the next weeks would bring. At one point, Yves delivered himself of a jeremiad against the technological experts and their supposed marvels. He and Martine had attended a seminar in Toulouse the previous fall at which, apparently, a young scientist had showed them that it was possible to calculate the yield of a parcel of vines meter by meter using satellite imagery and global positioning. "*À quoi bon?* What's the use of that, especially in a year like this?" he railed. He was not a Luddite; he bought the most modern equipment he could afford and the best genetically selected vines, but he had no use for supposed innovations that in the end seemed to serve no greater cause than keeping the government-funded agricultural institutes busy.

Two weeks later I was out in the vines with Jean-Luc, who was fatalistically assessing the coming harvest, the current state of the grapes. His vines had suffered in exactly the same way as Yves and Martine's. It was one thing to have a winemaker say, "My grapes are ruined." It was another to watch Jean-Luc's face as he walked dejectedly up and down the rows, yanking off a pathetic, burned bunch here, bending close two steps away to caress a fine cluster which had, for whatever reason, filled out magnificently.

"The outer row always suffers the most because it's so exposed," he remarked, his eyes sweeping along the row, gauging the extent of the damage. "But much of this is . . ." He paused, thrusting an arm out over the whole field. "It's gone. Just *gone*."

It was grotesque, almost sickening, and yet paradoxical, too. The leaves were still green, most of them, and the vines looked vigorous, until the eye traveled down to the lowest wire, where the grapes usually hung in such abundance, clearly visible as long triangular bunches of full purple-black globes, one after the other in a line all the way up the row, every row, wherever one looked. In that third week of August, however, many of the bunches were hardly perceptible, the grapes shriveled or, more pathetically, pea-size and immature, and so incapable of holding any juice.

"It was almost a hundred ten degrees here, and that has never happened before, not in my life," Jean-Luc said. "Then that hot wind blew through. It just *crisped* the grapes on the vine. Whether or not you did leaf-thinning around the bunches made no difference; the wind grilled everything. My neighbors didn't thin, and they got burned the way I did." Those who had thinned the leaves of the vines would actually pay more dearly that year, as leaves can shade the bunches from the sun. "Up in Floressas, you're two hundred fifty meters high and, sure, they've suffered, those vines, but they'll be okay. Below, the valley forms a big bowl, and the hot air just settled in and baked everything."

But some vines lower down than his seemed, I observed, greener, healthier. "Some people"—he looked away—"they dope their vines, and doped vines resisted the heat better, suffered less."

Doped? I asked, not understanding.

"Doped."

This is the same word the French use to describe athletes who take performance-enhancing drugs, so I was a bit confused. (Throughout that yearly French summer obsession, the Tour de France, which Lance Armstrong had won yet again in 2003, one of our more ungenerous friends had taken to calling him *le dopeur américain*.)

Doping your vines, Jean-Luc explained, means chemically fertilizing them or fertilizing them beyond the minimum required. Though it is not strictly a violation of the appellation's standards, the only fertilizer you find in all of the best vineyards (including Jean-Luc's, Yves and Martine's, and Philippe's) is composted cow manure.

"Around the vineyards, one thing I have noticed was that those vines that were 'doped,' they had more generous, greener foliage, and those leaves made the grapes better able to fill out." He looked down at the ground, kicking at the parched soil where even weeds were rare. "Those of us who worked the hardest, who made the effort to thin leaves and to cull the bunches, we'll suffer the most!" he finished bitterly.

At Clos la Coutale, not two miles from Jean-Luc's vineyard, Philippe was walking across the courtyard when I pulled in to see him later that afternoon. He was wearing a short-sleeved yellow button-down shirt streaked with sweat; shorts; and his usual flip-flops. His face was grim, and his sentences were even more sparse than usual. "I have never seen a year like this. I can't tell you when we will harvest. I can't tell you what the wine will be like. We don't know. We need rain, two or three inches at least, and that coming not too late." He shook his head and looked at his feet.

We walked to the edge of his vines, and he lifted a few pathetic bunches, looked at me, took a few ripening grapes, and crunched down on them. He grunted and spat. "You go anywhere out here and in some spots a third of the bunches are lost, in some state of dessication or already so hard and tough. And they're not even ripe! Taste them!" I did and found that they had only a hint of sour grape left in them, not even any sugar, not even the jammy sweetness of a raisin.

Up and down the river valley, the story that August was the same. A very few vineyards, through a peculiar combination of location, geological anomaly, and perhaps, some whispered, moonlight irrigation, would come through with two-thirds of their harvest intact. Most winemakers were predicting losses of half or more. There would be almost no white wine made, as those grapes ripen the earliest and had suffered the most dramatically. Paradoxically, the wholesalers were happy, for the moment, because in wine barns throughout the appellation, more than an entire year's worth of wine lay, unsold, from previous harvests. "It's not this year that we'll suffer," Yves had remarked when we had been out looking over his ranks of ruined white wine grapes. "But two, three years out, when we have nothing to sell, no wine or very little, that's when we'll suffer."

There was even talk of declassing the vintage—and this before the grapes had been harvested or a single bottle of wine made! Declassing a particular vintage in a particular appellation—declaring that no wine made in that year in that place is of sufficient quality to qualify as an *appellation contrôlée* but must instead be sold at a much lower price as bulk wine or *vin de table*—is a serious and quite rare maneuver used to protect the reputation of the whole appellation by removing its name from bad wine made in truly bad years. That it was the head of the Cahors winemakers' cooperative who was doing the talking, well, that was all the worse.

7

❧

HARVEST

In the first week of September 2003, seven days away from the grape harvest, Yves' rain gauge at Clos de Gamot recorded just under two and a half inches. "Sixty millimeters. *Beaucoup trop*"—much too much—Yves was telling me ten days later as we stood in front of the small wine barn just next to the tasting room. Except for more drought, lashings of rain were about the worst thing that could have happened just before they brought in the grapes.

It was the middle of September, and you couldn't drive a mile down any back road through the vineyards in this part of the Lot without having to slow for a lurching mechanical grape harvester turning between row ends and wheezing tractors and farm trucks of every vintage pulling brightly painted wagons of ripe, fragrant grapes on their way from vine to vat. On the outskirts of some villages, like St. Didier-Parnac, Mercuès, Prayssac, and Douelle, where the houses ended and the wine barns and vines began, the air was heavy with that musty, almost cloying smell of ripe grapes beginning to ferment, a sweet smell that always reminded me of my mother making strawberry jam in a hot kitchen. Another common sight that fall was a tractor backed up to a barn door, a conveyor spilling the grapes from the wagons onto a sorting table where nimble hands picked them over, throwing to one side those bunches too dessicated to do anything but make the wine taste like raisins. In the evenings, all the cafés and bars from Albas to Puy l'Evêque were filled with sunburned men and women whose clothes looked as if they'd been splashed with purple, their hands stained the particular shade of rich plum that showed they'd been picking.

Having expected a scene of supercharged chaos and excitement, over-flowing wagons lined up to discharge their loads, and the vines alive with the laughter of the pickers, I was a little surprised to find, on arriving early that morning, Yves and his son Franck—still recovering, his knee in a cum-bersome brace—standing around a wagon full of grapes talking quietly and not in the least harried. From time to time, one or the other would reach in to remove stray leaves or to pluck a grape from a particularly fine bunch for tasting. The ground underfoot was littered with purple clumps of grape skins and seeds, and various tubs and hoses and pumps awaited the start of the next operation, de-stemming, lightly crushing, and then pumping the resulting slurry up into one of the tanks where it would, everyone hoped, quickly begin to ferment.

"Sixty millimeters in a week!" Yves repeated. "The vines took up too much water in too little time. It was excessive in these conditions. And it made the grapes swell, so the skins burst more easily, while the heat has already eaten the acidity in them. That's why we're in a hurry to harvest. They're as ripe as they're going to get." He gestured offhandedly through the open door, where three cement fermenting tanks of between fifty and seventy hectoliters (1,322 to 1,855 gallons) awaited. "In three days we've harvested only eighty-five hectoliters," a little more than just the biggest tank. "This year we're already scrambling around to find small enough tanks for the parcels we vinify separately." The only reason they were not in a hurry this morning was that, with so few good grapes on each vine, it was taking the pickers longer to fill the bins. "And down the road we're going to see a huge lack in what we have to sell. That's why you always, always have to keep a good stock. Our society has forgotten that nature will occasionally take back what she has given. Wine is not an industrial product, but a natural product. You can't manufacture it." As if he'd heard his father beat this particular dead horse before, Franck rolled his eyes at me, grinning good-naturedly.

The meager harvest and the poor state of the grapes, though

obviously discouraging, were not a surprise. Toward the end of that difficult summer, I would often walk the vines with Yves. Martine always came along when they were taking samples because it was something they did together, an opportunity to keep in touch with the vines for Martine, who tended to divide her time between the office and the wine barns, and particularly to talk over with her husband any problems they found, away from other cares and distractions.

Three weeks earlier, just before I had left to take my wife and daughter back to America for the start of the school year, I had been out with Yves and Martine at Château de Cayrou, their largest vineyard, as they took samples of the grapes to determine their maturity, in particular to measure the amount of sugar, which predicts a final alcohol content; and the acidity, which is necessary to make a balanced wine that will age well. Yves was dragging a makeshift plywood rack that held his testing equipment, a motley and rather abused collection of plastic buckets; beakers; what appeared to be a food mill; a complicated jerry-rigged apparatus made of squeeze bottles, calibrated pipettes, and surgical tubing that dispensed metered doses of a chemical reagent; two refractometers, which looked like fat silver cigars but with an eyepiece at one end; and two or three plastic-covered conversion charts much creased and stained with use.

The local wine authority faxes bulletins every few days summarizing the test results of its own enologists, who are also out in the field, checking maturity levels from vineyards all over the valley and up on the plateaus, but Yves and Martine rely very little on others for information about what is happening in their own vines.

This is something Yves and Martine are fanatical about (Jean-Luc and Philippe, too): keeping on top of the health of their grapes and monitoring the ripening of the grapes themselves. They will be out in the vines testing, usually once a week and more frequently as harvest approaches, in forty different spots throughout the various parcels beginning about a month after the first color appears, usually at the start of August, through to the harvest in late September in a normal year.

Their equipment might look old-fashioned or ragtag, but in this, as in many other things, appearances are deceiving. Yves and Martine are slaves to the morning and evening weather forecasts on television and radio, but Yves still charts the rainfall and temperature on their own lands himself. He can tell you the elevation to the meter of landmarks all over the valley, not just those of his own parcels, and he knows where the hot spots are and where humidity lingers. He puts out his own insect traps and monitors his vines for various diseases obsessively, rather than relying on the agricultural service to tell him when and what to spray.

Also, like Philippe and Jean-Luc, the Jouffreaus subscribe to the idea of growing grapes and making wine as *la lutte raisonnée*. A concept hard to translate, it means essentially that all these winemakers take an almost organic approach to their vines, forgoing the use of chemical fertilizer and herbicides while encouraging nature to do what it does best. This is in contrast to a more industrial approach that follows the dictates of any predetermined, by-the-book regimen in fertilizing, dealing with insects and plant disease, and managing yield.

"There is always some disease—fungus, mildew, whatever—present in the vines, always insects, too," Jean-Luc told me one day that summer as we looked at a disease-ravaged grape leaf. "I read the bulletins from the agricultural service, sure, but if I am out here, watching, following, observing, I know how much is too much and so when and where or even if I need to treat. The goal is to use the fewest chemicals possible, and we've discovered that, by keeping our vines as healthy as possible—and that is more work, more labor—we can do that." This approach is not without risk, as, should he find a situation he had to respond to quickly, it would take him three full days just to spray his vines once.

I had heard nearly identical words about this notion of taking the middle course from Philippe, when I commented on the two tractor-trailers delivering huge bales of composted manure one day at Clos la Coutale. "You don't need to use chemicals to fertilize," he told me. "So why do it? Manure is what our parents used, no? Around here they used to walk the cows through the vines to and from their pasture," a natural manure-spreading operation.

Even as we had driven the narrow road that runs along several of their parcels that afternoon of testing in August, Yves had groaned and sighed. "Normally," he said, "when you drive up at this time of year, you see a thick band of black at the bottom." I had noticed this, too, at the harvest a year earlier: when you looked down a whole row of grapes, your eye immediately caught the contrast between the rich green leaves above and the dark bunches below, hanging like a thick, dark ribbon about two feet off the ground. But now, although I could see dark patches, they seemed separated by lots of space. As we pulled off the road and parked not ten feet from the nearest rows, I could make out the individual bunches, most of them short and many shriveled away to nothing. "This year, we'll be lucky if we get fifteen hectoliters to the hectare," which is about 165 gallons per acre of vines. "That's about two-thirds less than normal." We went into the vines, Yves and Martine pulling grapes from left and right and tasting them. We walked the length of a whole row to a break between the parcels, and at the other side Martine looked at her husband grimly. "I know," he said.

She turned to me, explaining, "The ends of the rows are OK, but the whole middle is burned up." She let out her breath and smiled up at me a little wistfully. "It's too bad. You'll come back in September, and we wanted to show you a lovely harvest. *C'est comme ça*. . . . There are no guarantees."

I wondered how the ends could be fine but the middle totally ruined. "The outer rows get more air, more circulation, and less heat, and are thus healthier. Also, Michael," Yves directed me, "look at the middle of the parcel. There's a berm [a ridge of soil] across the top that stops the water from flowing downhill here. And there, below, the vines are all *sur les galets*." The middle vines were planted on a bed of pebbles, unlike where we were standing at the edge, which had at least enough organic matter to nourish grass and weeds.

Yves moved through the vines, plucking thirty or forty grapes randomly along each marked row, which they had tagged with ribbon tied to the last picket. They had begun testing these rows weeks earlier, following the evolution of the grapes in what years of experience had taught them were representative places to sample. The grapes fell, each variety in its own plastic pitcher, on top of which Yves put a leaf from which he would later identify the parcel and variety. He went from malbec to tannat to merlot, from young vine parcels to old vine parcels, and then finally we returned to the edge of the field. *"Allons-y!"* he said, taking the first pitcher and dumping its contents into the food mill. Why not just squeeze the juice? I asked Martine as he ground away, a slurry of mashed skin, pulp, seed, and juice dripping into a beaker underneath it.

"We want to measure just as if it were in the tank," she answered. Measuring the sugar and acid of just the juice wasn't enough; the pulp, seeds, and skins all contribute, and all must be measured.

First, he took the sugar of the first parcel of merlot we had walked. This meant smearing a dab of juice from the beaker on the glass screen at one end of the aluminum cigar, the refractometer. He pointed it at the sun, looking through the eyepiece at the other end, and then handed it to me. I saw a scale in black mounting vertically, and a blue column that, Yves told me, was the sugar level. The blue rose to about 11.5, which was a rough indicator of the degree of alcohol these grapes would produce after fermentation in a finished wine. "Eleven point eight, eleven point three," Yves told Martine, who was recording the numbers in a field diary. He then sucked up a precise amount of juice with a pipette and put it into a clean beaker before dribbling a reagent from another precisely calibrated beaker. He swirled the solution, adding more reagent drop by drop, until it turned blue. He then looked to the chart to determine the acidity according to how much reagent he had poured. The merlot from this parcel was at 5.4.

"As the grape ripens, the sugar rises and the acid falls," Yves said. "But too much sun burns up the acidity. What we want is maybe 12.5 degrees of sugar and an acidity of 4.3. That's a good balance."

Some anomalies emerged as Yves ground away through the rest of the parcels, measuring and dictating to Martine. This is why they do it themselves, so they can catch the anomalies, which in turn dictate the order of attack when they harvest however many days or weeks later. One parcel was at a relatively low alcohol (10.5 degrees) while the acidity was still high. "That's not a good sign," Yves told me. "Sometimes the sugar increases but the acid doesn't move. These grapes need another ten days at least." A parcel of old vine malbec gave an almost clear juice, which disturbed him. "Look at this, Michael; the juice isn't even black, and by now it should be." Then, from a neighboring field of young malbec vines, he pushed the beaker under my nose. "See that? In a week it will be bright red. It's already redder than the other." It had good sugar, at 11.3 degrees, but its very low acidity—4.4—made Martine suck in her breath. "It shouldn't go below three," she said. "And in the last weeks it can really move down quickly."

Three weeks later, we watched the level of the grapes in the wagon fall as the rotating screw set into its bottom pushed them out one end and into the de-stemmer (*l'éraffloir*), which removes the stems, crushing the grapes lightly in the process. Yves held a long wooden stick, and from time to time he would lean into the wagon, clearing out the corners, where the grapes tended to clump up. This was the first wagon of the day, bearing the efforts of a dozen or so pickers who had been working in one corner of Gamot's parcels since seven-thirty that morning. There would be ten or more before the team quit at four P.M. or even five, if Marise—Martine's sister and the one who always organized and oversaw the pickers—could get them to work that long. It would take them, this meager year, a little less than two weeks to harvest Gamot's thirty-two acres, all by hand.

Between the noise of the tractor engine, whose power drove the screw emptying the wagon, and the racket of the *érafloir*, conversation was almost impossible. Yves had shown me this machine, pointing out that it was forty years old, was used less than two weeks a year, and was very expensive to replace. It is a very simple device consisting of two hollow steel drums set one inside the other, their tops cut away and both in a cradle on their sides. The metal of the inside drum is pierced at regular intervals with holes just slightly larger than the largest of grapes. Revolving inside it is a screw-shaped spindle from whose flanges protrude spikes at right angles. As the bunches go in at the top, the spindles force them gently against the sides of the drum, where the individual grapes, which are very ripe and loose on the stem, drop off and fall into the outer drum. From there, along with their juice, they are pumped up in to a tank for fermenting. The stems are too large to fit through the holes and are pushed out one end by the action of the turning screw.

"For the reds," Yves had told me, "you want to liberate the seed and crush the skin to release the matter trapped in it. You don't want to

crush the stems, because that would release too much of the green tannins in them. It used to be, thirty years ago, that we would also crush
the grapes, passing them between two rollers, but there has been an
evolution in both technology and taste. It used to be that the fashion
was for very tannic, very woody wines, but now people want more fruit.
As well, people drank stronger, more alcoholic wines, while now they
want something lighter, fresher. It is all this—science, experience, and
taste—that makes things evolve. Life is eternal change," he finished
philosophically, "Only in death do you find stasis."

An hour later, we pulled off the road at the Jouffreaus' larger property,
Château de Cayrou, at the end of a parcel. In the distance, we could see the
beefy Bernard, Yves' right-hand man, atop a tractor pulling a mechanical
harvester, while his lieutenant, Pierre, walked along on the other side of
the row. As we watched, Pierre darted in front of the harvester and pulled
something from the ground. He would also, from time to time, take a
secateur from his pocket and clip a bunch left behind, throwing them up
and into the bins on either side of the harvester.

I got an idea of the action of the harvester when, standing at a row
end, I saw the vines begin to shake violently right in front of me when
the machine was still 100 yards away. It works by straddling a row of
grapes. At the front, special *battes* on either side and low down embrace
the base of the vine and agitate it rapidly back and forth, so that the ripe
grapes fall off the stem onto two ridged conveyor belts that close
around both sides of the vine. The inside edges of the belts are made of
a soft rubber-like material, allowing the vine to pass without damaging
it, and are cut to fit together like the teeth of a zipper so that the grapes
don't fall through. The belts loop from just off the ground to carry the
grapes and their juice up and dump them into two compartments, one
on either side of the machine. The end result, when you look at a row of
vines, is rather weird: the green stems still hanging but minus their
grapes, a litter of leaves at their feet, as if a great wind had come through
and sucked off every last fruit. It is also immediately obvious where the
harvester has passed, because, beyond the obvious lack of grapes, the
lower leaves and vine stems are dripping with juice.

When they reached us, Bernard pointed to the wine barn in the distance, signaling that the bins were full, leaving Pierre to join us. His sudden dashes in front of the harvester were due to the occasional forgotten wooden stake, used to prop up young vines inserted here and there into the rows to replace older vines that had died. "The harvester eats them," Pierre explained, giving me a lopsided grin. "They clog up the works. Other than that, it's going well."

I asked Yves about the loss of all that juice in mechanical harvesting. "[With] the machine, yes, you lose some juice," Yves told me, "but the unripe grapes and the raisins stay on the vine and out of the vat." It wasn't possible to harvest this by hand? "Where would we find the personnel? Also, it costs us maybe 350,000 francs [$70,000] to buy a machine—and we can write it off. It costs us perhaps 450,000 francs *every year* to harvest by hand, and guess what? You can't write that off!" As we walked into the rows, he cut a few bunches that the harvester had missed. He held one out to me, pointing at the slight ridges and wrinkles on the skin of the grapes. "*Perlé,*" he said, blistery. "And that's why we have to harvest. When it blisters, the juice comes out and the rot comes in."

Later, inside the wine barn at Cayrou, Yves knocked his knuckles against a stainless steel tank. "Three tanks they've filled," he said, shaking his head. "Normally, we'd have filled the row, all eight of them, by now."

In one corner, Bernard was dumping a huge tangle of grape stems into a bucket of water to soak. "Our other worker, Marc, he'll make the *paillon,* the filter at the bottom of the tank," Yves explained. It is safe to say that many of his colleagues, Jean-Luc and Philippe included, would probably laugh at this. Making the *paillon* (or *paillou* in the local Occitan dialect) is the very old-fashioned practice of binding a bundle of stems tightly with grapevine to make a sort of plug that is propped with a weight against the pipe on the inside of the tank that leads to the spigot. When the tank is drained, the *paillon* catches the heavier sediments as well as keeping the spigot from getting blocked with the larger detritus of fermentation.

Yves left him with a few encouraging words, and then we hopped back into the car. "Bernard and Pierre and the new kid who's back at the barn preparing the tanks, the three of them will do nine acres today." All together it would take them a little more than a week to harvest Cayrou's sixty-eight acres by machine. Gamot's thirty-two acres would take a dozen harvesters, in a year with normal yields, twice that long.

As we approached Gamot, Yves slowed at the collection of beat-up cars pulled off the road where the pickers were working that morning. He grumbled to himself, then turned to me. "I'm counting heads. When you see their heads, it's a bad sign. They should be bending over picking."

His day was only going to get worse. Late that afternoon, with several wagons full of grapes oozing their precious juice, the de-stemmer would break down. Because the grapes might spoil or become contaminated with bad bacteria from the air, they couldn't just leave the grapes in the wagons overnight. He and Bernard would try to fix it for hours before giving up and hauling the one from Cayrou to Gamot to finish the job. They wouldn't get to bed until two-thirty in the morning, though that was early enough for a few hours of sleep before the pickers returned the next day, myself among them.

It was 43 degrees out when I got into the car at seven to drive to the vineyards. In a hurry, excited, and cursing myself for not having risen in time for a cup of coffee at a café en route, I sped along the back roads, driving far faster than I should have. Coming around a corner, I braked hard. Two hundred feet ahead of me a wild boar, a big male with yellow tusks and a dark, bristly coat, paused only briefly to stare at me before hurrying across the road. As I sat, shocked by this apparition, fourteen more—smaller females, young *marcassins,* and a half dozen babies looking exactly like their piglet cousins—followed. I took it as a good omen, but slowed down all the same. Crossing over the last ridge and down into the valley, I could see fog over the lower fields and on the river, a heavy dew on the grass of the verges.

There were a dozen or more rough-looking men and women gathered in front of the wine barns, sucking on cigarettes and drinking from water bottles, by the time Marise appeared. Marise Jouffreau is quite different from her sister, Martine. Her dark hair is cut short; she is slender and intense, very direct and energetic. That day, in worn khakis, a polo shirt, and high rubber boots, she looked like just another picker, very different from her usual elegant and businesslike appearance. She told us where we would be picking, and we dispersed.

The parcel we would be harvesting was across from a field of corn on one side, sunflowers on the other. A flock of pigeons settled on the heads of the sunflowers, which were a rich chocolate brown next to the vivid green of the vines. A farmer had lit a brushfire, and white smoke hung like a twisted ribbon in the sky. We began to harvest, and that was the last time I had the time or energy to notice much of anything until lunch.

Five hours later I had made the brutal discovery that, because I am a little over six feet tall and the grapes hang about two feet off the ground, there is no good grape-picking position for me. At first, I tried bending from the waist, until my knees were creaking, my lower back was protesting, and the tops of my thighs were burning. Then I tried squatting, picking while resting on my haunches, but my ankles and feet soon went numb. I went down on my knees for a while, until they were well and truly bruised from the rocky soil. No matter the position, my back ached and blisters formed on my palm. My jeans were covered with mud, and everything—hands and forearms, shirt, and thighs—was sticky with the red, sugary juice of the grapes.

Here is how you harvest. In your left hand you have a bucket. In your right you have a sharp metal secateur, like small garden clippers for deadheading roses—this one red-painted, no comfy neoprene grips, just bare metal, which will quickly become slippery with grape juice. You find a partner who will work the vine from the other side. If the vines have been leaf-thinned, in which case you can see more clearly, you can work only on one side, the one from which they tore off the leaves. You put the bucket under the vines to catch any wayward grapes. You rip away any leaves covering the grapes, which hang in bunches four to ten inches long about two feet off the ground. You cradle each bunch (or several bunches, if they are small and contiguous), and clip the thick stem, guiding them with your hand into the bucket. You shift the bucket left or right, kicking it along with your foot until it is so heavy with grapes that you have to pick it up. Move to next vine, repeat, without a break except to call for a new bucket, or to empty it yourself if you happen to be close to the wagon.

The bunches sometimes grow in tangles around the wire, and then you have to grope blindly with your left hand to find the stems in the tangle, and then snip them with your right hand without cutting your fingers, or, more embarrassing still, the fingers of your partner, who is snipping, often, only inches away. Good harvesters have a way of snipping once, then again lightly, catching the tip of the stem in the jaws of the secateur and flipping the bunch out of the leaves and into the bucket with a single motion.

I have thick fingers, and after a few hours it seemed harder and harder to see the stems, partly because the sweat was running into my eyes. I could feel the back of my neck hot with sunburn, and my forearms were bright red. By then, mid-morning, my knees had gone, and my back, to the point where straightening up was becoming an exercise in willpower. My socks were swimming in sweat, loose in my rubber boots. My shoulder began to ache from lugging the buckets and from that motion, repeated hundreds of times, of lifting the pail over the wire and hurling it forward until, with a final jerk, the grapes and juice fell into the wagon instead of going down the front of my shirt and jeans, these last gone almost purple, like my hands. This is to the winemaker a good sign, a sign that the grapes are ripe, that they have color and that the skins are releasing it.

If the picking is well run, the tractor driver advances the tractor in pace with the bulk of the workers, and he or his bucket runners appear regularly at your call of "*Sceau! Sceau, s'il vous plaît!*" Bucket! Bucket, please! They drop an empty bucket and collect your full one and those of your neighbors. If you're close to the wagon, buckets are ferried under or over the wires and vines by anyone handy. The etiquette requires that you never go to the wagon with a single bucket, but always grab someone else's full or nearly full one on the way.

At Clos de Gamot, Marise's team that year was mostly *voyageurs*— "travelers," polite French for Gypsies, in particular a local group called *les Manouches,* some of whom live in camping caravans at a spot on the riverbank which is known as Les Pescadoires and which the local authorities have been trying to eradicate for years without success. Most of them are young, in their twenties and thirties, but some look older, especially the women. Early marriage, many children, and living sometimes very roughly have taken their toll, especially on skin and teeth. They were a very merry, vocal bunch, and it didn't take long to figure out a few things. The women were working in general twice as hard as the men. The men seemed to miss no opportunity for slacking off for a smoke, a joke, a sip of water, especially when the rows we were working were almost finished and it was time to move on as a group. Then, they gathered around the tractor and its wagon, empty buckets dragging, until Marise rallied them either to help those who hadn't finished their rows or to get going on the next section. (When you're harvesting and you discover someone has done the end of your row, that's called a fat Sunday, slang for sleeping in and here meaning a bit of a break for you.)

Marise worked the team with a wisdom gleaned from years of harvests. She pushed them hard in the morning, always in their midst, popping up here and there, laughing at their jokes, speaking softly with many of the women. "It is always so hard to find good harvesters," she told me. "We used to have a group of people from the villages, mostly women, who came to help every year. No one wants to do this work anymore, and so you have to work with what you get. We try to hurry a bit now, when it is cool and they are fresh. After lunch, it will be a different story." Marise never complained, never made excuses, just kept on until the work was done—a quiet presence, but a presence all the same.

I would be humping along, brushing the sweat out of my eyes so that I could see enough not to cut a finger with the secateur, when she would appear beside me, her hands, protected by long rubber gloves, deftly separating grape from stem at a rate I could only admire. "Ça va, Michael?" she would ask, her dark eyes flashing. "There's water in the car if you need it." Then she was off to help the next laggard finish out a row, or to call for an empty wagon. Marc, the tractor driver, was always on top of it, very competent, fast, disappearing with loads of harvested grapes. He'd brought down two tractors with their wagons, and he pulled the empty one up into the rows before taking off with the full one so that you never knew he'd gone.

I found myself working with Dani, a lovely, dark-skinned, dark-haired, dark-eyed woman who had four kids, the youngest five years old, and whose sister was married to the shirtless, short, stout tattooed guy who produced more noise, scatological commentary, and waves of laughter in the others than buckets of picked grapes. Dani was a cheerful help and also gave me running translations of their impenetrable slang—about a girl who was about to get married too young, about the dawn arrest at gunpoint of one of their own suspected of robbery, at Les Pescadoires, a story I would read in the next day's paper—while blushingly refusing to translate some of the wilder propositions being bandied about between the rows.

Toward lunchtime, Yves arrived out of nowhere. He watched a harvester working toward him, then, suddenly, seeing the puddle of spilled grapes all along the young man's row, exploded in frustrated anger. He grabbed the harvester with one hand and with the other gestured violently at the fallen grapes. "You put the bucket under the vines, under the vines, understand? Jesus Christ!" The others came over to watch, Yves repeating the phrase like a mantra, looking from face to face. "Under the vine! Under the vine! The bucket goes under the vine!"

Although his approach was a bit strong, I could understand his emotion. By then he knew for sure what before he had only suspected, that this year the yield wouldn't be just half the usual, but perhaps even less. (In the end, it turned out to be about 40 percent of normal.) All over the valley, whole parcels were going unpicked because there were not enough healthy grapes to justify even the cost of the harvest. This was hardly a year to lose what little that was good to laziness. And it wasn't as if he were crying over the loss of a few grapes here and there, either. Unlike table grapes, which are firmer and less sweet, wine grapes are left on the vine until they are at their peak, and as a result they are also fragile. These grapes, so ripe and swollen by the recent rains, were delicate indeed, some bunches even blooming with the first spidery webs of mold, which was not necessarily a bad sign. As soon as you touched a bunch with fingers or secateur, it often exploded with a shower of juice and grapes, which, if you were doing as you were supposed to do, all fell into the bucket.

Later, I found myself next to Benjamin, a twenty-two-year-old local boy. Tall, dark-haired, and very tan, he was quiet and serious, talking mostly to his picking partner, Jean. The two worked at the same pace, and they were trailing most of the others because, when you looked at their vines, they were clean, and the ground underneath was clean, too, except for rotten or dry bunches and parts of bunches. Was this a good vineyard to pick at? I asked him. He shrugged, his fingers going from vine to mouth, sucking juice from the grapes. "One place we worked, they fed you at noon, gave you a bottle of red. My stomach is grumbling! My back aches, my hands. But there's no pause here; we go from seven-thirty or eight to twelve-thirty, then an hour and a half for lunch. I go to my parents, put my feet under the table, and I eat! An hour and a half, it passes quickly, too quickly. And then back to work for four or five hours without a break. It's physical work, hard labor. For the well-being of the worker we should get a break."

Some pickers always worked as teams, and this wasn't their first, or only, harvest. They were fast, talked only to each other, and kept to themselves at lunch. They would start in the south, sometimes as far south as Spain, and work their way north as the grapes ripened, picking the latest-ripening whites in November in Alsace. There were a few solitary harvesters, too, who didn't talk at all; they only picked. Benjamin had pointed one out to me earlier, a middle-aged man with the dark, leathery face of someone who spends a lot of time working outdoors and who was moving at a furious pace, always ahead. "Look at that guy! A robot. He must be on some kind of drug!"

And so we worked on past noon to the lunch break, the morning's exuberance fading a little as the day heated up and the novelty of the work wore off. There were cries of "Who's got a bucket? A bucket! A bucket for Jean!"—and the snick-snick of fifteen pairs of shears, the snapping of foliage as people ripped off bunches of leaves, the rattle of bucket handles, and the plonk-plonk of bunches of grapes falling into empty pails.

When lunch was called, we trailed back to our cars, then up to the wine barns. There was a picnic table set up outside in the shade, and the Manouches had soon loaded it with baguettes, pâté, sausage, and cheese. The stout guy brought out a bottle of Ricard, eighty-proof anisette, for his aperitif. When I left, Marise was delivering the wine, unlabeled bottles of red, plonking one down at each end of the table. She looked at the Ricard with a frown, and then went off for her own lunch.

Contrary to the folklore, there was no harvest feed put out every day by the vineyard, with the grannies serving up a hearty, home-cooked banquet and the winemakers pouring gallons of the new wine with a free hand. At Gamot, there had been such a spread some time ago, but Yves, Martine, and Marise couldn't remember exactly when the practice had stopped. It seemed to be tied up with the fact that the whole tradition of picking by hand, which used to be the norm all over France, was giving way to machine harvesting as people left the land. It used to be that everyone pitched in, young people not yet back to school or the university, all the relatives living in other cities returning home for the necessary week or two, retired people, housewives, and all the local surplus labor, too: groups of the same people coming together to work side by side in the same vineyards year after year.

Today, with the passing of the rural economy, those ties no longer exist. A readily available pool of labor willing to work in the vines for $9 or $10 an hour from first light to last, seven days a week, which was what the grapes demanded, had also disappeared. It was now against the law to ask for such long hours, and the government was no longer granting exceptions to the wine industry. The unemployed young weren't willing to do the work, and that left the North Africans, who today perform most of the jobs the French no longer want to do themselves.

To Yves and Martine, it seemed that machine harvesting had followed the social changes, the shift from a tradition of communal labor to individuals with machines, rather than the other way around. "Since women began working out of the home the same hours as the men, there's no time," Martine observed. "It used to be the women worked the harvest with the men. My grandmother, my mother, and I, we all worked both in the vines and in the wine barns when the grapes came in. I can remember when the men and women would sing in the fields. They were happy to be working together, getting the grapes in, today harvesting this one's land and the next day someone else's. Now, a lot of the young kids, they're plugged into their Walkman and don't even hear what the person across the row from them is saying."

Because the harvest was so early this year, the *magrebi*, as the French call the North Africans, were either not yet back from their late-summer furloughs or already working elsewhere. "Everything's

out of whack this year," Yves had complained when I asked if they usually had trouble finding harvesters. "That's why we don't have any
Moroccans this year. They're picking apples and plums farther south.
Or they're still on vacation. The chasselas [white table grapes, a local
delicacy grown in the neighboring Tarn-et-Garonne region], you must
have seen them coming up from Toulouse—they're all rotting on the
vine because they ripened so early. In the markets, everything has its
season, and the buyers weren't ready for them either. So, no lovely
chasselas grapes for us, and no North Africans to help us harvest. This
year we took what we could get."

Why don't they just harvest all their vines with the machine? The
vineyard of Clos de Gamot is ancient by modern standards, with fewer
than half of its parcels replanted in the last generation. When you walk
the vines, you notice right away that many are thick in the trunk and
trained lower to the ground. Here and there, a white grape vine pops
up among the red, planted to fill the gap long ago, in an era where you
couldn't go to a nursery to buy the right replacement but had to use
what you had on hand. Many of their vines are more than fifty years
old, and they even have one five-acre parcel of the famous *vieilles vignes,*
or ancient vines—squat, gnarled beasts whose twisted bases can be as
thick as a small tree trunk.

These vines, all malbec, are part of the living history of the vineyard, for they were hand-grafted to the first phylloxera-resistant rootstocks and planted by Martine's great-great-grandfather, Guillaume
Jouffreau; they are some of the few vines in the whole appellation to
bridge genetically the pre- and post-phylloxera eras. Their yield is pal-
try, 4,000 or 5,000 bottles, but quite special (and expensive), and their
grapes make, in the best years, an intense, long-lived wine, an old-
fashioned wine that has no equivalent in the entire valley.

The old vines and the ancient vines were planted long before the coming of mechanical harvesting, which works best on taller, younger vines
that grow straight up out of the ground, while the stocky trunks of these
old warriors veer this way and that between the ground and the trellis. For
all their girth, however, they are fairly fragile, as Yves showed me once
when he put his boot against the base of one old granddad and pushed.

The trunk, far from being massively rooted, as its size suggested, wiggled back and forth very loosely in the ground. Quite simply they are too delicate, too quirky. They have to be harvested by hand.

Philippe at Clos la Coutale not only doesn't have any old vines but doesn't see why anyone would bother with them. "There *are* no hundred-year-old vines," he had told me flatly one day as we walked his vineyard. "It's a myth. We rip them out after fifty years because they get sick! They get sick and so produce less, and you see it's time for new vines. There are viruses in the soil that attack weak vines, old vines. If you tell me you have hundred-year-old vines, I'd say, 'Show me the planting certificate.' Maybe, maybe they have a few that have been regrafted, after the phylloxera, but do they give any grapes? Enough to make a wine?" He shook his head. "I doubt it."

I have seen the Jouffreau planting certificate, an official document countersigned by the wine authority certifying that so many malbec vines grafted to this or that particular rootstock were planted in this defined place. The Jouffreau document shows that their old vines were planted in 1893, and, yes, they still produce both grapes and wine.

Jean-Luc has old vines at Clos Triguedina, too, planted in the time of his grandfather. I know them intimately, as, after a day at Gamot, harvesting this parcel was the next day's task. Another early rising, this one complicated by the fact that I could hardly move. Another motley crowd of pickers, but a crowd whose differences soon became apparent. They were professionals, much less voluble in their conversation if speedier in their picking. There was a mix of young and old, including a good number of professional migrant vineyard workers who spoke of their time in Bordeaux, doing the midwinter pruning, of planting and staking new vineyards in Languedoc in the spring, of their most recent jobs two months earlier thinning leaves and bunches further south in the Pyrénées foothills.

Jean-Luc joined us soon after we started, along with Sabine, his petite wife with her quiet, pretty smile and competent hands; and his three-year-old daughter, Juliette, a moppet lugging a wooden basket almost half her own size and a pair of nursery scissors. Sabine is from Burgundy, from a winemaking family, and she knows well the rhythms of vineyard work. I worked beside them for a while, watching as Sabine showed her daughter which grapes to cut and which to leave, Jean-Luc looking on with a rare smile and encouraging words when her spirit flagged. That morning, he seemed oddly at peace, given the poor harvest, with a lighter step and even the occasional bit of dry humor emerging from his lips.

It was much hotter than the day before, and somehow even more depressing, as Triguedina's old vines, the parcel we were harvesting, had suffered enormously in the previous months. Though I had been told that vines older than forty or fifty years produced fewer and fewer grapes, this was a shock, almost painful. The bunches were pathetically few, and in those that hadn't shriveled away to raisins, the individual grapes were separated within the bunch by huge spaces. Very occasionally, I came across a real keeper, a long bunch of fat grapes crowded together to the bursting point, each berry full of juice. It seemed more sobering, somehow, to have a single taunting instance of bounty when there were whole stretches of vines where you would carry your bucket ten, fifteen, even twenty feet without finding a single bunch that wasn't trash. Each vine might have borne six or eight bunches, every single one reduced to raisins, dark, black, and very sweet in the mouth but totally lacking in the juice necessary to make wine.

"They are sweet, no?" Jean-Luc asked when he saw me tasting one. "But actually, they are more apparently sweet than really sweet. If you put them in the tank, they are very acid, and you could get that *confit*, that cooked taste." This was the great fear of 2003 in the Lot, that the wine was going to end up a thick, syrupy, overly jammy, overly alcoholic concoction.

"It's the skins that are important because they contain the tannins, and they'll have to give them up in the vat during the maceration," Jean-Luc continued, maceration being that period after fermentation when the alcohol naturally liberates the tannins from the skins. I remembered Philippe, three weeks earlier when we had been out walking the vines, telling me, too, to suck the grape seeds, to feel that unripe, green woody taste on my tongue, to taste the sharp bite of the inside of the skin. I did, and they had reminded me a bit of the smell of newly mown grass, or boxwood hedge trimmings. I took one of Jean-Luc's very ripe grapes in my mouth, crunching down gently on the seeds again, and didn't find any of that astringency, that sharpness. "Everything has to be ripe, Michael," Philippe had said. "Good sugar and acid in the juice, ripe tannins in the skin and seeds. That's the start of making a good wine."

As we walked through the picked-over rows on our way to lunch, Jean-Luc's eyes were darting right and left with every step. He moved quickly between the rows, snipped a bunch that had gone unnoticed by the harvesters. "That's a half a glass of wine!" he said. A little farther along, he found another and then another. "That's a half a bottle. Maybe by the time we get to the end, I'll have a bottle." When we reached the lawn at the end of the row, he was cradling an armful of grapes, and I had some as well. "This year," he finished as we unloaded them and prepared to wash up at an outdoor faucet, "it really counts, let me tell you."

Less than three miles away, at the back of the valley pushed up against the *cévennes,* the ring of low hills that defines the southern edge of the Lot River, Philippe Bernède's grapes sat unpicked. At the beginning of September, when almost everyone else already had a week's worth of harvesting in the tank, he had been away, attending a wine expo in Montréal. Part of this was just laid-back Philippe not letting potential natural disaster interrupt a schedule planned months in advance, for any more rain would have certainly caused his grapes to rot, and quickly. Part is also the *terroir* of Clos la Coutale, which is very different from Triguedina even though so few miles separate them. "Here," he told me, "the grapes ripen later, and we always harvest later, too, when the grapes are very ripe, so that they have less acidity and rounder tannins."

When I finally caught up with Philippe (did this man always wear flip-flops?) shortly before I left France that fall, he was not overly pessimistic. "There will be less wine, sure, how can there not be with the state of the grapes?" He shrugged, as if to say, "These things happen." We were walking through his wine barns, passing from the front, where his huge oak *foudres* awaited the new wine after vinification, to the back, where two rows of stainless steel tanks sat, the red digital temperature gauges blinking up and down in those that were already filled and fermenting.

Did he know that most of his neighbors had already finished harvesting? "Sure. Some of them started harvesting a month ago. I realized some years back that harvesting later, when the grapes are fully ripe, gives fuller, smoother wines, a wine that is not aggressively tannic, not loaded with acid, not hard-edged [like other young Cahors]. When you start with grapes that are fully ripe, you don't have that problem of a green edge or a hard edge to the wine. Our *terroir* at Clos la Coutale, our land," he continued, "it has always made softer wine. And our wine has always had that image, of being a less tannic wine, and we have always made it that way, kept to that tradition. My father made it like that, and I have continued. You can make wine that you have to cellar for ten years before drinking, but I prefer to make the wine I make, which is the wine the *terroir* makes best."

We had paused in the short passage between the two barns. The tall doors on one side were open; a wagon was disgorging its contents onto a conveyor belt that would carry the grapes to a crusher. On either side, men in boiler suits hovered, their heads down, their hands plucking bunches either too dry or too rotten from the moving stream and tossing them to one side. Like all the other careful winemakers who harvest by machine, this year he had been forced, at a significant cost in time and money, to pick over every wagon by hand. "And the wine this year?" I asked, gesturing at the workers.

"*On verra.*" We will see.

8

VINIFICATION 2002

Making the Wine

Note: Although I had hoped to be able to write about the ripening, harvest, and vinification of the same year's grapes, a variety of circumstances prevented this. Because I don't like to be away from home for long periods during the school year, I had planned to arrive in time for the last week of harvest and the first week of winemaking. A hot spell in the early fall, though not nearly as extreme as the one in 2003, pushed up the harvest so that, by the time I got there, the grapes were already in. As it turned out, this was fortunate, as the winemaking of 2002 was much more interesting than that of 2003, as will be the wine.

Walk into any wine barn in France a week after the fall harvest has ended, and you're sure to notice a few things right away. First, the air is not just pungent, but so freighted with smell that it almost has texture. There is a prickling of something chemical in the nose, but mostly the odors are organic, with hints of compost heap and heady rot, a deeper muskiness like a wool blanket left out in the rain too long, all this overlaid with the sharp tang of ripe red fruit and hot fumes that bring back your first whiff of Daddy's evening scotch. Overhead, fruit flies and late-season bees whizz drunkenly about on their way to the constantly crackling blue-glowing bug zapper in one corner. The light is dim, and the humid air alive with strange gurglings and bubblings coming from the round silver tanks ranged on either side of a central aisle and rising up to the ceiling. You look up and see the steel grates of a catwalk running along their back along the wall, way up there in the gloom, and then you notice the stairs, also of steel grating. Pipes large and small rise out of the floor, some running at your feet horizontally, others climbing the walls at intervals, arcing overhead, tributaries branching off to each tank in turn.

Even though it is dim, you can see that everything is clean, the stainless steel tanks dully gleaming, the floors of concrete or tile freshly washed, no trash or bits of grape detritus in evidence. Someone somewhere is opening a squeaky faucet, water splashes into a bucket, and you see lengths of red-stained hose curled like oversized eels in huge tubs of clear water. In one corner, rakes, shovels, and pitchforks lie against a wall in ranks, all strange in appearance until you realize that their business ends, tangs, and handles are all coated in orange and red rubber or plastic sheaths. You put a hand to one tank and feel its warmth, lay your ear to its side and hear the muted rumblings, pings, and gaseous eruptions within, like a huge stomach digesting. Indeed, everything, but everything, here—the heat, the sounds, the smells—all this is part of that primordial process of digestion called fermentation happening in those tanks all around you.

A healthy, ripe grape is a little biochemical wonder, its every constituent seemingly designed, by nature, to play a necessary role in its subsequent transformation into wine. Wine is mostly water (82 to 85 percent), alcohol (10 to 18 percent), and acid (less than half a percent), with the actual matter responsible for the infinite variety we find in how different wines look, feel, taste, and smell representing a tiny proportion of the whole volume.

Good wine is a wholly natural product, meaning that the winemaker starts with grapes and adds nothing, or almost nothing. Sulfites, found in nearly all wines and added originally as sulfur dioxide, keep them from turning to vinegar. In France, unlike America, it is illegal to doctor any wine sold under an appellation label in any way, even with water. (It is permitted to use reverse osmosis filters, however, to remove water from the juice before fermentation and thus boost alcohol content, although this can deform the wine.) Except in the very northerly appellations—think of Alsace and Rhine wines—or in extreme years of poor weather, in most appellations the winemaker must always apply for special permission to chaptalize, to add sugar to increase the alcohol of the wine to the minimum level required. Even then, he's permitted to do this only when his wine is already very close to the right alcohol content—less than a degree short. In Cahors, this is increasingly rare, 1997 being the last year a rainy harvest diluted the juice in the grapes so much that some winemakers added sugar.

Everywhere in France, it is forbidden to add coloring agents or flavorings or spirits to manipulate appearance, taste, or smell, and the honest winemaker can't use any of the various preparations theoretically reserved for low-quality bulk wines and designed to raise or lower the acidity or residual sugar, to accentuate the mouth feel ("glossy" wine which feels almost slippery in the mouth being very popular these days). He can't inject carbon dioxide to make something fizzy that would otherwise be flat or use chemical binders or strippers to change aspects of the taste or smell. Winemakers, of course, do all these things and more to wine before, during, and after its making, with all the best enological products originating (surprise!) in France, Italy, and America, according, at least, to the winemakers with whom I've talked.

If you're an upstanding, honest winemaker in the Lot River valley and want that mark of quality—*Appellation d'Origine Contrôlée Vin de Cahors*—on your label, however, you've got the grape and, perhaps, a very few other natural products, to work with. Those products are generally concentrates or refinements of substances already present in the grape itself or otherwise of natural derivation and designed to enhance or attenuate any one of the various processes unleashed when ripe, sugary grapes meet yeast in the fermenting tank. (Pectinase, for example, and other natural enzymes help break down the grape pulp and skins to release the juice, tannins, and color pigments trapped in their cells. These may be added during the initial stage of fermentation or, at the end, to silt-heavy press wine to help it settle and clarify.) Hence the paramount importance of grapes that are, first of all, ripe; and, second, healthy—the product of vines that enjoyed good measures of sun and rain in the right seasons and weren't stressed by frost, heat, disease, or too much humidity throughout the growing year.

When Yves, Jean-Luc, and Philippe use the word "ripe," they mean not just that sufficient sugar and acid exist in the correct balance inside the grape, but that its skin and seeds are ripe as well, fully developed and in the necessary state to contribute what they must for a balanced wine. This is why Philippe, plucking a seemingly ripe grape from his vines in late August, crunches and then sucks on the seeds and pulp instead of just tasting the juice, which may be deceptively sweet while the innards are not. When he then talks about the tannins, largely contributed by the grape skins, as being green and astringent— "angular" in the winemaker's lexicon—I have my first concrete reference for this elusive term. Later, tasting both hard new wines that prickle the cheeks and mouth and softer wines sometimes only months older, whose tannins are said to be round or relaxed, I will remember this sensation and use it to judge what is in my mouth.

The idyllic conditions of perfectly ripe grapes from perfectly healthy, thriving vines, needless to say, almost never hold true, and the winemakers end up compensating for various lacks as best they can along the way as they harvest the grapes and make the wine. What distinguishes a good winemaker from a great one, in fact, is just that, the ability to make excellent wine every year, not only in the good years, from whatever hand nature has dealt. Sometimes this means making a slightly different kind of wine, sometimes it means making less wine, and sometimes, as in 2003 in Cahors, it means making a lot less wine.

Even when the yield of grapes is sufficient, hail, soaking rains at harvest, and other factors can, rarely, diminish its quality so much that the result isn't something the winemaker wants leaving the *chai* under his own label. Yves and Martine, facing just this situation in 1991, sold almost none of that wine under their own label. As Martine put it, "We'll sell it to you if you ask specifically, but it doesn't even appear in our brochures and catalogs as something we offer."

When I drove into the courtyard at Clos de Gamot on October 15, 2002, Yves was making one such compensation. More exactly, he was at the wheel of a forklift, inching up the incline from the big wine barn down below to the much smaller barn next to the tasting room. He was crawling along because balanced on the forks was a single 300-gallon fiberglass tank brimful of fermenting Clos St. Jean red wine. He stopped in front of the doors of the small barn, and Bernard and Jean-Marie, half of his full-time outdoor staff, slid them aside, revealing a tight space packed with five tanks. Three were of concrete, square, and built into the wall on the right-hand side, their fronts sculptured and painted to look like barrel-heads. Across from them were two much smaller vessels of stainless steel, technically not fermenting tanks, but *garde-vins*, holding tanks.

"Nothing but problems this year, Michael," he said after we'd caught up a bit on all the family news. "In parts of Bordeaux they had rain and hail. The cabernet wasn't ripe but they had to bring it in after the hail. In Burgundy, the pinot is excellent this year, apparently. There were floods in the southeast, while in Cahors, well, we've got good quality but a reduced harvest, not terrible, but smaller. So, a very irregular year in France." (I can only wonder what he would have said had he known the misery coming with the next harvest, the drought- and heat-plagued harvest of 2003.) He tapped the fiberglass tank, explaining that it was filled with malbec from "up on the mountain," from Clos St. Jean, his small traditional vineyard whose vines were just coming into their own. "We finished the harvest on October tenth, and these will ferment, probably for eighteen days. There were few grapes, and little juice. That rosé there"—he pointed to the big stainless steel tank against which he'd nestled the Clos St. Jean—"it is still fermenting, and the heat should help the Clos St. Jean to ferment, too."

With Yves, it is easy to come away with the first impression that he is always complaining, always doubtful about the final outcome of any single venture, a real Eeyore. After spending some time with him, however, I concluded that the glumness was a pose. It always dropped quickly away and his true self emerged, a jovial, lively personality fond of bad jokes, given to frequent jeremiads against socialism, and passionate about good food and, naturally, good wine and its making.

Such was the case that morning, and his doubts soon evaporated as he turned his concentration to the tasks at hand that day. They were various and many and would involve the collective labor, throughout the day, of his wife, Martine, and also Jean-Marie, Bernard, Pierre, Marc, and Saïd, a seasonal employee who spent six months of the year away from his family back in North Africa. That was just the winemaking crew, for the daily business of bottling, labeling, packing, shipping, and selling their wine didn't stop just because they had to make it. Marise, Martine's sister, took on more than her usual large share of administrative and marketing work with one secretary and another woman who packed and pasted labels (work still partly done by hand for their Clos de Gamot wines), running the day-to-day business and manning the tasting room, freeing up the others for the often sixty- to seventy-hour weeks that follow the harvest.

At Clos de Gamot, after the de-stemmed grapes go into the tank along with a dose of liquid sulfur dioxide to discourage the growth of bad bacteria, the natural yeasts on their skins and in the air begin to multiply in the "must"—what winemakers call the skins, seeds, and juice before it has become wine. The yeast in a sense "eats" the grape sugar, transforming it mostly into ethyl alcohol and producing carbon dioxide gas and thousands of by-products in the process, many of them useful in forming the taste and aroma of the wine.

This first transformation of sugar to alcohol is the alcoholic fermentation, and it will continue until there is no more sugar, or very little, left to digest, given the right conditions. The residual sugar—what we perceive as the relative sweetness of the wine after fermentation—in the dry reds of Cahors is minimal, unlike a Sauternes or some of the late-harvest Rhine whites, where a degree of sweetness is a desirable aspect of the wine's complexity.

Many winemakers use particular strains of laboratory-developed yeast that they feel better suit their wine; but for Yves, Philippe, and Jean-Luc, what nature has provided, wild yeasts, she provided for a good reason. Jean-Luc may occasionally use a cultured yeast to provoke the fermentation in the first tank and then, once it is well under way, seed the other tanks with some of that wine to help them ferment, too. But, as he points out, it is the natural yeasts which quickly dominate and which are responsible for the bulk of fermenting.

Yves was attempting to hasten the very slow fermentation of the small tank of Clos St. Jean with the ambient heat of a larger, neighboring tank already fermenting because heat jump-starts the action of the yeasts. Jean-Luc often heats his barn after the harvest if the weather is cold, and industrial winemakers go a step further, submerging immersion heaters into the must to help the process along.

(I visited several other wine barns in those weeks, including Château du Cèdre, halfway between Jean-Luc and Philippe. The front office there was deserted, so I went around to the *chai*. Hung on the door was a sign I'd seen in a few other places already: KEEP THE DOOR CLOSED! FERMENTING! Almost as soon as I had opened it and walked in, a voice boomed out, "Close the damned door!" A very tall, thin, sandy-haired young man popped his head out from behind a tank, saw me, and smiled, embarrassed. This was Le Cèdre's winemaker, Olivier Teissière, and he apologized. "Normally, I only yell at the secretaries, who are always forgetting! It's true, we're a little stressed during the vinification. But it's the little details, little things like that—keeping the heat in—that make the wine.")

In Gamot's big wine barn down below, our next stop, Yves halted next to one of the twenty-five-foot-tall, gleaming 4,000-gallon tanks and tapped it lightly with wine-stained fingers. "Last year we filled eight of these, this year four. This year the vines wanted to rest." He continued, "the summer wasn't very hot, or very wet. The vine regulates itself, adjusts its yield to its capacity." He put his ear to the tank, closed his eyes, listening, then walked to the next and the next, pausing at each. At the last, he looked up and beckoned. "Listen." The smooth metal was warm against my ear, and it took me a moment to block out the other noise in the vast barn. At first I heard nothing, then a muted tick, ticking, whiffles, snuffles, small burps, whispers of noise. Yves took me up the stairs and along the catwalk and opened the hatch of one tank. "Stick your nose into it," he said. Peering into the top of the tank, I could see, just a few feet below, a foamy, scummy carpet of crushed grapes. I stuck my head in, inadvertently breathing deeply and choking, finding Yves' hand on my shoulder pulling me back.

"*Eh, toi!* That's carbonic gas, you can't breathe it!" he said, laughing. "See?" He took out a cigarette lighter, lit it, and then submerged it to where my head had just been, and the flame abruptly went out. "One liter of fermenting must produces twenty-five liters of gas, and that's a lot in a small, confined space."

Over the tank beside us, what looked like a large circular showerhead dripped a steady stream of cool water, which flowed down the tank's sides in sheets, drawing off the heat of the fermentation and thus slowing it. Though fermentation needs heat and produces heat, too much not only kills the yeast but can lead to flabby wines of high alcohol content but not much depth. Pouring off samples and measuring morning and night, Yves and Martine try to keep the must at about seventy-eight degrees Fahrenheit, allowing a long, slow fermentation, generally between two and three weeks. "Toward the end, when there is almost no sugar left, it can go up to eighty-eight degrees, and that's OK, too. The higher temperature softens the last, potentially harder tannins and extracted matter," Martine said.

"You *can* ferment a wine in three days," Yves told me, a look of disapproval on his face. "But when we are fermenting the reds, we try by maceration to extract the tannins and other matter from the skin yet to stop before the woodiness, that green edge, comes out." Maceration is a process that takes place after the initial alcoholic fermentation: the winemaker lets the wine sit for some period of time in the tank with the skins, a kind of steeping in which the alcohol draws out all that is good from those parts of the grape that are not juice. "So we taste the wine every day. These tanks"—he gestured to first two in the row—"we tasted last night, and they're ready. So this afternoon, we'll pour them off and then press *le marc.*"

He was referring to the next stage, after the alcoholic fermentation was complete and the wine had sat on its skins, macerated, long enough in his estimation. At that point the wine is poured off (*l'écoulage*) from the tank. The wine that flows freely after the spigot is opened is called *vin de goutte,* free-run wine, and Yves will pump it into another tank, leaving it to rest, the solids to settle out over the winter.

What is left in the tank, the detritus, is no longer must but pomace, called *le marc,* and it, too, has a value. Most often, the winemaker will wring it gently in a *pressoir,* yielding "press wine," a usually more concentrated and very tannic wine useful for blending in small amounts to add body and substance to the more delicate free-run wine. "Press wine also has the bacteria you will need later, for the *malo,* so a little bit can be useful then, too." This is the secondary or malolactic fermentation of late November to early December, when bacteria in the wine, often given the nudge of a bit of heat, change the harsher malic acid in the wine to the softer lactic acid.

Earlier, Yves had made the distinction between *vins primeurs* and *vins de garde.* (*Primeurs,* a word found on the awnings of many French grocery stores, is also how the French identify the first young, fresh, and very delicate vegetables of spring.) The first young or spring wines are now made in almost every appellation of France; Beaujolais *nouveau* (the earliest of the early birds, arriving in November) is the prime example. These are generally lighter in color and body, fruitier, less tannic, and sometimes less alcoholic wines meant to be drunk young and thus usually released onto the market as soon as the spring after their making. Such experiments are often unsuccessful, and I can't help remembering the words of A. J. Liebling: "The vintner who handles only young wines is like an insurance company that will write policies only on children; [he] wants to risk nothing and at the same time to avoid tying up his money."

Vins de garde—Clos de Gamot and other Cahors, most fine Bordeaux, and many other wines—are more substantial, more structured, more complex wines that require cellaring for a number of years before they reach their full potential.

"A young wine is a free-run wine, usually of short fermentation," Yves had explained. Free-run wine is, simply, everything that runs out of the tank when you open the spigot, as opposed to press wine, which runs out of the press when the pomace is squeezed under pressure. "A wine to cellar is a wine of extraction, and press wine adds to its constitution. They need the extra tannins and other extracts from a longer fermentation and maceration."

Here, he was making a distinction in process. All red wine is fermented with juice, skins, and seeds, together in the tank sometimes for weeks, or it wouldn't be red in color and tannic in nature. For rosé, its lovely pale pink comes from an abbreviated marriage of the skins, seeds, and juice of red-wine grapes in the tank, from a few hours to a few days, after which the juice is poured off and left to finish fermenting. In white wines, the grapes are pressed lightly and the juice is then separated, usually after a day or less, from the skins; that is why white wine has little or no tannin and why most white wines, particularly the dry ones, don't age beyond a few years.

After the initial stage of fermentation, the alcohol produced begins to leach tannins (polyphenols) and pigments (anthocyanins) from the grape skins along with many other substances in the maceration process Yves was talking about. Malbec is a purple-black grape with, proportionally, a thicker skin and a smaller size than many other red-wine grapes. The length of maceration—how long the juice is in contact with the skins—directly affects how dark and how tannic the eventual wine will be (remember that Cahors is often called the black wine), and thus if and how it will age over time. Those same tannins and anthocyanins are also powerful antioxidants, as is the added sulfur dioxide, and all three help neutralize destructive chemical by-products like free radicals that over time lead to a wine's decomposition in the bottle.

Back down below, Yves and Martine had assembled a pump and sufficient hose for the daily task of "pumping over" (*le remontage*) the two tanks still fermenting. They positioned an empty plastic 100-liter tub below the fat spout of a tank, and Yves dropped one mesh-covered end of the hose into it. The hose fed an electric pump out of whose other end more hose, secured firmly to the catwalk railing for support by rope ties, climbed up to the tank's hatch. Yves grabbed a plum-stained wooden stick as long as he was tall, his *pigeur,* and climbed the stairs; soon we could hear him breathing heavily as he used it to beat a hole in the cap. Periodically breaking up the cap either mechanically or manually so that the skins and seeds are freed from the mass and sink by themselves is called *pigéage,* and it is an alternative to "pouring over," used in other appellations of France. (Philippe uses *pigéage* on his small-batch wine, as does Jean-Luc, who will also use *battonage* on his white wines, stirring up the lees, the sediment that falls out of the wine, during and after fermentation with a long wooden pole, with the goal of intensifying their flavor.)

During fermentation, the skins and seeds trap bubbles of carbon dioxide gas and tend to rise, floating in a cap (*le chapeau*) on top of the juice. I joined a sweaty Yves up top, watching as he labored, his face at the level of the hatch but turned to one side so he could breathe, both his arms, red to the elbow, plunging the stick up and down, agitating the surface of the cap. He straightened and drew out the stick, now dripping with grape skins and juice. "Pumping over we do to wet the cap so that the top of it doesn't dry out," he said, still breathing hard. "If that happened, you could have bad chemical reactions, bad microbes growing. It helps the wine ferment, too, and the maceration, if the liquid is more in contact with the solids than if they're floating on top."

"Eh, Martine!" he called. "You can start!" The pump began to whir and thump loudly, and at first a trickle, then a rush of wine came out of the hose Yves had put into the hatch. He moved it back and forth, as if he were watering a bed of flowers, for several minutes, and as he did so I noticed that my eyes were watering and my nose was tickling as the splashing wine stirred up the gas. Finally, he tied the hose, still spouting a steady stream of wine, firmly in place to wet the cap and sink it. Down below, Martine stood, one hand on the spigot handle to stop the outflow from the tank should anything go wrong. At her feet, brilliantly purple wine foamed into the tub, almost as quickly being sucked up for its round trip back into the tank. Here, too, the reek of the gas was strong. "It sparkles a bit," I ventured.

"That's the gas coming out," she replied. And exposing the wine to the air? Didn't they risk contaminating it with wild yeast or bacteria, or something? I asked. She chuckled. "We do this on purpose, oxygenate it. With the thick skin of the malbec grapes, there is more *matière* and less juice." *Matière* is all the tannins, coloring, and other solids available to be extracted by, or dissolved in, the alcohol and juice. "We adapt how and how long we oxygenate according to each vintage, because this helps avoid the wine hardening in taste. This we do seven days a week, but at the end of fermentation." She pointed to the slate propped on top of the hatch cover. "This tank was filled September thirtieth, so it's been fermenting fifteen days already. Also, we filled the tanks at harvest, one each day, but these two are still working, as we heard, while the others have finished fermenting. Why? They're the same grapes cultivated the same way but from different *terroirs*."

After five minutes or so, when Yves judged the cap had submerged once again under the wine pumped on top of it, Martine closed the big spigot. Soon the pump was sucking air and so shut off. Yves untied the other end of the hose from up top, descended, then carefully maneuvered its end over the tub. Martine held it in place while he moved to the far end, then marched toward us, creating a hump in the hose so that all the wine trapped in it would run into the tub and not onto the floor. "That," he said, eyeing my notebook, "is called walking off the hose." I smiled, and he said, "Hey, there's fifty liters of wine in there!" Winemakers waste nothing, certainly not wine, and every last drop from every operation, even the dregs from our tasting glasses, would end up in a tank somewhere, eventually to be bottled and sold.

"You can pump over for five minutes or for a half an hour, once, twice, or even three times a day," Martine remarked. "Five minutes at the very start and end of fermentation and maceration, that would be just to keep the cap wet. In full fermentation, though, perhaps when you wanted to cool the wine down and encourage the activity of the yeasts, you might go longer and more often. You do it by intuition, according to the grapes that year, too."

An hour later, the tanks had been pumped over and samples drawn off to go to the enologist's laboratory. As Yves went to pull the huge doors shut before we headed up to the house, he surveyed the very warm, very clean space. "Wine! It's a story of a thousand details, Michael." All the hoses he had coiled in tubs of fresh water to soak after rinsing, and the pump he cleaned, too, by cycling more fresh water through it. All the tools were washed and rinsed and put away; the floor was hosed down; stray bits of grape *marc* were washed into the narrow grates running the length of the *chai*. And then it was time for lunch.

When I returned the next morning, Yves said we had to run an errand first, "to go get some lipstick for the *pressoir* at Cayrou," actually nontoxic, food-grade industrial grease to lubricate the wine press that removes liquid remaining in the *marc* after everything else has run out of the tank. We took Yves' battered red Citroën—Martine would meet us there later—and set off for the Jouglas farm store on the outskirts of Puy l'Evêque across the valley. You could assemble a whole vineyard and winemaking operation with equipment used and new in the yard and on the shelves at the store, and as I wandered happily through the wares, I could hear Yves complaining to the saleswoman about the prices. In the car he showed me the lipstick, fat tubes like huge cigars at $42 each, and rolled his eyes.

As we drove through the vines toward Cayrou, Yves pointed out the window. "Those parcels, the ones that are still green, that's the tannat. The leaves of the malbec have already turned, the merlot, too." It was cool and lovely; the vineyards in October looked as if the brush of a Mondrian had left huge wide swaths of primal color, ribbons of green and gold and russet intersecting, a vast carpet of rectangles and squares with the meanders of the river the only curves running through it. Yves had a contented smile on his face, and I thought I could understand why. The harvest was in, the wine was working, and the weather, the change of season, were now things to be enjoyed rather than feared. Nature had done its part, and the rest was up to him.

In the *chai* at Cayrou, the tanks have an innovation that makes pumping over much easier. They are designed with an internal sprinkler inside the head of each tank to wet the cap. Yves still has to punch a hole in the cap so that it will slowly submerge itself in the liquid, but there is less manipulating of hoses involved. At the door he fished three wineglasses from a carton in one corner and rinsed them in cold water. At the first tank, in a ritual I was coming to know very well, he filled a single glass almost full from a small spigot placed high up in the tank, then put his palm over the top and shook it rapidly up and down. "To get the gas out," he said. When he took his hand away, the wine was foaming, looking almost carbonated. Then he poured the wine back and forth between the glasses until each of us had a scant third. "The water here has its own taste, and you have to get rid of that before you can truly taste the wine."

As I had the day before at Gamot, I first sniffed deeply, eyes closed, trying to get past the stink of fermentation. I tasted, swirled, aerated the wine by swooshing it back and forth across my tongue, held it in my mouth before finally spitting into the grate at my feet. New wine, I confess, defies easy assessment, and I was able to make only the grossest distinctions when pressed by Yves and Martine. By the time we got to the third tank, when Yves asked me my opinion, all I could muster was, "It tastes more like the first tank than the second."

"No," he said. "It's got more fruit, more red fruit."

"It has changed," Martine added. "The acid has left and the fruit has come out. But it is too concentrated, still."

At the next tank, Yves and Martine exchanged a glance as I inhaled deeply, nose in glass. "Peppers," Yves said, and then, in a rare burst of mangled English, "Here we have a wine of vegetable." What he meant was a wine whose predominant aromas were in the realm of the vegetal or herbaceous (rather than floral, fruit, mineral, or animal), which in France embraces everything from the smell of new-mown hay though leaf mold, truffle, fern, mushroom, and the sharp tang of green pepper.

"This is an experiment for us," Martine explained. "Usually, we never ferment different varietals together, usually not even the same varietal from parcels that are too different from each other if we can help it."

"We don't buy grapes from others," Yves interrupted. "We make do with what we have. It's harder, but it's more honest." The problem, one that all winemakers have, is that you need containers of the correct size for fermentation and everything that comes after. Tanks have to be filled almost to the top with the grape slurry, both to let the slurry ferment properly and to avoid exposing it to too much air and the oxygen and contaminants that air may contain. In this case, after they had filled one tank of merlot, the diminished yield had left them with but half a tank each of both the merlot and the tannat grapes, and they simply didn't have enough small vessels to ferment them both separately.

"It happened, also," he continued, "because we had been out in the vines tasting the grapes from the twelfth of September. And one day we were up there, the merlot had a very high acid but a sugar just sufficient. The tannat was very high in sugar but with a meager acidity. We were talking about it. . . ."

"And Yves kicked the base of a vine and all the grapes fell off!" Martine broke in with a laugh. "Whoops! Better harvest, we said. And that's how you discover things."

Newly fermented wine is a weird animal. It is not "colorfast," so to speak; the pigment, though in such fine particles as to seem part of the liquid, is not yet bound to it. Pigment sticks in a pink film to the sides of the glass—sticks, in fact, to anything and everything it touches. My hands, my notebook, shirt, pants, socks, and boots, even my eyeglasses, I found later, were tinged with its rosy hue. The wine, one could say, is also not yet "tastefast," its constituent parts still separate and the grosser elements (often the only distinctions evident to this tyro taster) sometimes overpoweringly so. The alcohol is volatile, making the wine seem stronger in the mouth and nose than it will be several months hence, and the dominant tastes and smells—whether sugar, fruit, licorice, tannin, or blackberry—exist in layers, in isolation from one another rather than knit into a complex whole. A few things stood out, perhaps pounded into my head through Yves' exhortations. The tannat and the malbec were noticeably more drying to the mouth, more tannic. At one point, he had me stick my head into a tank still half full of malbec *marc*. "Smell the fruit! Red fruit!" That I could sense, too, the dominant raspberry-plum-red currant aromas so typical of French malbec.

All the while Martine stood calmly by, taking samples, measuring the sugar, but also tasting, dispensing corrective comments to Yves' more blunt observations. She is, I think, a more subtle taster than he, and he will defer to her in this realm as in no other, calling her the *maître du chai* or cellarmaster, the one traditionally responsible in a vineyard for making the final decisions about fermenting, blending, and aging wine. She is also quite thoughtful. "There are no nuances in the technical analysis—so much sugar, acid, et cetera," she told me. "The nuance is in the palate, in the senses. We try to strike a balance in our wines, to keep some of the fruit while having also sufficient *matière* and tannins so the wine will age well. We're a little bit like the doctor and the nurse, and here's our maternity ward. For wine is a living thing. And," she finished, looking down shyly, "for us it has more meaning because this is what brought us together!"

Our tasting was interrupted by the arrival of Monsieur Thiollet, the local enologist whose lab just down the road does the chemical analyses for most of the area's winemakers. Yves and Martine measure the temperature and density, following how much grape sugar has been consumed, and the enologist not only confirms this, but also tracks malic acid, volatile acidity, residual sugar, and alcohol content.

Monsieur Thiollet is tall for a Frenchman, with a good head of shaggy gray hair and a narrow, rather austere face. That day, with his bifocals askew and his shirt, pants, and white sneakers all amply splotched with red, he looked rather like a mad scientist, particularly since he was holding a plastic liter sample flask in one hand and a clipboard in the other. He filled the flask from a tank, then peered at the wine, smelled it, then sipped delicately before spitting. "This one still has some sugar," he said.

"Yes. It's still fermenting," Yves replied. Both men, one tall and thin, the other short and plump, put their ears simultaneously to the tank, then just as abruptly drew back. As the enologist went from tank to tank and took his samples, he carried on a running commentary with the two winemakers, a technical assessment of how much fruit each had, its acidity and structure, how finished it was, and whether it might merit more time on the skins or not.

"The press wine this year," he said, "with such a small yield, I am finding the juice very concentrated already."

"We won't be adding much back to the free-run," Yves agreed. "Maybe one liter to fifty in this tank." He turned to me. "Otherwise, the press wine, which has a bit of greenness, a hard edge to it at the end of the palate, that could ruin the whole wine."

After Monsieur Thiollet had left, I asked if they had known him a long time. "Since forever!" Martine said. "Papa sent me to him when I was fifteen for my first wine-tasting course." I tried to imagine any fifteen-year-old American kid I knew being sent off by her father to learn how to taste wine. Martine had told me once that she had been "born in a wine barrel," as they say here, and this was just one more proof of that, a youth built of experiences intimately linked to the vineyard and the grape.

As we had been tasting, Bernard, Jean-Marie, and Saïd had run off one tank, and it was time to remove the *marc* and press it. Bernard, clearly in charge, had his back against a press and was urging on the other two beside him. He has been working with Yves since 1979, and I have seen them have an entire conversation laying out a full day's work for five men with forty words and ten gestures and no one but the two of them the wiser.

There are two presses at Cayrou, both Vaslin Véritas 32s, old but functional yellow-enameled monsters eight feet wide, fifteen feet long, and about as tall as Yves. They weigh a ton, and are difficult to shift on their small steel wheels. Yves and I hurried over and put our backs into it too, shifting press alongside the tanks with enough room in between for the conveyor with its pouched belt. Yves looked at the relic and laid a hand to it. "Three hundred and fifty thousand francs [$50,000] for this thing, and we only use it five days a year."

Each tank has three hatches: the very large round hatch on its top, and two smaller square hatches on its face, one at the bottom and the other about halfway up. Jean-Marie, whippet-thin, intense, and full of youthful energy, had already run up top to open the round hatch and dangled a light inside. When he then opened the hatch set high into the tank's side, the air around us became instantly thick with the reek of old socks and sulfurous carbon dioxide overlaid with an intense pong of alcohol.

Jean-Marie turned to me. "When you first go in and it's full of *marc*," he said shyly, "you can't lean down too far, not below the level of the upper hatch. You have to remember that. But after, the gas leaves through the bottom hatch, and then it's the alcohol and the heat that get you."

"Remember," Yves put in, "when I threw out my back in that tank?" He turned to me. "They had to help me out through the top. Christ, that was hard. And then, straight to the doctor."

Bernard, who looks like a character actor in a French film noir, dark, thick, and stocky, with hands like dinner plates, rolled the mechanical lifter in front of the lower hatch and then placed a plastic bin under its mouth to capture any liquid. The lifter, cousin to that familiar piece of farm equipment used to raise bales of hay from wagon to loft, is nothing more than a ridged conveyor belt, on wheels and adjustable in angle, to carry the *marc* up and into the open hatch of the press at its other end.

Though I didn't yet understand why, the three workers looked dressed for a nor'easter, in high Wellies and waterproof overalls coming almost up to their necks. Bernard was tying a sheet of plastic around his waist like an apron.

After they opened the large square door at the bottom of the tank, the shoveling began. "No metal in that!" Bernard barked to Jean-Marie, and the young man mutely waved the plastic-coated rake at him. The conveyor started with a clunk, and first he cleared out the mouth of the tank, reaching in as far as he could, pulling clots of carmine grape skins onto the conveyor. After ten minutes, when the hatch was clear and he couldn't easily reach more with the rake (and after the worst of the gas had dissipated), he gestured to Saïd to take his spot, and then, in an artfully gymnastic move, pulled himself backward and up into the tank, disappearing into the wide mouth of the lower hatch. Saïd handed in a pitchfork, and soon the *marc* was flowing once again. I climbed onto a box and looked in the upper hatch to see Jean-Marie up to his waist in grape skins, his face red and running sweat. Bernard had donned his costume for a very good reason I saw, too, when I looked to the other end of the conveyor. He was standing inside the drum of the press, using a stubby rake and his feet to evenly distribute the river of marc, some of which flowed, at times, almost down his chest and onto his apron.

I grabbed a handful of the *marc* and spread it between my fingers. I saw mostly whole grape skins crushed and emptied but not disintegrated, the seeds glistening almost white, and a few bits of stalk.

When they were nearly finished, Yves told me to stick my head into the nearly empty tank. I did and saw two strange objects at the very bottom, against the drain hole of the spigot. Directly against the drain was what appeared to be a bundle of grape stems bound tightly with grapevine. Holding this in place was "a very important piece of equipment," Yves told me. It was a large rock, which emerged completely purple. Yves kicked the stems lightly with one foot. "That's a *paillon—paillou* in patois—a filter that helps keep the *marc* in the tank while we run off the wine. We could dry them and sell them for a fortune in America, eh? For barbecuing?" he joked. "And that," he said, kicking the rock and eyeing my scribbling pen with a mischievous grin, "that's a rock. That scum on it, that's all the lees, what comes from the effects of fermentation, what feeds it, what becomes of the pulp of the grape, everything inside of it that is not seed or skin, dead yeast cells, too."

With the tank empty, Saïd fed Jean-Marie a series of brushes big and small, a curved squeegee, and, finally, a high-pressure hose to wash down the tank walls to remove the last of the *marc,* which ran out the hatch and was flushed into the grates over the drains set into the floor below.

"The wine in the next tank, it hasn't finished fermenting but it's time to get it off the skins, so that will go into this tank once it's clean," Yves said. I asked him if he didn't have to disinfect it first. "That's a little bit the American syndrome, isn't it?" he asked me rhetorically. "If I clean the tank too much, sterilize it, I kill all the good microbes, and then maybe I'd have to add some artificial product to help the other wine finish fermenting. But I know, if everything's in order of course [with the previous wine that came out of the vat], that I don't have to add anything."

The crew takes turns working inside the tank, and, curious, I asked if I could see what it was like working in there. Two minutes later, kitted out in my own garbage bag skirt, I found myself slithering backward up the hatch of an almost full tank to join Saïd, who had already cleared the entrance. Inside, the floor is sloped just gently enough that you have to think about keeping your balance. When I stood, I was up to my waist in the densely aromatic *marc,* Saïd working away with a shovel and his feet right beside me. I followed his example, pushing the grape skins out the hatch with my feet. After a minute, I was sweating heavily, and not from the work, which didn't take after all that much exertion. No, the air inside was very hot, more heat rising off the grape skins all around us, too. I tried to take a deep breath and coughed. My God, I thought, this is nothing but alcoholized carbon dioxide in here. It was like being inside a bottle of whiskey. Outside, someone hit the tank with a metal tool, and it reverberated mightily inside. I looked up at the tiny light hanging above and was happy I wasn't claustrophobic. Or was I?

I looked through the eye-level hatch to see Yves, Martine, and Bernard all staring at me from across the floor. "*Ça va?*" Martine mouthed over the noise of the conveyor. You OK? I nodded and smiled reassuringly, at the same time thinking how easily someone could get a little weird in here, slip, hit his head on the stainless steel wall, fall face-down in the moist *marc,* and choke to death before anyone realized what was happening. I was remembering all the stories they had all told me about working around the tanks, the gas, the fumes, that each year some hapless winemaker or worker was found dead, asphyxiated or drowned in fermenting wine. It was also why the crew was forbidden to do this kind of work alone, ever, and why they took turns in the tanks.

Ten minutes later, I was ready for that tank to be empty, and thankful that it was. When I emerged after only fifteen minutes, I was completely purple. There is just no good way to climb in and out of a tank full of grape skins, its every smooth surface running with wine, without staining your clothes. Later that afternoon, cleaning up, I would find skins in my rubber boots and socks, in my cuffs, even stuck to my back inside my T-shirt and in my hair. Just after I climbed out, my throat was very dry and raw, my eyes and nose were stinging, my sinuses running. I had the impression that someone had coated my face with Vicks VapoRub, with, in the place of eucalyptus, the reeking ether I remembered from high school biology class. I was a little unsteady on my feet and went to stand outside, trying to put a finger on the variety of strangeness that had overtaken me until I realized quite simply that I was drunk. Not the enduring happy high of a glass of wine or two, but a dopey, unsteady unpleasantness that passed, happily, after a few minutes of fresh air.

"You get used to it," Yves remarked. "But maybe now you can understand why most winemakers are finished by sixty and dead by seventy." Between that work and the tasting, I guess I could, I told him.

"You have to be careful when you are a winemaker," Martine added, "that the tasting part is your job and not a need. My father was very vigilant about that with us. You *have* to spit, or in three years you're finished. And after, at table, to have a few glasses, something everyone likes to do now and then with a good meal, you have to make sure it remains a pleasure and not a need. With our meals, unless it is a special occasion, we take water, only water."

That I had noticed already. On my frequent visits, they most often invited me to lunch, and though sometimes Yves would open a bottle to illustrate a point, to teach me something, generally it was water, lots and lots of water, that we drank with the food Martine prepared those days. (Jean-Luc and Philippe also partook at table very modestly—again, opening a bottle usually to demonstrate something we'd been talking about that day.) Even when Yves did pop a cork, half a glass was usually all anyone wanted after a morning spent tasting from the tanks.

For me, this was not because I felt inebriated, but because tasting new wine is hard on the mouth, throat, and nose, and hard on the brain, too (my brain, anyway). It demands a particular kind of concentration and a focus on the senses very rarely required of us in other aspects of life. At a very good restaurant, the chef may ask you if the plate of fine food in front of you tastes good, but you're not expected to then declaim the provenance of the meat, the manner in which it was prepared, and the seasonings used in that preparation. Chefs often do this when eating out by instinct, however, tasting and then deconstructing dishes so they can reconstruct them in their own kitchens later.

In those first weeks of tasting, Yves and Martine began to teach me not the subtler points of fine wine, but the more obvious benchmarks they use every day to follow the evolution of their wine and to make decisions about how to blend and age it. Fruit, sugar, color, acidity, the state of the tannins—these were the bases we touched over and over again, and finally I began to internalize the benchmarks to the point where I could refer to them mentally.

By the time my head had cleared, Bernard had filled the press, which holds just half the *marc* of each big tank. It is a fairly simple piece of machinery in the form of a hollow horizontal drum, its exterior perforated with narrow slits from which the juice will run, dripping into a catch basin below. The two ends of the drum are not fixed, but move toward the middle on long threaded bolts, compacting the grape skins and seeds between them to the desired pressure and thus squeezing out their liquid.

"We just wring out the skins," Yves told me. "You shouldn't actually press them too much, because then the press wine becomes astringent. The grape seeds, you don't want to crush them, because they contain a bitter oil." Yves pushed a button and the press started with a clank and a shudder. The drum began to revolve very slowly, and I imagined its ends moving toward the center like two plungers. Immediately, bloodred wine ran from the slits in the drum, sheeting down it and into the catch basin. "See how slowly the press moves? How gently?" Yves said. "It's as if we're wringing out the *marc*, not crushing it."

I noticed that I was breathing more shallowly as waves of alcohol fumes came off the press, and I looked to the others working around me. Again, I could only imagine the cumulative effect on them, working around this all day every day for weeks on end.

"What we'll do with this press wine we don't yet know," Martine said, echoing her husband's opinion. "But most of it gets left out of the final blending. Last year, much of it was blended into the Clos de Gamot. It is blended into the tanks we judge the weakest, so to speak. It fortifies them, bucks them up." They would let it settle first in the stainless steel tanks over the winter and, then, after pouring it off the resulting lees, leave it to mellow in the great oak tuns out back, in the aging barn. "We'll taste it and see after." As the wine from various parcels evolved over the winter and spring, they might return more press wine to any batch they felt could use the extra oomph.

Other winemakers follow different protocols. Philippe adds back all the press wine to the free-run wine of that tank. Jean-Luc, finding the press wine coarser and too tannic, uses almost none, blending it instead into his second-label wines.

Yves dipped a glass out of the catch basin and handed it to me. In appearance, it was a milky soup. I swirled it, and it left inky streaks on the sides of the glass the hue of the pink carnival glass my grandmother used to collect. It smelled fierce, all the strong odors I had met earlier, but concentrated. I tasted hesitantly. It was overwhelmingly tannic, like sucking three lemons, and I could feel the insides of my cheeks drying out.

"You can't leave the *marc* out in the air too long, either," Yves told me. "It gets unpleasant. All the alcohol evaporates, and it's open to the air. Remember, some of it is getting mixed later with the rest of the wine, and you don't want bad microbes to contaminate it."

Even after pressing, what is left still has its uses. In some parts of France, most notably Burgundy, *le marc* the grape detritus is distilled into *le marc* the oak-aged, eighty-proof, grapey, often earthy distilled after-dinner drink that is France's more refined answer to Italian grappa. Not too many decades ago, particularly in the poorer, less renowned regions, distillers would even add water, sugar, and yeast and referment the mix-ture to produce a thin, sour brew that was the cheapest plonk on which to drink oneself stupid in the neighborhood dive.

These days, the fate of the *marc* is much more prosaic and inti-mately tied up with that most French of things—taxes. French wine-makers are required to pay three different taxes on the wine they pro-duce: the 19.5 percent value-added tax, one on the overall yield from each year's harvest, and six cents per bottle as a tax stamp (Marianne in all her glory) that appears as part of the metal capsule on the top of the bottle as it leaves the vineyard after being sold to an individual or wholesaler.

In a wrinkle originating between the wars as a control against fraud, the second tax is assessed not in money, but rather in liters of pure alcohol distilled from the *marc* and due to be rendered unto Cae-sar after the winemaker officially declares his yield each year. French winemakers are required to call the distiller to come and take away the *marc* after it is pressed. The distiller is licensed by the state. He weighs the *marc*, measures the alcohol still remaining in it, and then assesses the winemaker according to norms established about how much pure alcohol should be derived after he distills it from a given amount of *marc* (and lees). When the winemaker's *marc* lacks sufficient alcohol, he will end up owing the distiller money to fill out his assessment.

This unusual system of taxing the *marc* came about first as a way for the government to ensure that it would have a sufficient strategic stock of alcohol for industrial and other purposes. The system quickly evolved into something else, however. Once upon a time, before the distillers got into the act, there were whole oceans of wine sold under the label of renowned vineyards capable of producing only small lakes. Some of this was fraud by counterfeiters, but some winemakers were regularly reporting yields far higher than others in their region. Where were these grapes (and there was sometimes doubt that grapes were even involved in the making of this "wine") coming from? Other wine regions suffering from a surplus that year? Spain? Italy? Algeria? ("All of the above" is apparently the correct answer.) By obliging every wine-maker to document the quantity and alcohol content of his *marc* and lees and using the distiller to verify the reported results, the government could calculate the yield from the leftovers of fermentation and then determine whose production was suspiciously out of whack in the appellation, given their acreage.

As I stood beside the slowly turning press, I could judge how far the ends had telescoped by watching where the wine was emerging from the slits. At the start, with the *marc* distributed evenly along the whole length of the press, the red stuff poured from the slits from one end to the other; ten minutes later, with the ends separated by only a few feet, it was only those slits at the center that bled. Yves didn't let them get much closer than that before shutting the press down. He could read the pressure gauges on the control panel to check his intuition, but he knew from experience not to compact the *marc* too much.

"Do you want me to run the next batch?" Jean-Marie asked when he saw us gathering up our things.

"Do you know what you're doing?" Yves responded.

"Yes. Sure."

"Well then, go ahead and do it yourself!" As we drove off, Yves turned to me. "He's a good kid, a hard worker. That's unusual today." He sighed loudly. "So, we're well under way at Cayrou. They'll put the free run from the next tank into the one they're cleaning now. Then, this afternoon, Martine and I will start the first blending, choosing which malbec from what parcel to mix with another so we get the balance we want."

They always did the initial blending of different tanks of the same varietal just after pouring them off, and always into stainless steel. Months later, after the heavier sediment, the lees, had settled out and the wine had been "racked off"—separated from its lees—once or twice more, they would blend into the malbec, for the wines of Cayrou, nearly a third as much of softer merlot and a much smaller amount, never more than 10 percent, of the more tannic tannat. The result would then be left to age in the great iron-banded oak *foudres,* the 2,500-gallon tuns, in the cool, dark L off the back of the *chai* before being bottled a year to a year and a half after its fermentation.

How often you have to rack off (*soutirer*) the wine depends on the wine and the weather. "You always wait to do the first racking after the malolactic fermentation. So usually in December," Martine told me. "But how often and how much lees comes out of the wine, that depends on the weather. Very cold weather makes the wine precipitate more, and so you'd rack off more often than in a mild winter."

Back at Gamot, Yves, suddenly smiling mysteriously and humming to himself, guided me through the bottling room and to a stairway which I had never seen before and whose entrance was blocked by a gate of thick iron bars. "Let's go visit the capital," he said, taking a very large, very old skeleton key from his belt and bending to the equally massive and aged lock. In the truck, he had been ranting that the accumulation of capital—in his case holding stocks of wine for sale years after the harvest—was almost against the law in France in the modern era, or was taxed so heavily that the result was the same. Theirs was a system whereby everyone had to share everything and no one was allowed to have more than anyone else, and it was crushing them under its weight, turning the country into a static backwater where initiative and personal responsibility were lost and people looked to the functionaries of the state to fulfill their needs. From what I had seen just of the complexities of hiring and firing employees, the man did have some legitimate points.

The gate swung open on creaking hinges, and we proceeded down two flights of stairs that ran beside the shaft of a freight elevator. He switched on lights as we went, and the air got noticeably cooler. At the bottom, another steel door, another key, another light switched on, and before me as far as I could see in the gloom pallets and pallets and pallets of wine rising to the high ceiling. High up on the wall at intervals were red-painted signs with the vintage; under them were wheeled pallets holding 100,000 bottles of recent vintages back to 1995 and, in one corner, perhaps 10,000 bottles of even older wines from 1980, 1982, 1983, 1985, 1988, 1989, 1990. He walked across the floor to the smaller stacks of unlabeled bottles, brushed the dust off one, and returned, handing it out to me. "*That* is the capital, Michael. Don't drop it!" He had seen that I was still in a state of awe and wonder, for being in the presence of so much old wine is like staring history in the face, in this case the very personal and intimate history of the Jouffreau family and all they've worked for.

"This cellar holds a quarter of a million bottles, this space, but as you see there aren't even half that many here. We have about the same number at Cayrou, too, but I've had to sell stock," he said, a note of regret in his voice. "What good does it do if you can't pass it on to your children? I remember my father-in-law saying to me, 'While I'm alive, you don't touch the centenarian vines!' And we didn't. History is respect for your elders, for what has come before. We can't do otherwise. I have perhaps ten, fifteen years left." I looked at him, surprised by this turn in the conversation. He stared back frankly, without a hint of melodrama. "I am not cynical, just pessimistic. I have ten, fifteen years left to take care of things, arrange for the parents, for the children." To accumulate the necessary capital, he meant, to pay the inheritance taxes so that the next generation, his and Martine's and Marise's children, would at least have the choice to continue on as winemakers.

Our mission accomplished—bottle in hand—it was time for something that had become one of my favorite rituals of the days I spent at Yves and Martine's: lunch. Yves and Martine don't live in the big house in the center of the compound with her mother; they live at the back of the property, in a smaller stone house renovated into large, airy rooms with warm tile floors, everywhere the chaos of a place that is well lived in. At one end of the kitchen are sliding glass doors, giving out onto a small yard bordered by a profusion of rosebushes and exotic trees. The Jouffreaus don't do anything in a hurry, and first, after washing up, we might take a look at something in the yard—a mimosa badly frostburned come gloriously back to life, Martine's yellow pear-shaped heirloom tomatoes—or even take a short walk to observe what a neighbor was up to in his vines, Yves' wry commentary always enlivening the occasion.

Then it was time for a serious lunch, their big meal of the day, which consisted of a small first course, meat or fowl with trimmings, and then a cheese and sometimes an uncomplicated dessert. Usually, Martine prepared very simple, very sustaining things. To start, depending on the season, we might have local melon with thin slices of country ham, or avocados or peach halves (yes, peaches) filled with lightly-dressed tuna, a brothy vegetable soup, or tomatoes or radishes from their garden. Then it might be a roast of lamb, pork, or beef with chunks of potato or stuffed peppers or tomatoes, and creamed spinach—or perhaps a rich stew on a colder day.

That hour an a half always yielded up a rich harvest of things I otherwise would never have known about them, or them about me, for it was a chance for us to deepen our relationship beyond the obvious. We talked about our families, our countries, politics, religion, Iraq and Bin Laden, Bush and Chirac and the troubled Franco-American relationship (it was the "freedom fries" era, remember). And we talked about wine, about the current drop in sales of French wine in America, about the crisis in the appellation of Cahors, both in its leadership and in the financial health of its winemakers.

It was around that table that Yves spoke with both fondness and bitterness of his youth in Algeria, his father's vineyard where he grew up, the neighbors wounded in a terrorist attack on a cinema, and his subsequent arrival in Bordeaux in 1962 as a penniless nine-year-old refugee when his family had had to abandon their vineyards, their house, and all their other property there. I learned that he had originally trained as an agricultural engineer with a background in viticulture and had taken wine-tasting courses with Émile Peynaud, the best-known French enologist, researcher, and wine writer of our time, in Bordeaux in the early 1970s.

In that kitchen, I got to know Martine's father, Jean, through her stories of growing up with him, and heard her first memories of the vineyard. "Washing the bottles, that was always the first job you could do. Once, I fell into the tub and they had to fish me out!" It was where I learned that their daughter, Isabelle, was getting married, and where, a year and a half later, exhorted to shush by Martine with a finger to the lips, I met their first grandchild, Juliette, sleeping in a bassinet on the table.

Over many meals there I came to know Martine as a serious person with a contagious sense of humor and a warmth that can't help overflowing, touching those around her, many of whom she looks after in one way or another. She works in the office, travels to wine shows all over Europe, puts in long hours in the *chai*, and accompanies Yves out in the vines to follow the ripening grapes. She and her sister, Marise, both take loving care of their mother, who will probably stay in the big house on the winery grounds close to children and grandchildren until the day she dies. When Martine and Yves' younger child, Franck, now a student at a university, had to have his knee ligaments repaired recently, it was Martine who arranged everything, and it was to his parents' home he came from the hospital and from rehabilitation.

That particular day in October, after the boots had come off and the hands had been washed, after the first thirst had been slaked with mineral water, Yves handed the bottle to Martine, who took one look at it and smiled and blushed. "Ah, the 1977, that's the wine of our love," she said, looking at Yves fondly. "We first met in the fall of 1976, out in the vines."

"We were young then!" Yves said.

"He was here as an enologist, taking samples just before the harvest. We were married in June of 1977, and Isabelle was born the first day of the harvest, September twenty-sixth, 1978!"

"We didn't lose any time, you see," Yves added, stating a fact.

Everyone was quiet as we sat and Yves poured the wine. In the glass it had the brown-tinged robe of age but offered up to the nose a rich plum fragrance, almost that of jam, reflected again in the mouth with that first sip and then fading to an earthier, darker note.

"Do you remember the 1976 yesterday, Michael?" Yves asked. "I wanted you to taste it to see that even in a year of drought the grapes can make a very special, a very intense wine. That was a wine *sur le gras,*" a very rich, full-bodied wine with lots of concentrated fruit. "And there was the 1980."

"And you said it was a year of paradox," I put in.

"Paradox, yes, because it was a small harvest, not from drought but because of the frost in the spring which pushes back the maturity, the harvest, everything. It is a wine therefore which develops much more slowly in the bottle. The 1980 has all of what we think of as reflecting the *terroir* in an old Gamot—that red fruit, yes, but with characteristics too of undergrowth, or black truffle. This is somewhere between the two, I find."

And that is how we spent those hours, not always or even usually, but sometimes with Yves having snuck off during the morning to stash a bottle along the way, only to bring it out to teach. Mornings and afternoons in the vines, in the *chais,* were about the present and the future, but lunch was reserved for the past. The lessons were as much about history, their personal history—the vagaries of this year and that, each wine capturing for them a twelvemonth lived—as about tasting wine. It was then that I began to understand why they talked about their wine in the way they did, for it embodied so many things to them. It was their living, certainly, but it was born of the land they loved, a symbol of the family faith, its color, smell, and taste holding every echo of the time and labor in its making, time in a bottle.

Much later that afternoon, I drove down the long drive attempting to digest not just lunch but all the new experiences of the day. How rich was their life, I thought, and yet what a price they paid for being, as Yves had said one day, rooted in their vineyards—nailed to the land were his exact words—by the needs of the vines and the wine.

9

Vines in Winter

Out in the wide world in the winter of 2002, it was an odd time when everything seemed in flux, a time of entropy, of tragedy, of things falling out of the sky and natural disasters. All the news was bad, the war with Iraq, at that point merely hopelessly inevitable, staining every conversation. France and Germany, in the persons of Jacques Chirac and Helmut Schmidt, were tripping over each other in a contest to see who could excoriate Monsieur Bush most furiously, while his own drum-banging speeches and crusader rhetoric only further inflamed those who had been, a few short months earlier, our allies.

In Maine, we were in the middle of the worst winter in decades, certainly in the ten years that we had lived there, with record snowfalls and a bitter arctic cold that had blasted in before Christmas and never left. When the snow on the porch roof accumulated to a depth of three feet, I had had, for the first time, to climb out my daughter's bedroom window, shovel in hand, and spend three hours in the morning and the same again in the afternoon shifting it onto the ground below in a pile that grew as tall as a man and that would not finally melt away until April 15. I had discovered the temperature below which my car refused to start (–14 degrees), and our twenty-year-old cat, Jade, had gone abruptly into a steep decline.

My departure in February on a trip to visit my winemaking friends was a hasty one, too, as a big storm was creeping its way up the east coast and wreaking havoc on airports, buses, trains, and entire cities. When I got to Boston's Logan Airport, the place was a madhouse, the waiting areas around the Delta gates packed with people trying to go south. In search of a sandwich, I made the classic error of waiting until I had gone through security only to find that the crowds, like locusts, had vacuumed up everything but the candy bars and cheesy gifts in every kiosk and restaurant throughout the terminal. My plane was one of the last to leave Boston before a blizzard dropped a foot and a half of snow on New England, closing down the last major airport open on the eastern seaboard from Washington north.

I was hoping to find, on the other side of the Atlantic, balmier climes certainly, but also that particular calm and sense of otherworldliness that the wild, empty landscape of the Lot valley always inspires in me. I also hoped to find the winemakers more relaxed, their work a far cry from either the frenzied days of the harvest itself or the equally intense months that follow, when every waking hour is spent in the wine barns, worrying over the progress of the fermentations and the young wine's early evolution after that.

For winemakers, winter, particularly the period from January to March, is supposed to be a time of relative peace. Outside, the winter winds strip the last leaves from the vines, and the colder air forces the sap down into the roots. The canes go woody and dry, and, aided by the colder weather, the whole plant rests, a necessary yearly pause if it is to give good fruit the next fall. It is the lack of a prolonged dormant season, together with dry, hot conditions necessitating irrigation (for example, in parts of Australia, Argentina, and South Africa, and much of California and Washington State) that makes subtropical vines tend to overproduce inferior grapes and live far less long, their harvest also requiring more enological manipulation to make balanced, long-lasting wines. That winter southwestern France had seen weeks when the temperature had hovered around 20 degrees, a good thing, and a midwinter warm spell, which can occur in the Lot when hotter air moves up from Africa, worrying the winemaker lest the vines get confused and bud early, just in time for the spring frosts to kill them.

In the wine barn, the cellarmaster, *le maître de chai,* enters into a more contemplative rhythm, his work now more of the mind, mouth, and nose than the hand. This year's wine, in the stainless steel tanks and huge wooden *foudres,* will be racked off—separated from—the lees several times over the months. As the dead yeast cells and other leftover solids of fermentation are eliminated from the wine, its cloudiness disappears, and it begins to take on those characteristics of smell and taste which belong more to a finished wine. Where the vineyard produces a blend of different grape varieties and the result is not destined to be aged in small oak barrels, as in most of Cahors, early winter or early spring may be the moment when this wine is mixed and then left to sit again, the different varietals melding for several months before bottling.

Some winemakers will also fine their wine, and the French term, *le collage,* a word whose root connotes glue or stickiness, helps define the process. Usually activated charcoal, egg white, or a refined clay called bentonite (and, in the old days, animal blood) will be used to clarify the wine by attracting the impurities and binding with them before settling, over time, to the bottom of the tank or barrel. Of course, fining doesn't just remove impurities that might later lead to off-tastes or off-smells; it pulls out of the wine all particles of a certain size and nature, some of which may be beneficial to the wine as it ages, making it more complex, more interesting.

"We don't fine our wine," Martine told me flatly one February day. "The wholesalers do it, using chemistry to freeze the wine in time so that it never moves, never changes, never ages. It is biologically dead, of course, and incapable of ever becoming other than what it is at that moment." Jean-Luc and Philippe don't fine their wines, either, all of them believing that to do so removes too much of the biologically and chemically active material which makes Cahors, over time, evolve into its characteristic self.

None of these winemakers filter their wine, either, by passing it under slight pressure through screens to catch the largest particles. This process, which can be very finely tuned by varying the width of the holes in the filter, can be much gentler on the wine than fining. Still, the pendulum today is swinging away from filtering and fining, answering the market's desire for more natural, nearly organic, wines which have been manipulated and fussed with as little as possible. Some French bottles now have "unfiltered" on their labels, and as a consequence also carry the reminder that, with age, the wine might show a completely natural deposit, visible as small particles at the bottom of the bottle.

Last year's wine, the best maturing in the oak barrels called *barriques* or *fûts*, the standard size holding about 280 bottles, has its own demands. Certainly, barrels occasionally leak (and you can bet the barrel maker hears about that). There is the ongoing task of keeping the barrels, lying on their sides in special cradles so that air circulates around them, topped up, as throughout the course of a year a minimal percentage of the wine will be lost to ullage—evaporation—rather poetically called the "angels' share" though the winemakers wish these heavenly visitors weren't so thirsty. The goal is to keep the level of wine in the cask as close to full as possible, right up to the bunghole. The lower the level in the barrel, the greater the surface area of wine exposed to the air, the greater the potential for evaporation. While some oxygen is desirable, even necessary, for the wine to evolve and develop in tandem with the oak, overoxidation can spoil the wine. One of the magical properties of oak is in fact the just sufficient amount of air, a truly minuscule amount, its pores allow to migrate into the barrel. The winemaker will also be tasting periodically from barrels from all the different parcels to follow the evolution of each varietal over time.

In much of Cahors, where family-owned vineyards are still the norm, most winemakers consider the position of cellarmaster more of a Bordeaux affectation, as his tasks are performed by members of family and always have been. At Clos de Gamot, you'll find Yves, together with Bernard and Pierre, his two full-time employees, overseeing the wine barns, racking off, blending, and keeping things topped up. You won't find the small new oak *barriques* in their aging barns, however; you'll find the huge, old *foudres,* or tuns, which, though made of oak, are long past the stage where their wood could contribute anything to the wine. What the wood does do is allow oxygen to penetrate to the interior of the tun, helping to mature the wine. (Yves is experimenting with *muids,* new oak barrels that hold twice, even three times, what a small *barrique* holds, for the small batches of wine from Clos St. Jean, their experimental hillside vineyard. Being larger, these barrels lend a less forceful though still perceptible oakiness to the taste and smell of this wine.) When it is time to blend the wines, Martine, Marise, and their mother, Jacqueline, will join Yves, all tasting and making notes and giving their opinions before arriving at a decision together.

Philippe, who always tries to bring out the softer, rounder aspect that his Clos la Coutale is known for, adds another step even before he puts his wine in oak. When I asked about why his wine was so different in nature from other Cahors, he first noted the *terroir*, and noted that his grapes ripen later and that he lets them get very ripe. Also, "I use micro-oxygenation," he told me. "After the alcoholic fermentation, between October and January, we put a ceramic diffuser hooked up to a tank of pure oxygen into the bottom of the tank. It releases very, very small bubbles of oxygen, and not very many of them at that. They are so small that they dissolve in the wine before they even get to the top of the tank. The process fixes the anthocyanins, the body, the fruit of the wine, stabilizes it so it is not susceptible to wide variations. The harsher side of the tannins disappears, and the wine is more supple; that way, you can taste more of the range of flavors in the wine. The wine stays young longer, and has more fruit to it instead of the sometimes animal aromas you can get with the malbec. When you pump over the wine [the more traditional way of oxygenating the wine, and the usual practice in Cahors], you lose the more delicate fruit in the nose, in what you smell. Micro-oxygenation is more delicate, less rough on the wine." This is one of Philippe's innovations, and there are not many others in Cahors who use what is a new and fairly radical process.

Afterward, seeking the softness that oak aging can give but not wanting to overpower the natural fruit of his grapes, he puts the wine in oak barrels, but he uses only one-third new barrels every year. The other barrels, which may have aged one or two wines already, are capable of leaching less of their oak flavors and tannins and attenuate the effect of the new oak when the whole vintage is blended together before bottling.

Jean-Luc, because his Triguedina vineyards produce so many different wines and some whose distinction depends on his subtlety in their oak aging, probably has the most complicated time of it, juggling the very different demands of a dry and a sweet white, a rosé, and the five other reds he makes. Some of his wine, which has rested since vinification in oak for anywhere from six months to a year and a half, is ready for the *assemblage*, the blending, in the winter months. Cahors wine must by law contain at least 70 percent malbec; the proportions of the other two permitted grapes, merlot and tannat, vary with the winemaker's decision, though the softening aspect of the former means that it usually accounts for a further 20 to 25 percent. Between parcels of the same grape in the same vineyard under the same sun and weather there will also be variations that must be taken into account. (Remember, it's the *terroir*, stupid!)

Jean-Luc has the reputation of possessing a very fine hand in judging the ripeness of the wine in the oak, how long to leave any particular wine in contact with the wood. Too little time, and the winemaker might as well have thrown away the money he shelled out for expensive barrels. On the other hand, if he leaves the wine too long in the wood, particularly new wood, he risks destroying the balance of the wine with too much of the oak overtones in the nose and the mouth. And, complexity upon complexity, he also knows that two batches of wine from the same parcel but aged in barrels from different makers may evolve differently, sometimes markedly so. Rather than seeking uniformity and thus using a single barrel maker, most vineyards will use barrels from different makers precisely because they know they will get a range of results and thus a wider palette when it comes time to blend.

White wine, having almost no tannins of its own, is particularly susceptible to being overoaked, an experience familiar to anyone who has downed a glass of certain California and airline-service chardonnay and then spent the next hours waiting for his tongue to unshrivel. Too much oak, again generally more detectable in the whites, can give the wine an aggressive reek of the wood and a cloying sweetness, overwhelming the perfume of the actual grapes that is, one might assume, fundamental to the experience of drinking wine. (To see and smell the difference, open a $12 to $15 Kendall-Jackson or Turning Leaf chardonnay, one that refers to the oak on its label; and a bottle of $15 white Burgundy or Maconnais chardonnay side by side. The former have likely been dosed with oak chips or even extracts of oak tannins early in their short lives, whereas the latter most likely have had no, or very little, contact with oak. For the reds, the absolute best way to understand the influence, good and bad, of oak is to taste new wine directly from the barrel at the vineyard.)

The winemaker will also be waiting for the secondary fermentation, or malolactic fermentation, to take place in the new wine. Winemakers call this the "malo" for short. It happens spontaneously, generally in the cool weather as fall turns to winter, or more rarely in the early spring, days and sometimes weeks when the wine begins to work again. Yves told me that in late November and early December, he and Martine will go into the wine barn either first thing in the morning or late in the afternoon, when all is peaceful, and just sit, side by side, listening. "If you are quiet enough," Yves told me, "you'll hear the whisper of a bubble of gas making its way to the top of the tank, the faintest burps and rumbles that tell you the wine is working again."

Whereas in the first fermentation yeast cells converted fruit sugar into alcohol, in the secondary fermentation bacteria convert a significant by-product of that first process, malic acid, into lactic acid, producing carbon dioxide in the process. Today it is the work of the enologist in the laboratory to track the start and end of this process through regular sampling; but in Cahors, even in the earlier days of Martine and Marise's Papa, it was still in some sense a mystery.

"They didn't always know the whys of things," Yves told me one February day as he was teaching me about this. "But they knew *that* something was happening. 'In the spring the wine begins to work,' my father-in-law would say. Still, they made mistakes, sometimes! Jean told me a story once, before they regularly tested for the malo. It was 1969, and the malo took place in the bottle." There was a fine pastry shop in the nearby town of Figeac that always did a beautiful display in its front window around Easter. "You know, this is a time of christenings and first communions in the church, and so this window had beautiful, delicate white linens of the dresses for the little girls," as well as the rich cakes and confections that would make the feast after the mass. "Well, apparently, Jean had bottled the wine in the early spring before the malo, and in this window were some bottles of fine Gamot—which exploded!" The heat from the sun made the wine work, producing the carbon dioxide that blew up the bottles. "Jean got this call from the *patissière,* who was quite upset, yelling that her beautiful white window, everything in it was now purple!"

It is important for the malolactic fermentation to finish before bottling, not just to avoid making a sparkling wine unintentionally or exploding bottles all over town, but for reasons of taste. Winemakers have known for centuries that something magical happens over the winter, for the very rough edge of the new wine of the fall would generally disappear by spring, and the wine would be softer on the tongue though still quite tannic and puckery in the mouth.

Malolactic fermentation aside, the cold of winter brings, for long periods, a relative chemical quiet to the wine, new and old, as well, slowing reactions which require heat to take place, and encouraging the heavier particles in the new wine (dead yeast cells, microscopic bits of pulp and grape skin, crystals of tartaric acid) to precipitate out and sink to the bottom of the tanks. Low pressure, as is usual with cloudy and rainy weather, is also beneficial to this process.

With the wine resting quietly, the winemaker ought to be able to rest as well. Aside from the demands of the aging barrels, there is the pruning to think of in February and March, but this is measured, deliberate work usually carried out by a crew led by a few of the vineyard's old hands and leavened with experienced seasonal workers. These are men who have watched and worked enough seasons to understand the sometimes minuscule variations between and within this parcel or that as well as what effect last year's weather, growth, and harvest must have on this year's pruning knife.

Otherwise it is a blessed time of relaxation when the winemaker can sit back and reflect, plan for the new year, and perhaps take a vacation to a warmer climate, content in the knowledge that the vines are sleeping and that the weather, as long as it is moderately cold with some rain, really doesn't matter very much.

But when I arrived in the Lot that winter, instead of an island of serenity I found my friends stuck in a deep funk, possessed of an uncharacteristic uneasiness, not at all relaxed, and not only because of the situation in the wider world. With the economic decline that had settled over Europe as well as the United States, the price of wine had plummeted, with no bottom in sight. America, which represents France's fifth largest export market, seemed to be poised to turn its back on French wine just at the time when the winemakers needed to sell the most. The Californians, in turn, were crying over their own sagging sales and lower prices from over-production as thousands of new vineyard acres planted in the speculative frenzy of the dot-com era (some of whose millionaires had apparently planted vines instead of lawns), came into production. Overall, the importers of French wines were cutting back, and the exporters, in response, were ratcheting down the prices they were offering to winemak-ers for wine which was more or less the same in quality as the previous year's and which certainly hadn't cost any less to make.

In the world of French wine, it is hard to understate the importance of the mighty *négociants*—wholesale buyers, blenders, bottlers, and mar-keters—of Bordeaux, the middlemen who for hundreds of years have wielded an enormous influence on the direction of the market throughout the whole of France. It is the Bordelais who set the price for new bulk wine in their appellation in early winter, a benchmark from which all others are derived. It is not too strong to say that the price of Bordeaux acts like a puff of wind on a still pond, the ripples spreading to every appellation in France and even echoing distantly abroad. For those in the southwest, on Bordeaux's doorstep, the influence is great-est. The largest of these neighboring appellations are Gaillac, Bergerac, Buzet, Madiran, and Cahors, and their relative importance in the world of wine may be judged by the fact that the average American wine con-sumer has probably never heard of most of them.

For the hapless winemaker, sitting in his barn contemplating his full stainless steel tanks, his costly brimful barrels, and his empty wal-let, this time of year can be either hopeful or depressing. Through the late fall and early winter, the latter held true: Gaillac was selling in bulk for fifty cents a liter, Madiran and Bergerac for thirty cents a liter, Cahors for about a dollar a liter. Translation: winemakers who had to sell their wine to the wholesalers in bulk or bottle to generate cash flow were making very little profit for their labor. The prices of branded wines sold in the bottle, known as the "châteaus and domaines aver-age," were also pathetic, with Cahors at less than $1.50 a bottle.

On the supermarket shelves, at the retail level, you could find a bottle of Bergerac for 1 euro, then about $1.05 (2002). "I know what it all costs—the bottle, the cork, the label, and the wine—and they can't be making any money at all. It's depressing!" Jean-Luc told me.

On top of a very poor market, it was just two months since, at a cataclysmic meeting of the Cahors wine trade, the entire political, economic, and marketing structure of the appellation had collapsed. The leaders of the two most important groups had resigned, one walking out in disgust after being whistled down (whistling being the French equivalent of booing) at their annual meeting. The wholesalers were now refusing to buy any wine, and the winemakers were in open revolt against a proposal to reduce future harvests and increase quality by ripping out vines growing in the most marginal areas of the appellation. It was a mess.

Every December, after the harvest numbers are in, there is a great convocation of grape growers, winemakers, and wholesalers in the town hall of Puy l'Evêque, the large town that overlooks much of the appellation from its place high on the northern ridge. They belong to the Interprofessional Union of Vin de Cahors, which has about 600 members, and this is their yearly meeting. Leading them are delegates chosen from the two major professional associations—the Syndicate of Producers and the Syndicate of Wine Traders, two bodies normally in constant conflict with each other over the basic issues of quality, production, and price. Almost half of the growers are also members of a third powerful group, the Cooperative Winemakers of Cahors, known as Les Côtes d'Olt from the location of their massive winemaking, aging, and bottling operation. The issues aren't that complicated, but here we must pause to make a few important distinctions.

The grape grower, *le récoltant*, who grows grapes and only grows grapes, does not necessarily have the same interests as the winemaker, *le vigneron*; and both their interests will differ from those of the wine wholesaler or trader, *le négociant*. In Cahors, there are about 200 growers, many of them working less than 10 acres, family plots which are passed from generation to generation and whose yield, while not making them wealthy, contributes a steady part of their yearly income. The grape growers seek to push their yields up (this known colloquially as "making the vines piss wine," which growers and makers did in past decades) and to sell the harvest either to the cooperative or to the traders at the highest price. They don't have to make or sell the resulting wine, so quality—lower yields making better wine, all other things being equal—is to them only as much an issue as the buyers make it.

Growers who are members of the cooperative, by definition, are not allowed to sell to the highest bidder but must sell to the cooperative, and they do so at prices fixed by yearly contracts, with higher-quality grapes yielding a bonus. The cooperative then makes the grapes into wine and markets that wine, about 20 percent of the appellation's entire production, functioning much like a *négociant* in these respects.

The winemakers, about 300 of them, generally grow their own grapes, making wine, and then either bottling it and selling it under their own domaine and château labels (two-thirds) or selling it in bulk (one-third), from the tanks, to traders. If you don't bottle and sell your own wine, you want a high bulk price but probably don't really care about those higher-end domaine and château winemakers or the traders as long as their products aren't priced so low as to compete with yours.

The independent winemaker, like Jouffreau, Baldès, and Bernède, has the toughest row to hoe. He has all the costs of producing his own wine under his own labels, and he has the costs of marketing it, too. Unlike the grape grower, he has no guaranteed purchaser, and he sells in bulk to the middlemen only occasionally, perhaps to relieve the pressure of too much stock before the new harvest comes in or to provide short-term cash flow, or when the wine is of a quality not up to the standard of his own label. He may sell 60 to 70 percent of all the wine he makes every year to a group of loyal customers—individuals, restaurateurs, and retailers—from all over France and Europe, to locals, and to the important summer tourist trade. To him, the bulk price of Cahors is an important benchmark, but his concern is more long-term, with the reputation of the appellation as a reliable producer of good wine at a certain price. He wants Cahors to be known for an ever-improving quality and a rising price that reflects its quality, and he doesn't want the market flooded with quantities of inferior wine. He would prefer to sell fewer bottles at a higher price rather than see the market flooded with lower-quality wine sold at cut-rate prices because other winemakers need cash or space in the wine barn. It's like the old joke: What do you call the guy who finishes last in his medical school class? Doctor. Here, the crappiest, cheapest bottle and the most expensive in the appellation still say the same thing on the label: AOC Cahors.

The traders, *les négociants,* have the most power. They buy grapes and make wine sold under their own labels. They buy bulk wine and may sell it in bulk. In many European countries, you can take your own containers to a wineshop or market and have them filled from small stainless steel or fiberglass tanks. The *négociant* may also blend the wine of different producers and bottle the result under his own brands. Many *négociants* also own their own vineyards. They may sell under thirty or forty different labels, the cheapest at 80 cents a liter in bottles with plastic caps, the minis served on planes and trains, the multiliter refillable cubitainers (boxed wine with a plastic bladder inside) for the restaurant trade, multitiered supermarket brands, and finally, on top of that, another line of premium wines for sale in the better wineshops. They may be thus grower, winemaker, wholesaler, and even retailer all at once.

The traders have the most power because they have the capital and the infrastructure to vinify, blend, bottle, move, store, and trade huge quantities of wine, in fact the majority of the 30 million bottles produced in the appellation each year. They have the most power because they can abruptly close the faucet—stop buying wine, period, often for months at a time, hobbling the operations of those they buy from.

And did I mention that it is the traders who set that bulk price? In essence, each fall when the new vintage is in, the producers' syndicate and the traders' syndicate meet to negotiate a target price. The traders will support the price as long as the retail demand is there. What invariably happens, however, is that the price floats downward as the date of the next harvest—the point of greatest pressure for the winemakers—approaches, reaching a nadir in October, which is not coincidentally when all the big supermarkets and department stores have their wine sales. Also, in years of plenty, when every appellation is selling lots of good-quality wine, high prices are unsustainable.

Cahors may be less typical than other small appellations simply because, whereas in the late 1990s there were twenty middlemen, in 2004 there are fewer than ten, and several of these are conglomerates for which Cahors is but one link in a chain of a hundred labels, and a negligible link at that.

Another player in this game is the French state, in the guise of the National Institute of Appellations of Origin (INAO), a very powerful institution whose task is to foster the good image of French wine at home and abroad, to help the industry improve on all levels by making and enforcing the laws, and to rationalize production over time by strictly controlling the planting of vines. In most of France, today, it is illegal to plant vines. (What you buy when you buy a vineyard, along with the actual land, is the *droit de plantation,* the right to plant so many vines on that defined parcel.) In recent years, INAO's first priority has been a huge push to make some of France's 440 or more appellations smaller in area by forcing winemakers to take their more marginal lands out of production forever. This is what it has been trying to encourage in Cahors.

The rationale is very commonsensical. The French are drinking less wine, and the domestic market is therefore shrinking. Overproduction puts a downward pressure on prices, hurting everyone. In the face of burgeoning production in lower-cost places like South America, Australia, and South Africa, and closer to home in Spain, Greece, and Russia, French winemakers should abandon the low ground (literally and figuratively), letting the newcomers make and sell the plonk while the French make and sell less wine but wine of a higher quality and price. By harnessing the full power of the rich history and good reputation of French winemaking, the industry can, on the one hand, persuade the French to drink higher-priced wine, even if they drink less, and on the other hand export its way to more secure long-term health.

Although this is a simplistic explanation of a complex situation, a local example suffices to demonstrate the logic. At the prices and maximum permitted yield that applied in 2002, a Cahors winemaker would have been paid for bulk AOC wine, all costs aside, about $2,650 per acre of production. Even if he reduced his yield by 20 percent and added $1.50 a liter in extra cost (for oak aging, bottle, cork, and label), he would reap $3,600 an acre at an export price of $4 a bottle for a wine that would turn up on an American wineshop at $12 to $14. Although these numbers are approximate, it doesn't take much effort to see that quality as reflected in a higher price trumps quantity very quickly, particularly given that the winemaker cannot generate more profit simply by planting more vines to make more wine.

The final player in Cahors winemaking is (or was) one man, a force unto himself, Alain Dominique Perrin, or just ADP, as the press calls him. (And the press calls him a lot, photojournalists, television reporters, and newspaper writers being to this man what a grand piano was to Vladimir Horowitz.) Perrin was, until his retirement in 2002, CEO of the Richemont group of luxury goods companies. He rose to that position as, by many accounts, a brilliant marketer of such marquee names as Cartier, Piaget, Baume & Mercier, Van Cleef & Arpels, Montblanc, and a handful of European cigarette brands (later sold) like Rothmans and Peter Stuyvesant. He came to Cahors looking not for a vineyard but for a château, which he duly found in the early 1980s: Château Lagrézette, just outside Cahors.

He was also, until he resigned and walked off in protest at the yearly December meeting in Puy l'Evêque in 2002, the head of the *négociants* syndicate and a strong advocate for the controversial plan to reclassify all the land in the appellation. As the head of the wholesalers, he had pushed for and then supported higher prices for Cahors wine. He was the honorary grand marshal of the Confrérie, the Brotherhood of Wine, and an important force behind the Seigneurs de Cahors (Lords of Cahors), a marketing association of a handful of the most elite vineyards who agreed to strictures on yield and vinification to ensure the highest quality—with a corresponding price. He sells the most expensive Cahors—Le Pigeonnier, at $75 or more a bottle—which Robert Parker, for what it's worth, has found "outstanding."

Depending on whom you talk to, Perrin is either the savior of the appellation, dragging its image up from the depths and into the public eye and making it a wine to watch, or a Machiavellian spider who sucked what good he could from the appellation to his own ends and abandoned it when the going got difficult. Never have I encountered a single person about whom so many hold such strong opinions. Most of the winemakers of Cahors have one or both feet squarely in the peasant culture of rural France. They are a reticent bunch by nature, and almost never will you hear Monsieur X speak badly of Monsieur Y, whom he detests for whatever reason. Even if you ask him directly, Monsieur X will close his mouth and turn away, which is generally all you have to know.

Mention Perrin to anyone in the wine business in Cahors, however, and it is as if you were out in the middle of a field holding a lightning rod in a raging electrical storm. People have told me that he is, variously, "a foreigner," "an interloper," "a rank opportunist," "a snake," "an elitist," and "a diamond merchant," and have called him, less kindly, "His Highness," "a fat prick," and "that big fat Parisian turd" (though he is actually from Burgundy). Others are quick to point out that his mother is apparently Corsican, imputing his supposed vindictiveness and business cunning to that blood. Note: The people who made these comments and some that follow will remain anonymous—necessarily, as France is still a country where the rich will have their way in the courts and in the press at the expense of other people's reputations. Or, as one winemaker put it, "What can you do against someone like him? He has the French and English prime ministers to dinner at his house!"

When I arrived at Lagrézette for an interview, it was hard not to feel a bit like a supplicant before the lord of the manor, such are the surroundings. You arrive at a medieval-looking gatehouse and continue into a neatly graveled and landscaped parking lot on whose far side the road continues, wending its way through a handsome park, past various meticulously restored barns and outbuildings, to arrive at the back of a château that could have been the model for the Disneyland castle. On one side all is vines, descending in orderly rows on various terraces; again, everything is beautifully groomed and maintained, with not a piece of trash or crumbling wall in sight. The parkland hides a secret, however, for underneath, Perrin has undertaken, in his words, "a pharaonic endeavor," hollowing out a series of caverns that hold the entirety of his winemaking operation.

When Perrin arrived in 1980, the vineyards of Lagrézette were, like his château, in ruins and lacking even a functional winemaking operation. "Make no mistake about it," he told me, "I have invested enormous quantities of money in Lagrézette. I have invested somewhere between $12 million and $15 million here."

We were sitting in his home office, which is the completely round ground floor of one of the château's thin, graceful towers. The floor is of old tile, the walls are of dressed stone, and the fireplace is a spectacular showpiece of the mason's art, curving as it does to follow the tower's shape. He sat behind a wooden desk cluttered with papers, the phone constantly ringing ("I'm selling my London house"), and he told me his side of the story, how he came to be so dominant in the appellation, which could be summed up as *veni, vidi, vici* with perhaps an *exuent* at the end.

"In 1985," he began, "I got a visit from three men, M. Baudel, the count of Montpezat, and I think Jean-Luc's father, Jean Baldès."

These were all very influential men in the appellation at the time, but noticeably absent was Martine's father, Jean Jouffreau, who had long enjoyed the role of the knowledgeable, thoughtful elder statesman of the appellation, one whose opinion was sought in the media on this or that topic. He was, apparently, about to be replaced.

"They came because they had read about me in the papers, and they asked if I would agree to speak before the press about *vin de Cahors* and if I would be the Grand Master of the Confrérie." This last is the honorary head of the Cahors Brotherhood of Wine, whose members don crimson robes and funny hats for various wine ceremonies. "I refused. I told them that I had come here to relax, to in fact escape that sort of exhausting life filled with media attention. They came back again, seeking me out a year later, insisting very strongly, notably the count of Montpezat, and I caved in. I agreed to become the Grand Master of the Confrérie, and to take care of public relations and communications for the *vin de Cahors*. But I told them I'll do it with one condition—that I do it alone. I did not want that it be twelve voices all speaking, but that one voice do the talking. You have to have a single language, and the message has to be homogeneous. And it went very well: inductions into the Confrérie of important people, media attention, et cetera, I got involved as a wholesaler. I became good friends with Jean Marie Sigaud [head of the Producers' Syndicate], a guy I like a lot, whom I esteem quite highly, and together we made the price of Cahors in bulk climb from 5 francs to 8.40 francs [a liter] over three or four years. One thing is sure—I made the price go up 60 percent. Everyone profited from that. The quality went up, and little by little people came to have confidence in that quality."

As I sat in my comfortable chair in that luxurious medieval room listening to this neat recitation, several thoughts occurred simultaneously. Though his ego is ample and his manner often offensive when it comes to criticizing others, he is hard not to like for the sheer force of his oversize, very American media-steeped personality. He is also a consummate communicator who has a message and sticks to it, who delivers entire paragraphs of perfect, flowing prose, deflecting awkward questions and, when necessary, overlooking contrary facts however undeniable.

I was also remembering the other side of his triumphal rise to power, which had left some bitterness in its wake.

When Perrin first came, he had no place to make his wine. He became a member of the cooperative. Unhappy with the results there, he complained loudly and publicly and brought in Michel Rolland, a very well known Bordeaux enologist. When the underground winery at Lagrézette was rebuilt, he resigned, taking Rolland with him. Then, as an independent winemaker, he sought to join forces with other likeminded souls to create the Seigneurs de Cahors, a very exclusive dozen or so Cahors labels that all agreed to various quality-assuring strictures and who launched their venture with all manner of hype and promotion, even including a glossy book.

Here, of course, he was turning his back very pointedly, and also publicly, on Jean Jouffreau, who was closely associated with the Confédération des Caves Particulières (Confederation of Distinctive Cellars), which already existed and had existed for a number of years with exactly the same goals and requirements, if with less exclusivity. Not content with making his own wine in his own winery, Perrin then started a wholesale business and became, after a loud and very public battle with his most important rival wholesaler, the head of the Syndicate of Wine Traders.

"He divided to rule," a winemaker told me. "He started out working with the cooperative and spat on the wholesalers. He left the cooperative and made his own wine and then spat on the co-op and the wholesalers. He bought a wholesaler and spat on the other whole-salers, the cooperative, and the independent winemakers like us."

Perrin defends himself quite well. "If you drink Cahors from, say, 1990, you don't have to go back that far, it's not very good, hunh?" he told me. "It's not good. It was shit. It was rustic, coarse. It started to get better about then, some of it, but still, Cahors was a wine lacking elegance and with lots of faults. I think that at the same time the quality was going up the price went with it. Everyone will tell you, and everyone knows, and the wholesalers will confirm it, I made the price go up because I was the president of the wholesalers, and I asked them to support me in making the price rise. At any rate, the result was there; by December 2002, the price was at 8.40 to 8.50 francs a liter. Very high, and higher than our neighbors in Gaillac, Bergerac, Fronton, Madiran, very high in price, even higher in price than ordinary bulk Bordeaux."

The chef of a highly regarded restaurant in the region agreed with him. "It's good to have competition," the chef told me. "Perrin raised the bar and without him, most of the others would have been content to make wine as they always had, sell it to the cooperative, not go any further. Now, they all have stainless steel, they send their kids off to learn something about enology, and the wine is better."

So what happened in December 2002 that prompted his by all accounts very sudden and dramatic resignation and subsequent withdrawal from any political association with the appellation? The meeting of winemakers and traders would have been much like its predecessors had they not been voting on a plan to reclassify the vineyards of the appellation. In what is called a system of *zones de cru*, the best parcels would be formally identified and the wine from those grapes, judged therefore superior, would sell at a premium, perhaps even a huge premium, above wine from parcels identified as inferior. On something like 10 percent of the vineyard area—its very worst land, all on the lowest terrace—the vines would be uprooted. The government would not permit Cahors to inaugurate those highly prestigious *crus* unless the poorer land was declassed as unfit for grapes. All this would take place over twenty or thirty years, and generous subsidies for replanting would, theoretically, be available.

At that meeting, the head of the producers' syndicate, Sigaud, first read off the grim statistics—declining prices, "marketing challenges," and the telltale fact that at present, Cahors winemakers were still holding one and a half year's supply of wine from previous vintages in their *chais,* wine which should have been sold long ago. He urged them to vote for the reclassification, and then Perrin did the same, if at greater length and with some very pointed criticism of, essentially, most of their wines. He assured them that he had spoken not only repeatedly with the head of the National Institute of Appellations, but also with the prime minister himself, who was receptive to the idea of *crus* in Cahors and had the dossier at the top of the pile on his desk.

Two winemakers stood up to reply, earnest in their peasant accents, and Perrin's moment of reckoning was at hand. They were suspicious (and judging by the approbation of the crowd, so were many others) that this initiative was going to be very expensive for them in the short term and held little benefit for them in the long term. The first even read out the dictionary definition of "elitism," in the midst of talking about "this person who knows who he is," leaving no doubt about whom he was speaking.

The second speaker said, with the tortured eloquence of a simple man unused to addressing a crowd: "I don't know if you can reclassify the appellation every twenty years knowing that we are not planting peas, but vines, and that we are committed to the long term. We ourselves are committed. We commit our children, too, in their professional studies as well. Some of us have fifteen-year-olds who are off to enroll in agricultural and viticultural studies, who have made this choice, who are going to work all the way through to their retirement, that is to say, forty, forty-five years. They have made investments in their education and formation, and it takes a lifetime to pay them off. And we have made, since 1990 or 1995 or 2000 or as even as recently as yesterday, financial investments. We have planted, we have built wine barns and bought equipment, expenses that need to be amortized, if not over generations, than over a certain number of decades."

This was the voice of the little guy, who perhaps didn't have the best land, but it was his land and always had been. Now, without rock-solid assurances of compensation, new and better land, and the capital to replant, why should he vote to impoverish himself? And especially, why should he vote for something that he perceived would only make the rich richer, reinforcing the so-called elite of Perrin and his group in their position at the top because they alone had the capital, the resources, and the time to develop the new prestigious *crus* to which the plan would lead?

There was some more back and forth, and then the whistling began, and not a single winemaker stood up to defend the plan. Among Perrin's fellow *négociants,* the only voice was in fact the rival he had forced out to become head of the wholesalers, and this man's words, while defending the idea of Cahors *crus,* could only in the most diplomatic of interpretations be called a defense of Perrin. The vote went against the reclassification, and Perrin let it be known that, as well as resigning his posts, he would no longer use his resources to promote Cahors. Not content with this, however, he went on to suggest that he might withdraw from the appellation altogether, relying on the marquee value of Lagrézette and his name and relegating its association with Cahors to the back label on the bottle.

Many winemakers are of the opinion that Perrin planned the whole episode, down to the last melodramatic walk up the long aisle. ("You could have heard a pin drop," he told me, "such was the silence.") Given that he is such a master of communication, and that the explosive failure of the whole plan seems to come down to the long simmering, quite bitter, resentments of a large number of peasants of modest means against a small perceived elite combined with an equally massive failure in communication, I tend to agree. At the very least, now that Perrin has removed himself from the mix, this idea of redefining the appellation might move forward in some other form, perhaps one less ambitious but also less polemicized.

Perrin and those other Cahors winemakers, elite or not, who believe in getting rid of poorer land and constantly improving the quality of the wine (and thus raising its price) are right. He pointed out to them in his speech that the government had given workers the "gift of the thirty-five-hour workweek," which had already so increased costs as to prevent the winemakers from ever being able to compete on price alone. That leaves quality, and imposing a system of *crus* would be a huge step in that direction. It would also, it is true, probably drive some smaller, undercapitalized winemakers out of business and force all the other winemakers to change, sometimes significantly, the way they plant and work their vines and make their wine. The best among them are already preparing, replanting at higher densities of vine in their superior parcels, investing in better equipment. They foresee the day when the choice is no longer theirs but imposed from above. It remains to be seen whether Perrin's divisive legacy prevents the others from realizing, too, that it is only a matter of time before they must change or sell out. To begin to do that, they're first going to have to learn how to work together truly for the greater good and abandon their more parochial interests.

10

❧

A Visit to the Cooper

The barrel doesn't make the wine any more than
a habit makes a monk.
—Émile Peynaud, renowned
twentieth-century Bordeaux enologist

If the evolution of wine in the bottle over decades is still in some measure a mystery, the role of the oak barrel in which the wine was aged on the way to that bottle is an enigma wrapped in a mystery. For all our scientific know-how, we still don't know exactly why one wine, of these grapes, grown in this place under these conditions, aged in new oak barrels, then bottled, will ten, twenty, even thirty years later have evolved into liquid gold surrendering up to the nose and mouth in a single mouthful its entire accumulated excellence—while the same wine, treated identically but without the oak, emerges as an also-ran, good but not great, lacking the depth, the finesse, and the complexity of the first.

A few thousand years of winemaking have taught the winemakers a few things, however, and modern science is finally getting around to working out some of the explanations behind observations made down through the ages. It turns out that the material of the various containers through which wine passes in its evolution can be very important to the end result.

To back up a bit, you have to store wine in something, and for almost two millennia before the use of cement, glass, plastic, fiberglass, and stainless steel to make tanks, that something was wood—locust, cherry, beech, chestnut, and particularly oak. Even earlier, the Romans and Greeks had used clay amphorae sealed with pine resin against leakage. (Buy a bottle of *retsina,* the Greek wine still flavored with pine pitch, and you might experience what that wine tasted like after sloshing around over bad roads and on choppy seas in such containers.) Fittingly, it was the Gauls, the original Frenchmen, who seem to have first developed the barrel, its form evolving over time into the shape we universally recognize today. It was sturdy enough to withstand the rigors of transport in an era when that meant oxcart and a ship's cargo hold; it could be stacked handily, turned on its side, and rolled easily by a single man; and was made of a material that naturally adapted to changing conditions of heat and humidity without rupturing. As well, in a kind of natural protection system, the wood encourages the growth of tartaric acid crystals that precipitate out of the wine on the barrel's insides, a phenomenon later shown to serve as a kind of cordon sanitaire against microbes and particularly acetobacters, the bacteria that turn the alcohol in wine slowly to vinegar.

While these days we take the use of oak in winemaking as almost a given and assume that unoaked wines must be inferior in quality (as they usually are in price), this is wrong on two accounts. First, in the grand scheme of things, the notion of barrel-aging in oak as a necessary and integral part of winemaking is a nonstarter. The closest most of the wine consumed in the world has come to oak in its short life is probably when the tanker truck drove past an oak tree on the way from winery to bottling plant. Most of the wine the world consumes could not be sold at a price justifying the expense of aging in oak even if its quality merited this treatment and there were enough oak trees and barrels to accommodate it.

Second, we have only recently, in the last fifty years or so, come to appreciate that oak—and only oak—can imbue some wines with a magical ability to transform themselves over time, a transformation not possible with other woods or aging methods. This latent appreciation (more of a rediscovery, but we'll get to that) has as much to do with practical considerations as with matters of taste quite simply because, for most of its history, wine has been a highly variable, unstable, and perishable commodity rushed to market in a race against time, with the possibility of its remaining drinkable longer than one or two years remote at best. Though there have been isolated pockets of winemakers, in France and Germany particularly, whose wine was made from such high-quality grapes and with such care that it was known for its aging ability more than 300 years ago—Samuel Pepys refers to an excellent Haut Brion, for example, in his sixteenth-century diary, and Thomas Jefferson was apparently fond of old Château d'Yquem—such wine was the exception. As well, these wines were often sweet—Sauternes and German late-harvest whites, for example—or fortified with alcohol, as were port, sherry, and the so-called cooked wines of the Mediterranean. Sick wines were the rule: wines that had off-odors and off-tastes and that were fortified with alcohol or brandy or doctored with herbs and other strong flavorings just before drinking, even when quite young.

It needed the brilliance of Louis Pasteur, one of the world's first microbiologists, working in the 1850s, to largely explain the nature of alcoholic fermentation and bacterial and microbial contamination in winemaking. Though today we associate Pasteur's particular innovation, the process that bears his name, with rendering milk safe for children to drink, it was originally widely used in stabilizing bulk wines. His work led to changes in the way wines were made and kept so that they would be more likely to be stable and healthy enough to age at all. Aside from pasteurizing wine, he advocated storing new wine in cool places to inhibit bacterial growth; "ullage," or the regular topping up of barrels to reduce the contact of wine with the air as it evaporated; "racking off," or draining the clear wine off its lees, the sediment of fermentation at the bottom of the barrel; and also "wicking" the barrel, *mèchage* in French, before filling it.

This last, long a practice of winemakers already and still how they do it today, means burning a sulfur "candle," a twist of paper impregnated with sulfur, inside the overturned barrel before filling, and would turn out, with another fifty years of research and refinement, to be the key to helping wines of even moderate quality live on for years, dying a natural death, so to speak, rather than perishing from disease.

The pasteurization of wine—bringing the fermented wine to a high temperature for a short period of time to kill the microbes that might contaminate it—was generally practiced only until wine scientists mastered sulfur application. Even at the time, reputed winemakers, particularly *les grands Bordelais,* were reluctant to assault their wines with such violence, it being recognized that this was a brutal shock to a newborn vintage. They learned in the meantime to filter and fine their wines; these processes, if riskier, had somewhat the same effect as pasteurization, but they achieved the effect by physically removing the contaminants from the wine rather than killing them outright.

Both bottle and cork had been available as far back as the mid-eighteenth century in major wine markets like France, Holland, the Iberian Peninsula, and London, where a huge amount of Bordeaux, the Brits' beloved "claret," was actually bottled well into the twentieth century; bottling was more generally the responsibility of the end consumer or reseller after shipping, not the winemaker in his vineyard. Wine was still largely fermented in barrels, stored in barrels, shipped in barrels, and consumed from barrels, sojourning briefly in bottle, flask, or carafe between cellar and table. The idea of aging wine for even a few years was impractical, expensive, and unnecessary, and thus still largely confined to a smaller, rarer group of what we would call vintage wines.

We arrive at the turn of the twentieth century, then, an era of innovation in many things. Thanks to modern industrial processes, we now have glass bottles cheap and strong enough to be commercially viable for the export of wine near and far, railroads and steamships connecting the growing cities, and a healthy market of those prosperous enough to afford wine. We have high-quality, mass-produced corks to stopper those bottles, and many more wines to put in them that, being well-made and "clean," might last, and even improve, over time. From there, ironically enough, it was all downhill for the coopers and their barrels. Their downfall began with the hammer blow of phylloxera, the vine pest that was then well on its way to annihilating almost every French vineyard—and thus eliminating the need for barrels to make and age wine. The situation got worse with the new fashion, all the rage between the wars, of forming tanks of cement for making and keeping wine.

My personal odyssey to nail down the significance of the oak I trace back to almost the first time I set foot in the bowels of a winery, in particular the subterranean *chai d'élevage,* the maturing barn, of Jean-Luc Baldès at Triguedina in the spring of 2001. That year I had been writing a book about a small village and its restaurant, La Récréation, just across the ridge from the vineyards of the Lot. As with so many life-changing experiences that year, this one was in the company—and at the behest—of Jacques Ratier, the restaurant's chef-owner, and his wife, Noëlle. We had all been invited to this tasting and winery visit along with a motley group including two hunters, their boots still muddy from the woods, and a brace of yuppie couples wearing expensive clothes and ample cologne, a faux pas at a wine tasting.

The aging barn, a vast space blasted out of the limestone just adjacent to the wine-making barn with its ranks of stainless steel tanks, is the single most significant, expensive—and visible—change Jean-Luc has made to his father's operation, and it was natural for him to want to show it off. As we made our way down the stone stairs from the tasting room into this barn, two things became immediately apparent. At the same time I noticed that the air was suddenly cool and dry, my nostrils began to quiver at the sharp odor of new oak, an acrid smell familiar to anyone who has ever cut this wood for the fireplace or ripped a length of oak board on a table saw.

I turned the sharp corner at the bottom of the stairs, and before me spread out a carpet of oak barrels stacked in pyramids two and sometimes three layers deep, the rows stretching away the length of a football field. Above, intricately joined oak beams soared, while windows set high into the stone walls on one side let in gauzy natural light. Underfoot, clean gravel crunched. This peculiar space had, all at once, something of the cathedral, the bank vault, and the sanitarium about it—a fitting combination, as it held at least several million dollars' worth of wine being nursed through adolescence before graduating to the bottle and from there out onto the sales floor.

Nine hundred barrels of oak, one-third of them fresh from the cooper's mallet, put out a powerful reek. That pong, together with the heavy perfume of evaporating wine, combined to create in my head an olfactory "Eureka!" This was what all those wine writers were talking about when they talked about "new oak" or "new wood" as an element of taste and smell. Even though I lacked a glass in hand, the sensation was so pronounced that I found myself smacking my lips and inhaling deeply.

Jean-Luc also made a remark whose significance I nearly missed at the time. He was talking about his barrels, where the oak came from and how they were toasted. *Toasté* is the actual French word, and I immediately imagined a huge toaster into which barrel staves were inserted. They burn the inside of the barrels? I asked. "No," he said patiently. "They are put over a fire, and, um, more like roasted. My barrels are toasted *douce à moyenne*," light to medium, "this to bring out the flavors of the oak." He moved on to other things, and I was left to add yet another complication to what had seemed at first to be so straightforward.

A few moments later we were back upstairs, gathered in the gloom of the tasting room as Jean-Luc filled our glasses from a heavy glass carafe which he had pipetted straight from the barrel. This was the 2000 Probus, he informed us, and it was going to be an extraordinary wine. In the glass it was still viscous, almost black, the color adhering in sheets to the side of the glass as it will with new wine. I inhaled, nose in glass, and images of ripe summer berries came to mind; then I took a sip and felt the faint acrid touch of the oak roll over the berries, recalling exactly the experience below, but this time in the nose and mouth.

Tasting a young wine fresh from the oak is a very good way to establish a taste memory of what wine people mean when they talk about a strongly oaked wine; it smells and tastes of wood, a sharp, almost bittersweet odor like the odor of cutting brush in the spring. In a wine that is further down the road in age and in which the oak characteristics have had time to blend and mellow with those of the wine itself, you may still detect the faint echoes of the oak in the so-called vanilla and clove notes.

In a wine of great age, what the oak may have given the wine may remain in the vestiges of tannin that prickle the tongue and cheeks, but probably its taste and smell will rest more wholly on the grapes themselves.

Now a full-blown visit and wine tasting by invitation *sur place* is a bit of theater where each has his role. That afternoon, Jean-Luc was in full professional winemaker mode, letting fall pronouncements that provoked nods and murmurs of approval from the others, though I couldn't make head or tail of them. "The tannins are very well-rounded." "The wood binds the flavors, adds to the aromas of forest glade and truffle, but it's already quite well balanced." He was talking, as winemakers so often do, of what the wine *would* become, judging from its first unveiling. The import of his comments was only some-what diminished by the fact that, at the same time he was dropping his pearls one by one before us, he was attempting to distract his then two-year-old daughter, Juliette, by waving a large pink stuffed rabbit haphazardly about. Others around me sipped and smacked lips and whooshed and gargled, afterward looking knowingly at their friends and muttering similarly opaque phrases.

"You could drink this with the Christmas foie gras this year, and it wouldn't be shamed!" Jean-Luc said toward the end of his presenta-tion. Across the room Jacques lifted an eyebrow and gave me a know-ing glance. "You could," it said, "but I might want to wait a few years!"

That was my first religious experience with oak, and whenever I found myself in the next years in the company of likely victims—winemakers, enologists, sommeliers, or chefs—I asked them to explain to me what they knew of this phenomenon. I had found that the food and wine journal-ists, generally content to state baldly that this or that wine is "oaky," "lightly oaked," or "overoaked" and assume that the reader knows what such terms mean, are particularly useless on this point. After I had pestered Jean-Luc once too often about his barrels and their effect on his wine, he had asked me if I would like to meet his cooper. Aside from the loveliness of the phrase—Today, I'm going to meet my cooper!—I didn't think there would be too many other occasions in my life like this and readily agreed. The English, by the way, use the terms "cooperage" and "cooper" while Americans tend to favor "barrelmaker." I prefer the former, good old-fashioned words for a profession whose artisanal roots are still very much alive and healthy.

And so I found myself climbing into his Audi wagon far too early one cold, wet February morning, our destination a nine o'clock meeting with Monsieur Sylvain, the young proprietor of La Tonnellerie Sylvain—the Sylvain Cooperage—near Saint-Émilion in Bordeaux, two hours to the north of the Lot.

On the way up, I asked Jean-Luc how important oak was to his own wines, and how he had come to rely so heavily on it, given that it was such a pain in the ass. I already knew that the barrels are expensive and wear out after a few years. They take up space and require a particular environment if the wine in them is to remain stable and healthy. Barrels can leak, and some of the wine in them will evaporate over time. Because there is evaporation, a few times a month every single barrel has to be carefully topped up to avoid exposing too much of the wine to oxygen in the unfilled space in the cask, and generally with wine from the same grapes as in the barrel, meaning more logistical and manpower headaches. Why do the winemakers bother given all these burdens? And why do they bother in, of all places, a region like Cahors, whose wine will never command the sky-high prices of Bordeaux and Burgundy?

"My father put the 1976 Prince Probus vintage in oak," Jean-Luc told me, referring to his top-of-the-line offering, as we drove through the endless acres of cabernet and merlot and sauvignon blanc in Bergerac and up into Bordeaux. "That was a first at our vineyard. And it was *good*. He recognized right away, as did those who bought it, that the oak gave to the wine, which was already very good, something extra it otherwise would lack. Not all Cahors wine merits oak. But good oak is the cherry on the cake, giving that little bit more to the wine. New oak can also unbalance a wine, however, and I'm sure you've tasted wines like that: they can smell and taste woody, bitter, and harsh on your tongue.

"Originally, the barrels were the only means to transport wine, but we soon discovered that there was a natural harmony between wine and wood. Specifically oak—and only oak, which is the best wood for wine. It has that quality of vanilla, and its tannins marry well with the tannins of the wine. Chestnut is not neutral like oak, which imparts agreeable aromas to the wine as well. The barrel itself is very important, because it allows a slight permeability, a very small amount of air to come into contact with the wine."

This is a very controversial concept among winemakers and scientists, that, for wine to evolve over time, it needs to come into contact with just sufficient amounts of oxygen; sealed off completely in a vacuum, many believe, the wine stops evolving and may quickly die. The idea comes up often in the debate over cork versus screw cap, too, as a good cork is thought to allow the same exchange once the wine is in the bottle whereas a screw cap is impermeable. The counterargument is that the tiny bit of air left between wine and cap is sufficient to allow the wine to age and that screw caps eliminate the possibility that the cork, through contamination, will give the wine a moldy odor, which is either very common or less so, depending on which industry expert you're listening to. Further evidence, and more persuasive to many, is that some of the great Bordeaux châteaux have taken to keeping their stocks of old wine in screw-cap bottles.

"Some Cahors winemakers still say 'Oh, I don't oak my wine because its not worth it.' Don't forget, too," Jean-Luc continued, invoking the thriftiness of the peasant world to which most winemakers in the Lot trace their roots, "that some of the wine evaporates during the aging, between two and five percent over a year. If you put a thousand liters in a stainless steel tank, two years later, you still have a thousand liters. Stainless steel is simpler and cheaper, and the wine behaves better in it, too, with less risk that some external factor entering the barrel will have a bad effect over time."

Do winemakers change coopers from year to year, as a farmer might change seed variety or kind of fertilizer? He shrugged. "Every year, I experiment," he said, "seeing how this wine does in barrels from this maker or that. But mostly I keep to my regulars. My cooper does not have the right to make a mistake. This is why relationships between winemakers and their coopers go back and back. There is a lot of trust." Considering that the standard barrel holds 225 liters, or around 280 standard-size bottles of wine, a bad barrel could mean a retail loss at Triguedina of anywhere from $2,500 to $5,000, depending on the wine. That's a lot of trust, I would say.

"If you're going to oak your wine, too, you have to have *un chai d'élevage* [a maturing barn]. All those barrels take up a lot of space, they have to be looked after, topped up from time to time, tasted and analyzed periodically. The *chai* has to be cool, dry, and neutral in terms of changes in humidity and temperature." Wine is 85 percent water and 11 to 14 percent alcohol. Both evaporate, but how much of each depends on the surrounding environment. Jean-Luc's aging barn is cool but not hermetically sealed, sufficiently vented so that some air circulates. He finds that his wine loses more water than alcohol. As a winemaker, you would rather that be the case, especially because every appellation states the minimum alcohol permissible for wine sold under its aegis.

He went on to point out that, aside from the initial cost of the barrels, there were all sorts of other financial implications and risks. The farmer doesn't wait two or three years to sell his grain. He sells it after the harvest. At Triguedina, the harvest doesn't mean an instant return. As much as three years of capital may be tied up in a single barrel of wine, the year that went into its making and the eighteen months to two years it rests on the oak. And after that period, he is forced to sell most of it over a few months, whatever the market conditions, because every fall means another harvest, a significant percentage of which needs to go into those barrels, which have to be stored in that *chai*.

No winemaker is so flush as to run out and buy new barrels for every harvest (nor would he want to, as the wine might then have too much oak); and very, very few, despite what the media image is, have vast cellars holding hundreds of thousands of bottles of their wine for speculation in price over the years. Remember that Jean-Luc has more than 100 acres of vines, and that one acre can produce, in moderate production, around 2,000 bottles of wine, or 166 cases. Storing just one-tenth of his production in any one year would take up space equivalent to a 10,000-square-foot house, about the size of a deluxe McMansion.

When Jean-Luc took over the winery shortly before his father's death in 1986, only the Prince Probus, a tenth of the total harvest, was aged in oak. Beginning in 1990, he bought his first lot of fifteen barrels, and in 1991 he bought ninety barrels, until today he finds himself with almost 900 barrels, 300 of them new each year, the whole representing nearly half a million dollars in investment. Each year he has aged in oak an increasingly larger percentage of all the wine he makes. Currently, that means all of his finest wines: the Prince Probus, the Clos Triguedina, and the New Black Wine; his fine white chenin blanc dessert wine; and the dry white Vin de Lune, as well, or about 250,000 bottles of wine.

As we had been talking, Jean-Luc had gotten caught up in his tale, his hooded eyes sparkling, his usually soft voice a bit louder and more animated. Abruptly he fell silent, looked around, peering through the streaky windshield at the passing countryside. "Shit!" he blurted out, quite unusually for him. "I don't recognize this. I think I drove past the road to the autoroute." He fished a piece of paper out of one pocket, his cell phone out of another, all while driving, then, after several attempts, punched in the number of the cooperage to tell them we would be late and to ask for directions.

An hour later, as we got closer, I asked Jean-Luc what we were looking for. "We're looking for a place with a hell of a lot of barrel staves stacked up outside it," he said. A few minutes later, sure enough, a complex of buildings about the size of a large department store but clad in green and white metal loomed out of the mist, around it what seemed like acres of narrow boards stacked flat in cubes as tall as a man and marching off into the distance, where piles of tree trunks three and four feet in diameter rose higher than the roof of the building. Outside the car, the air smelled of oak, but also quite pleasantly of the campfire.

Two minutes later we were ushered into the presence of Monsieur Sylvain, who owns and runs this business, the Sylvain Cooperage in the town of Libourne in Bordeaux. Sylvain makes oak barrels for scores of clients in France, Europe, Asia, South America, and South Africa—in short, across the winemaking world. His customers include everyone from Château Cheval Blanc and Château Angelus in Bordeaux to Cakebread, Kendall-Jackson, and Mondavi in California. Not one for small talk or lingering over a welcoming coffee, he clapped his hands together and launched right into it.

"In 1900 there were three thousand coopers in the Bordeaux region. By the time I came into my father's business, there were fewer than a hundred of us." As he said this with a huge grin, and as we were standing in the plush foyer of his obviously thriving business, I was reassured that the story had a happy ending and settled in for a tale at once personal, professional, and vinicultural.

At age forty-four, Sylvain is thin and intense, more attractive and regular-featured than truly handsome, but so energetic, so enthusiastic, a slim bundle of energy just bursting to bend your ear for hours about barrels, barrels, barrels. One look at his casual but expensive lush brown leather jacket, beige cords, and open-necked shirt, and I guessed at once that he had the keys to the brand-new sparkling silver SUV, a BMW X5, parked right in front of the entrance. SUVs are still rare in France, the price of gasoline there generally hovering above $4 a gallon, and owning and driving one makes a strong statement—that you have arrived. In Sylvain's case, not only has he arrived, resuscitating through twenty years of hard work what was a dying enterprise and turning it into the favored cooperage of some of the greatest Bordeaux wineries, but he clearly intends to stay, judging from his plans. As someone who positively oozes success, it's not surprising that he has won a number of industry and national awards for his work. The crowning achievement came in 1996, when he was chosen as France's Artisan of the Year, receiving the award from the hands of Jean-Pierre Raffarin, then minister of trade and at this writing prime minister. France regards its artisans, a dying breed, very highly; an apt comparison would be, in America, a Kennedy Center Arts Award from the hand of Ted Kennedy.

Sylvain talks very quickly, sometimes running a hand absently through his thinning brown hair flecked with gray. He moves quickly, too, in the long strides of someone who has spent half his working life hiking through forests of oak in search of the perfect tree. I would spend the next hours chasing after him as he loped ahead of Jean-Luc and me, talking all the while.

"Wine is the last bastion of the barrel maker," M. Sylvain said, and went on to sketch the family history. "When I joined my father in the early 1980s, we restored barrels and we made a limited number of barrels of chestnut." Gradually, with the rebirth of the industry, they moved wholly into making new barrels and only barrels of oak for the wine industry. "A hundred years ago [the only container we had for winemaking] was the barrel. There was a reason, but we forgot it." Sylvain grinned. "We forgot everything! Next we had concrete tanks starting in the time between the wars, and everyone said, 'Barrels are finished, over.' They are too much work, so the winemakers burned everything up. By 1950 people were beginning to realize that wood was good, but all those barrels had gone up in smoke and meanwhile the masons had made a fortune making cement fermenting and aging tanks that lasted forever and had been very expensive to construct." And then came stainless steel, he explained, which had the advantage of being absolutely neutral and easy to maintain. With stainless steel, you could even do things like float a layer of inert gas on top of the finished wine, sealing it off from any contact with the outside air.

"It was the Enological Institute [of Bordeaux] that started the renaissance of the oak barrel as being an integral part of the maturation of wine. And then Pontallier, in 1979, came in as the new director of Château Margaux, and he had done a thesis on what the barrel gives to the wine. That was the start of a new road of research. Wine scientists and winemakers began asking questions like where the oak came from, what variety it was, who cut it, its origin, how it grew, on what land, how much moisture was left in it, and what all those things might allow you to say about the style of wine that might result from that given barrel. We are still learning, refining our knowledge. We have a limited range of ideas now, about the effects of origin, the actual grain of the wood, how it is dried, toasted. It is the drying of the staves, we've learned, that has the most influence on the wine."

The whole time he had been talking, we had been hurrying past the stacks of staves on one side, the factory walls on the other. We stopped at the far corner of the building where piles of oak trunks, most three to five feet in diameter, climbed three stories into the sky. Sylvain & Son had moved here in 1989, buying almost fourteen acres, most of which were taken up entirely by the wood in its various states on the way to becoming a barrel. The air reeked particularly strongly of oak, that cat box smell which wrinkles the nostrils. Part of the reason for that I saw at our feet, industrial-sized sprinklers that were watering whole, uncut tree trunks, many up to fifty or sixty feet long.

The forests from which the wood in front of us had come had their own pedigree, I learned, and you sometimes even saw the names of the individual forests mentioned on wine labels—Allier, Perche-Trappe, Tronçais, Saint Palais. All located in the middle of France, they are strictly controlled by the Office National de Forêts, as they have been for more than 350 years, since Louis XIV's minister of state, Jean-Baptiste Colbert, took over their administration as part of his program to rebuild the French navy.

"Our trees, what we buy," Sylvain was saying, "are one hundred fifty years old minimum, and two hundred fifty years old is not uncommon in many of these cultivated oak forests, which are grown according to principles of density. The state holds a Dutch auction once a year of standing wood, and you buy lots according to your needs." He used to spend half the week in the woods, selecting the best of what had been harvested for his purposes, making the long drive up on Wednesday and coming home for the weekend. "Only fifteen percent of what you buy is good enough for barrels. Maybe a tree has too many eyes [where the branches grew out], or it is twisted, so you look at the quality of the growth, all this of course without having seen anything but the exterior of the tree."

The best barrels, he believes, are made of very fine-grained wood, from trees that grow up, in height, rather than out, in diameter. As the tree matures, the lower branches fall off by themselves, naturally. There are two oak varieties used in French barrels, the sessile and the pedonculate; the first is more slow-growing and favors shade, often existing under the canopy of the more aggressive pedonculate. At maturity, fewer than three-quarters are harvested, leaving the rest to sow new trees, also naturally. He turned to Jean-Luc and grinned. "You see, we take as much time with the barrels as you take with the wine."

We approached a pile, and Sylvain bent to inspect the tag nailed to its trunk. "See, this is a 1998 harvest. We age them, and we water them to keep off the insects and so the sun doesn't dry them out." His cell phone rang, and he walked a few steps away. He fussed with a trunk, picking off a section of bark and looking at the wood underneath, as he talked. "They drill a core sample," he continued on his return, and many trees fail. "In a fifty-acre parcel, there might be only a hundred twenty-five trees good enough for us."

He led us around the building to the first workshop, where men were cutting the trunks into sections the length of a barrel stave, or about thirty-eight inches. Sketching on the freshly cut end grain of one such length, he showed us that outer fruitwood, because it is soft, isn't good, and the inner heart isn't either. Looking at a three-foot length on end, which may be three to five feet in diameter, imagine that it is marked like a dartboard, but with only three concentric bands. The bulls-eye, the foot of diameter surrounding it, and the outer foot to two feet are thrown away. It is from the middle ring that is left, cut into so many pie-piece shaped slices following the length of the log, that the staves will be shaped. There are about thirty staves of varying widths in a barrel, so each three-foot length of oak log might produce enough for one and a half barrels, with the other 80 percent of the wood as waste.

"One of the biggest differences between French and American barrels, aside from the variety of oak, is the waste," he continued. "American barrels are cheaper, but they use fifty percent of the log because the wood is so expensive there."

At the next station, Sylvain had to shout over the rhythmic whine of a hydraulic splitter that forced a wedge into the end grain of the log, splitting off long, triangular lengths. He picked up a length that had been split again to the rough shape of a stave and pointed to a deviation, a whorl in the grain where a tree branch had grown out. "This is the first control," he said, "where, if you have a fault like this in the middle of the stave, the fault is cut out and the two pieces are used for barrel ends instead." He tossed the piece onto a reject pile, all the while explaining about the care he took with quality at every step.

"The secondary control is about the quality of the growth. You can look at the end grain and see that either the piece comes from a part of the tree where it underwent moderate growth, wide rings; or, the best quality, very slow growth with very tight, almost indistinguishable rings. That has the finest grain and is what you want. About five percent of the barrels we sell are of second quality," he finished, their staves predominantly moderate-growth.

"Now, we know from chemical analyses," he continued, "that there are four major characteristics of the wood that interest us in terms of wine. That is, four groups of distinct chemical substances in the oak that we perceive in the wine. There are the tannins, which you feel in the mouth, of course; and there are three groups of volatile compounds, which are vanillans, the taste of the oak itself, and also another flavor which we call clove, like the spice. Different varieties of tree have different characteristics. The sessile is poor in tannin but rich in the volatiles. The pedonculate is rich in tannin but poor in the others. You don't want too much tannin, because that gives a taste of greenness, of bitterness."

We passed through a facility where a computer-guided laser takes the rough staves and gives them their characteristic shape. That is a plank from two to four inches wide in the middle and tapering slightly in width toward the ends to reflect the shape of the barrel. Through another door, and we found ourselves outside again, this time in a lot filled with acres and acres of staves, weathered gray, stacked on pallets six feet high, each layer running at right angles and each two staves with an inch of space between. The stacks are thus quite open to the passage of air—and rain, which led me to ask why they don't rot.

He smiled at my question, which, it turns out, has been at the center of a great coopers' debate.

"We've been doing studies of what actually happens during the drying outside, under the weather," Sylvain began, "because for a long time we thought that the rain somehow leached out the tannins during the two years that it takes for them to be dry enough to work. What we found was that water enters the wood not profoundly, but quite shallowly. The water in the cells of the wood, eighty to ninety percent of it, leaches out. Rain enters only the surface wood, and that layer is removed before the stave is given its final form and then becomes part of a barrel. It's like Gore-Tex fabric, where the water can only go out, in one direction, rather than in and out. We lay the pallets out here, on the eastern, open side of the park because in this region it is a wind from the west that predominates, that will help in the drying."

We passed into another building where aged staves take their final form. They are sawed to the correct length, the gray-tinged exterior wood is planed off, the ends are tapered, and finally the interior and exterior faces are milled with a slight concavity, a cup, and the sides beveled. Again, if you imagine a barrel from above, it makes sense that the sides of each stave will need a bevel to form a circle once they're all put together, and that the faces will need to be rounded for the interior and exterior faces of the staves to form a tight circle when the hoops are put on. I was surprised to find no tongue and groove joining stave to stave, but Sylvain told us that, no, it was the fineness of the milling and the pressure of the encircling hoops that made the barrel watertight.

"We have learned that barrels of only sessile oak give some wine too much tannin," he remarked. "Those we do sell, in Argentina, where the wine needs more tannin to soften—round out, we say—the harsher tannin of the grapes grown there. And in California, which takes half the barrels we make. So, we are even starting to understand the qualities of the different forests, whose trees do yield wood with substantial differences in how they age and so how they affect wine."

There we also saw the barrelheads being assembled. The edges of each are milled with a tongue and groove, and to create an even tighter seal between pieces, a paper-thin reed, *le jonc,* is inserted between them. We also passed square chest-high crates filled with scraps, all cut to exact shapes and lengths. And those? I asked.

"We consume almost all the wood waste here—to make the fires that toast the barrels!" he replied. "The size and shape of the scrap determine the temperature of the fire, so!"

In the main assembly area, the pleasant scent of wood smoke, the aggressive reek of wet oak, and the coffee-like aroma of toasting wood greeted us, as did the strange sight of open fires burning in steel buckets. The whole central area is overhung by an enormous steel hood, which functions as a chimney. The closer we approached, the hotter it got, and the men working in and around the fires were all sweating profusely, the skin of their hands and forearms red-tinged from the heat.

The whole room, about 500 feet on a side, is laid out to facilitate the flow of work. On one side, the individual staves are selected, the proportion of sessile to pedonculate and the amount of fine grain to semifine selected according to the customer's order and M. Sylvain's recommendations.

"We mix staves from different forests in the barrel, too. Why? Because each forest has its own particular characteristics. And the exact proportion of each, and the grain, is something I determine with the customer, usually the winery's enologist or the winemaker himself if he is the owner. When a big château hires a new enologist, that's something he can do right off, change the barrels, to put his own stamp on the wine. And they do, sometimes." He shrugged, smiling as if to add, and they'll regret it!

On a table in front of us a worker was assembling the staves flat, running almost six and a half feet across its surface, for a final inspection. Then the process of assembly began, a worker taking the staves and ringing them around the inside of a temporary hoop, then adding two more temporary hoops to keep the staves aligned and pounding the hoops down to bring the staves together. Now the barrel, half-formed, looked as if the unfinished end had exploded, the staves all sprung.

At this point, we came to see the importance of the fire, for the barrel moved under the hood, where the floor is divided into four squares, each the domain of a single master artisan. At his feet are three low steel pails perhaps six inches tall in which fires of varying intensity are burning, from red-glowing coals to vigorous flames rising almost to his hip. The barrel is first placed over a hot fire, then removed at intervals and hosed down regularly inside and out with water, causing great clouds of rank steam to rise off it. The heat and moisture render the wood supple enough to bend, for otherwise the staves would simply snap in half on bending. After the wood has become less rigid, the barrel passes to an adjacent station where a worker loops a steel cable around the splayed staves, then tightens it, gathering them in. He adds more temporary hoops, gradually pounding the hoops down and forcing the splayed staves closed. This process takes about twenty minutes before the barrel comes to rest over the lowest fire for another twenty minutes to encourage the staves to relax into their new shape after they cool. At any one time the worker will be manipulating a number of barrels over the various fires, wielding hose and mallet, all this over flames which can be as hot as 500 degrees.

The barrel, still without its ends, now passes to the "toasting" station, where still more fires flicker in another series of pails.

"This is *la chauffe*, where we toast the inside of the barrel," Sylvain told us. "Heat brings out and modifies some of the qualities inherent in the wood. You can order barrels with a light, medium, or high toasting, depending on your wine's needs." We were standing next to a barrel inverted over a fire, its open end covered by a steel disk to prevent the smoke from escaping. Every barrel is toasted for approximately ten minutes, medium and high toasts being defined as twenty minutes and thirty minutes respectively. The air stank of burning oak.

What does the inside look like after toasting? It looks not burned or charred, but roasted, and, indeed, if you thrust your head inside a barrel and inhale, you can imagine quite easily these aromas, or their little brothers, rising off the wine in your glass several years down the road.

While the idea of burning the inside of a barrel to impart particular qualities to the wine which will rest inside it may be counterintuitive, the process has a parallel in the kitchen, in both browning and caramelizing. Searing a pork roast in a very hot pan with a little butter or oil before it goes in the oven, we all know, has a way of bringing out certain qualities in the flavor of the meat. Caramelizing onions, which are high in sugar, removes the sharp or astringent taste, breaks down those sugars which themselves undergo chemical reactions, and results in the rich flavors and colors we don't associate with the onion in its raw state.

Oak is a wood, and wood is primarily cellulose, also a form of complex sugar. Applying high heat to—or "toasting"—the oak "caramelizes" the outer layers of the wood, causing the same kinds of chemical reactions in the cellulose that happen in the onion and thus releases flavors which will eventually find their way into the finished wine. Remember all those recipes in which the cook is exhorted to scrape up all those lovely browned bits at the bottom of the pan after searing, to use as a base for sauce or gravy? That's not a bad way to think of the toasting, as adding a final richness that the meat alone would not otherwise have.

After so much heat and humidity, the barrels are swollen, still without their permanent hoops and lids. After they cool, the round barrel ends are fitted into a groove cut into the inside of each stave-end, the seal accomplished by the pressure of the hoop but also with a paste made of peanut and wheat flour and glue. When this has set, the seal of each barrel is tested: a worker inserts a hose into the bunghole and pours in a few liters of water, after which he then pumps in compressed air.

We pass to a corner where twenty barrels are resting after this process, and Sylvain points out several where a stave has cracked, usually in the middle, and one or two with the telltale dark stain of water forced out along the seams by the air pressure inside. About 40 percent of the barrels fail at this stage and have to be taken apart and reassembled with new staves or ends.

Fully tested, the barrels are then sanded smooth, and their final hoops are pounded on before being moved to the shipping room just around the corner. It is filled floor to ceiling with barrels in various states of packing, each marked with its destination vineyard and country. I pointed to one stack of barrels and raised my eyebrows. Each sported hoops finished with a smooth enamel of baby blue.

"Some guy in California; apparently everything in his vineyard is that color," Sylvain answered. "You can get them in any color. Most just take the galvanized iron." He turned and guided us to one corner, where a craftsman was working with narrow bands of one wood, binding them together with strips of a lighter material that he took, wet, from a bucket at his side. "Those are bands of chestnut wrapped in reed. They go on either end to protect the barrel when you roll it. You'd be surprised how many châteaux order some of their barrels finished that way even though it is not strictly necessary."

Jean-Luc turned to me and smiled. He had been asking almost as many questions as I had, for it was his first visit to this cooperage. He waved an arm at the elemental hand-forged tools the worker was using, each specific to its task, at the lengths of split wood and the soaking reeds. "What a lovely job to have!" he said, almost wistfully, perhaps seeing in its simplicity everything his life was not.

"We ship according to the season of harvest," Sylvain continued, "which is different in each hemisphere. So, in the fall, September-October, it is to countries like South Africa and Chile and Argentina. January through March, our barrels are going to Germany, Spain, France, America. We have customers in fifteen countries." He pointed to an enormous barrel, far larger than any other. "This is a three-hundred-liter barrel, for the South African market. The two hundred twenty-five liters are for here, for Bordeaux, and the two hundred twenty-eights go to Burgundy."

I ask about the cost of the huge barrel. "Well, we make only thirty thousand barrels a year, and quality has its price. This one [the largest], this is a second-quality barrel and it will cost about $450. Yes, you can buy a bigger barrel, but watch out! Your wine will be less oaked. You have to either use a smaller barrel, or leave the wine in the barrel longer. That has its risks, too. And remember, a new oak barrel imparts its qualities to the wine in an ever-diminishing fashion."

Beside me, Jean-Luc nodded in agreement. "After three years," he observed, "the barrel does not have much left to give the wine. So? New barrels." He smiled grimly, a man currently sitting on 900 of the suckers, representing almost a quarter of a million dollars in investment over three years. He pays $450 for every 225-liter new oak barrel. Over three years, that barrel will oak about 840 bottles of wine, which means he pays fifty-four cents per bottle in the quest to make wine of an ever-higher quality. This is more than he pays for the cork, the labeling, or the bottle. He is also responding to the demands of the market.

The extreme expression of this idea—if oak is good, more oak must be better—is found, as are the extremes of so many things, in America. Today, there is a whole generation of Americans, evidently largely female, who have come to associate the words "white wine" with the oceans of chardonnay and sauvignon blanc flowing out of California that have been imbued with oak so thoroughly that this is the only readily distinguishing thing about their taste and smell. These wines will not age, and aren't meant to. The oak is present strictly as an easily recognizable element of taste, that sweetness and vanilla aroma identified on the label most often as "buttery."

Only quite rarely and on the most expensive bottles will you find a mention of aging in oak barrels on the label. We do make barrels in America, of white oak, but not in nearly the numbers required for that flood of wine. So, whence the oak? Of course, our American ingenuity being what it is, industrial winemakers have learned how to use oak chips and tannin powders and other concoctions in the tanks and thus have disposed altogether with those pesky barrels and the required "aging" (read "nonmaximal asset allocation"), which is supposed to be a long, gentle steeping process. "Essence of oak," derived from oak tannins, already exists as a flavoring one could add to wine. In France, the maker of an AOC wine would be arrested, if not pilloried, for such bald adulteration, but in America no law prohibits it, nor do we require such disclosure. What seems to be in France a genuine attempt to make good wine better, and this by resurrecting old technologies and traditions, we have turned into just another industrial process.

Wines whose makers, in places like Spain, Italy, Portugal, South Africa, and Central Europe, would even five or ten years ago have scoffed at using new wood are now undergoing a baptism in oak because, it appears, the market wants oak. Even in Cahors, what distinguishes the bottle at $6 from the bottle at $12 is most often a little phrase in small letters on the front label—*Elevé en fûts de chêne,* matured in oak casks.

Of course, the French being the French, they are now beginning to take this rediscovered tradition one step further. In 2002 I returned to France two weeks after the harvest to find all the winemakers haunting their fermenting barns, worrying over the sometimes violent, sometimes delicate process of fermentation. And I found a few surprises.

In Jean-Luc's barn sat twelve enormous new oak barrels far larger than those for aging. Crowded together in one corner, they were covered loosely by a heavy plastic tarp, a blue-light bug zapper hanging above crackling regularly as it incinerated fruit flies. The barrels were open to the air and held a mass of crushed grapes whose gentle roils filled the air with that unmistakable aroma of ferment. I must have looked surprised, for Jean-Luc said, almost bashfully, "I'm trying something new this year. Fermenting in new oak. All the work has to be done by hand, of course, but . . . perhaps it will make a *grande cuvée*?"

This is a wine that is so superior, so special, that it rises far above the winemaker's usual offerings. It is the winemaker himself who declares that part of the vintage is a *grande cuvée,* and, oddly, this self-policing seems to work, limiting the declaration to only the best years lest his colleagues laugh him out of the market. I found the same at Clos la Coutale, Philippe Bernède having used a small portion of his best grapes, hand-picked and carefully selected, for his experiment, his *grande cuvée,* Le Grand Coutale. Just as they had returned to oak for the aging, how it was being used for the fermenting. I still haven't tried these wines and won't for many years, when, perhaps, having lifted glass to lips and tasted, I'll be able to add a new experience to my knowledge of wine . . . *so that's a barrel-fermented grande cuvée.*

And then there is Clos de Gamot. At Gamot and Cayrou, Yves and Martine eschew the use of new oak almost entirely, the exception being the 1,500 bottles of Clos St. Jean. Even then, they use *muids,* barrels twice the size of the normal Bordeaux barrel, and they use these *muids* for the particular purpose of softening the harder edge of grapes grown up on the steep hillside, rather than to add the flavor and nose of oak to the wine.

There, you won't see ranks of the forty-gallon hogsheads in the maturing barn or any experiments with fermenting in oak, either. They are most definitely not of the new generation of winemakers who believe that a wine without some oak overtones in nose and mouth is a wine both unsalable and "rustic" (winespeak for dowdy, old-fashioned, uninteresting). Though they might seem stick-in-the-muds, the issue goes more deeply for them than defying the current fashion in taste out of pride alone.

One day Martine and I had been talking about the varietal of Cahors, the malbec grape, about why it was best suited to a *vin de garde,* a wine to age, rather than a *vin de primeur,* a young-drinking wine. Seventy percent of the wine in any bottle of Cahors must come from this grape, and it is therefore not as if the winemaker can escape its influence or character.

"You have better fruit, more superior fruit with grapes like the gamay and the pinot noir," Martine began. "Cabernet sauvignon, that's a grape that gives relatively little fruit, and so it's a wine to age.

Malbec is also not a grape that lends itself to a young, fruity wine, and you have to therefore force it a little bit into that image." Here she smiled mischievously, about the closest she comes to criticizing the choices of other winemakers.

"After the vinification, you can make the wine age faster. There is the phenomenon of using new oak barrels, for example, putting the wine into new barrels for a few months, and then you can sell it the next year; or accelerations of the aging by micro-oxygenation." Contact with oxygen promotes aging in wine and promotes it particularly quickly in a small barrel, which exposes a large surface area of the wine to the wood through which oxygen can migrate. Micro-oxygenation, which Philippe practices, is a more high-tech manipulation and involves bubbling bottled oxygen through the wine with an aerator placed in the bottom of the tank or barrel.

"But again these are going to be wines that are very ephemeral," Martine continued, "and you can't put them in the cellar and forget them for five years. These are choices that the winemaker makes. It's true that financially it can be more profitable to sell all of what you produce right away, and that way not have the costs of storing your wine. But wine like that, it has more to do with technology than with the winemaker's art. And the storage is very important."

In their maturing barn, one of the original, stone-walled structures onto which the new wine barn was built in the 1970s, the Jouffreaus rest their Gamot wine for eighteen to twenty-four months in enormous 2,500-gallon oak *foudres* before bottling. Some of their casks are decades old, and any "oakiness" they could possibly give to the wine today is long past. Instead, the role of the oak is strictly as the best medium of maturation for a wine that needs none of the "additives" or "extractives" or "age-enhancing" that lots of new oak provides. In their literature, in fact, they treat this aspect of their wine matter-of-factly, as just the way it is. "In their younger years," the Clos de Gamot brochure states baldly, "these wines often stay closed up and concentrated, sometimes even unpleasantly so. But their complexity expresses itself, blooms, with the years, which confer on them harmony, power, and body. They are therefore best for drinking between eight and twelve years of age."

How can it be reasonable to ask the consumer to buy something today that they can't drink for a decade? Again departing from modern thinking about winemaking, Yves and Martine actually take on much of this burden, and capital risk, themselves, holding hundreds of thousands of bottles in happy obscurity in their cellar. "Right now, for example," Yves told me (in 2002), "in the Clos de Gamot we still have 1990s, 1988s, and a little bit of the 1985, though all in small quantities because Clos de Gamot just isn't that big in area. In Château de Cayrou, which is larger and so permits us greater depth in years, we have all the way back to 1983. So it is our pleasure to offer people a choice of ten or twelve vintages."

"To oak or not to oak" would seem to be, from my amateur investigations, not the right question at all. As Yves and Martine, Jean-Luc, and Philippe, in his own way, said to me over and over in various situations, to make the best wine one does what the grapes want rather than forcing the wine into some kind of mold. Sometimes new wood is the fillip, sometimes it is merely gratuitous, sometimes it is absolutely wrong. It has its place, but, as those utterly smooth, complex old Clos de Gamots reveal, its place is not everywhere. Likewise, rushing to oak every $7 table wine, particularly the whites, by whatever means limits rather than expands the experience of the everyday wine drinker.

11

❧

Wine at the Restaurant Table
A Few Hours with Laurent Marre
at Le Balandre

Along a sycamore-shaded boulevard just up from the train station in the capital of the Lot, Cahors, stands a modest brick-and-stone hotel and restaurant, of a provincial type that is, sadly, not found so much in France any more. It is owned and run by a family, the Marre brothers, Gilles and Laurent, together with their wives. Gilles mans the stoves while Laurent is the sommelier—the wine steward—taking care of the wine cellar and also overseeing the waitstaff. Gilles' wife, Jacqueline, and Laurent's, Corinne, between them handle most of the management and administration of both hotel and restaurant, though it is very much the kind of place where everyone lends a hand. You might find Angel, the sprightly Spanish headwaiter, for example, at ten in the morning bustling about in jeans and sweatshirt, his arms filled with bunches of flowers for the day's arrangements. At lunch or dinner, however, he'll reappear at your table in his best waiter's black, not only serving adroitly and with much good humor, but also wheeling in the cheese cart. This is his other main duty—master of the cheeses, the one who selects them personally, sees to their ripening, and then educates you as to their provenance and particular qualities before your dessert.

Where Gilles is dark and solid through the middle, Laurent is blond and slender. Gilles prefers to sit back quietly and has a certain gravity not generally found in a forty-five-year-old; Laurent is a talker, his rather severe features belying a humor which is never far from the surface, and which often emerges in a characteristic smile and bob of the head that make him seem quite boyish, reminding you that he is only thirty-five. They are as Mutt and Jeff as two brothers can be, but their differences seem complementary rather than divisive, as anyone who has ever eaten at their restaurant can attest.

The restaurant, Le Balandre, has a long and illustrious history, the boys' grandfather, Pierre Marre, having been the first chef in the Lot region, in 1922, to win a mention in the Michelin guide. During World War II, the *Feld Gendarmerie,* the German military police, apparently having developed a keen eye for the best billet and grub from their experience in previous occupations, made the Grand Hôtel Terminus their regional headquarters, a move which apparently prompted Pierre to bury a few very special cases of his best vintages and aged spirits in a subbasement. Laurent's discovery of them caused a minor stir a few years back. After a pause between the generations, Gilles, the elder brother, reopened the hotel's restaurant as Le Balandre in June of 1984. Laurent joined him as sommelier eight years later after completing his studies and various apprenticeships all over France. (The restaurant takes its name from its location not far from the site of an ancient ferry, the *balandre* being the kind of system where bargemen crossed the river using a rope slung overhead to hold on to.) Pierre's legacy lives on in his grandchildren's faithful re-creation of the intimacy and comfort of an old-fashioned hotel with an excellent kitchen; it is also there quite literally, on the menu, in *oeuf Pierre Marre,* a simple poached egg topped with pan-seared fresh foie gras in a sauce flecked with bits of black truffle and paper-thin slices of that same dark wonder fanned across its top.

Fifteen years ago, when my wife and I ran off to France to be married, it was by the purest of coincidences that we celebrated in this restaurant on the eve of our nuptials. At that time, we knew nothing of the Lot or Cahors, or of the region's gastronomy or wines; indeed, I hadn't been back to France since my college days in Paris in the early 1980s. I consider that it was at Le Balandre that my adult gastronomic education began, with the eight-course tasting menu and a much younger Gilles coming out of the kitchen to explain how he prepared his sweetbreads, and that of course we could finish the meal without foundering, as the portions were kept small.

Although Yves and Martine, Jean-Luc, and Philippe had ushered me into their intense world of grapes and winemaking, it was at le Balandre, in the hands of Laurent, that another, necessary part of my vinous education began: understanding wine as a complement to a meal, particularly wine as one part of that grand French tradition of consecrating five hours and the contents of your purse to the god of the restaurant table.

My wife mocks me when I say it, but Laurent Marre is quite simply my favorite sommelier. She is right to mock me, as I know only three sommeliers well enough to judge, but then I am used to it, and one should never get too pompous about wine or food, particularly around French people, as they can out-pompous you any day of the week in these areas.

First off, let it be said that one can take enormous pleasure in a good meal at a good restaurant in convivial company without any wine or alcohol at all. We have found that, particularly in the heat of summer, or if we have to be able to do a reasonable imitation of sentient beings any time in the afternoon and will not have access to a bed for napping, it is in fact wise to forgo alcohol at lunch, particularly with a heavy meal. As Laurent has reminded me several times, "One should never feel obligated to order wine if you don't like it. You can drink water! If it gives you pleasure to drink Coca-Cola at the table, if that is your taste, your pleasure, do it! You should never go to a restaurant and end up feeling that you're a prisoner of some immutable system or of some trend, [and this] I think Americans are good at resisting."

Dinner without wine? That's heresy, anathema, from the mouth of a sommelier, and yet it embodies but one of the reasons why Laurent pleases me so. When it comes to wine, he proceeds almost completely without dogma, quoting received wisdom only to question it, and is far more interested in having you come away from the table with your knowledge increased rather than your prejudices confirmed. If he has a single credo, it is, in his words, that "wine should always be *une affaire de plaisir*. There are rules, often dictated by people's snobbism, but it should be about enjoyment, about pleasure. When I put my nose in the glass, it smells wonderful, and I want to take a sip. I take a sip—ah!—and I want to take another sip. That's what wine should be about. If it's just a question of big bucks or of rules preestablished by people who don't know everything, then, and pardon my language, but we're going down the toilet and it makes me sick."

One morning in October of 2003, I found myself ensconced in a comfortable chair in the hotel bar, very happy to be a bit early for a meeting with Laurent that I had been trying to organize for more than a year. I was happy because this establishment is not one where you can sit for more than two minutes before one of the staff comes over and offers you a cup of pungent coffee with hot milk—which, coming off a week of very early risings to pick grapes and do my work among the harvesters, I desperately needed. And I was happy because the room itself is so pleasant, evoking the memory of so many very good dinners and awakening anticipation, to my mind half the pleasure of any good meal, of my next experience there.

At ten in the morning, the hotel bar is still a sleepy place, one corner given over to a few tables at which late-rising guests are enjoying their croissants and brioche and coffee while casually clad young men and women set about their morning tasks of polishing brass, arranging chairs, watering plants, vacuuming, seeing to the thousands of little details that you would notice only if they were absent as you sipped champagne before your five-course meal that evening.

The bar is of dull, silvery zinc polished by a thousand elbows; the windows are of restrained, geometrical stained glass in Art Deco style; the carpet and upholstery are of subtle, pleasing patterns of turquoise and caramel; the walls are paneled in some soothing material the color of cured tobacco and lit at intervals by the soft light of frosted lamps with sculptured zinc bases echoing the 1920s theme.

The headwaiter, Angel, who possesses all the presence of an English butler, wandered through, a pot of roses in his arms, and looked outside, where a heavy wind was tossing the trees about. "Ah, this wind!" he said. "And rain coming with it. We can only hope the Atlantic wind will come and push this mess away!" He passed to one side of the bar, through the short hall to the dining room, elbowing open tall oak doors inset with more stained glass portraying a calm spray of rose blossoms and leaves, these leading into a restrained, high-ceilinged room whose walls are hung with bright oils breaking up the cream-colored plasterwork. The space is shaped like a T, a modest wing protruding at one end, and quite ample for the dozen or so tables. I noticed that no table was more than a few feet away from one of the small buffets scattered throughout the room. This is where each table's wine rests during the meal, and also provides a staging area for the more elaborate service sometimes required in the serving of Gilles' dishes, as you would never put a tray—and rarely leave a bottle of wine—on a table at which people are seated.

Laurent appeared, and we headed upstairs to a quiet conference room to talk. He had arranged for me to see the restaurant *cave*, the best restaurant wine cellar in the region, with his apprentice, Vivian, some days earlier. I told him of my adventures in the vines, and he began to talk of the pitiful harvest. "It's normal that nature takes its due from time to time. It's a shame for the winemakers, but it's been almost ten years that we've had only good vintages. Only the Bordelais [the winemakers of Bordeaux] are going to make the vintage of the century this year!" he said mockingly. "It's unbelievable, because on the sixteenth of August," when they began to harvest in Bordeaux, "the grapes were either burned up or underripe, and of this they're going to make the vintage of the century?"

This in fact was one of my questions, for I had indeed read and watched on TV as a parade of Bordeaux wine barons pontificated on the supposed excellence of their 2003 vintage. Anyone who had looked at the weather map that summer had seen that they had suffered through the same conditions as the entire south and southwest, and Bordeaux is, after all, less than two hours away by car. Was there some enological magic I didn't know about by which they were going to escape the fate of winemakers in the rest of the country?

"They're a bunch of bandits," Laurent observed. "I was in Saint-Émilion when they had just picked. It's indefensible. They were so scared of losing everything with this heat wave that they harvested very early; it was not the right time. Then they started making such a noise in the media, in the newspapers, on the radio and television, how it was going to be a great vintage. It was the same [weather conditions] everywhere in France. Here in Cahors there were lots and lots of parcels where there was nothing to harvest. But at least what was harvested and culled, that will make good wine because the grapes were ripe. In Bordeaux, they are going to make real crap, but still sell it for a high price because they've told people it is a great year. It's sad, a shame, because eventually people won't believe them any more. Eventually, to sell at a hundred bucks a bottle something that's worth five—and because it is Bordeaux that is the first image associated with French wine—it's France that is going to suffer, not just the Bordelais."

"They'd also have you understand," he continued with heavy irony, "that they've lowered their prices; excuse me, but their prices have not gone down. Sure, they put the price down by maybe twenty-five percent, but since it had gone up in recent years three hundred percent . . ." He sat back and laughed. "I'm really anti-Bordeaux, now. There are good things, sure, still lots of good wines, but they're bandits. There is a proverb that says, 'In Bordeaux, there is no wine to taste, but it's all for sale. In Burgundy, you can taste everything, but nothing's for sale.' In Burgundy," he explained, "usually the wine is available in such small quantities" that it is all spoken for before the grapes are even harvested. "But in the wine cellars, the winemakers always welcome you in to taste. In Bordeaux, you aren't permitted to taste at most châteaux, only buy. It's very representative of their kind of thinking," he finished, throwing up his hands.

Our talk turned more directly to his work, and I began to ask him all the questions that had crowded my mind as I watched him go about his job in the dining room, as well as some that had always puzzled me. He has been working with wine in restaurants for more than a decade and a half, having started when he was sixteen in his first apprenticeship. He had followed the classic route, deciding at age four-teen (when all French children must pick a road) to head in the direc-tion of a *métier* rather than a university education, in his case a few years at a hotel and restaurant school learning the basics of the hospi-tality industry, followed by a one-year course specializing in *sommel-lerie*—the art of the wine waiter. "It's a long year," he told me with a wry grin, "and during it, you study the wine varietals, the geography of winegrowing and winemaking, enology, and tasting. This year has two internships, one month with a winemaker to better understand how wine is made, and two months in a restaurant with a working somme-lier to better understand how wine works in a restaurant. At the end of the year you have a diploma, which doesn't mean a hell of a lot, because after your education you've got to go work in different restau-rants, in different regions, and taste their wines. Therefore, the best sommelier is the one who has just retired; that's the ideal, because he's the one who knows the most."

He lit a cigarette as we talked, looking at it and shrugging his shoulders when he saw my surprise. "I permit myself only a few a day, and I mean a few, and never before a tasting!"

In the seven years before he came home to work with his brother at Le Balandre in 1994, he worked in the Atlantic Pyrénées, in Alsace, in Cannes, in the French Alps, building a résumé that reads like a mini-guide to the some of the best restaurants of the era—Au Bon Coin du Lac, Le Relais de la Poste, L'Auberge de Lille (with Serge Dubs, who has been judged the World's Best Sommelier), the three-star L'Aubergade in Puymirol, La Palme d'Or, and Le Bateau Ivre.

I said I could only imagine what it must have been like, at sixteen, to leave home, a newly minted sommelier with no experience bound for parts unknown. "*Oui, oui!* I was young," he said with a big grin. "In my profession, it's better not to do fifteen years of study. It's a profes-sion of the hands, where one learns the most from contact with the customer out on the floor. You need the basics, but now I see that they're giving waiters eight years of studies, and I ask myself what the hell they could be learning for eight years. It must be all the professors' strikes that make them lose so much study time!"

Though his *métier* has something in common with other wine trades, he is careful to set apart the work of a sommelier. "To be a *caviste* is not to be a sommelier. A *caviste* is someone who manages a wine store, a *cave*, and who has contact with his customers but not at all the same contact as a sommelier. A *caviste* will recommend a bottle for the customer to drink in two days or two years or ten years. Someone who works in a *cave* is often called a sommelier, but for me he's not a sommelier. An enologist is also not a sommelier. An enologist is a wine technician; someone who 'fabricates' wine—I don't really like that word, but it is true. Wine, like cuisine, has a healthy dose of chemistry to it. The fact that at a certain temperature the must begins to ferment, that's pure chemistry. So, an enologist knows how to do a vinification—how to make the wine—and he knows much more technical things than a sommelier: the dosage of sulfur dioxide, the effects of sulfur, why one harvests grapes today at this certain level of sugar in the grape—he's a technician. The work of a sommelier, he's at the same time a *caviste*, an enologist, and certainly he has a huge amount of contact with the customer.

"Here, I'll show you what my day looks like," he said, rising. We went downstairs and through a narrow passage to a small back kitchen with a table and chairs at which the help eats, the rest of the long narrow space lined wall to wall with large, freestanding, glass-fronted cabinets holding hundreds of bottles of wine in an environment controlled for temperature and humidity. In the morning of a sommelier's typical day, Laurent explained, he will take care of his wine cellar, reorder what needs to be reordered, and prepare everything for the lunch and dinner service. He'll restock the upstairs stores by bringing up bottles from the main cellar below. "Here we use Euro-caves, which is just a brand name for these units." He pointed to the glass cabinets. "The wines in the downstairs cellar, mostly the whites, are not at the appropriate temperature to be drunk. So we keep at least one bottle of every white wine stocked upstairs, in the Eurocaves, so it will be at the right temperature at the right time. It's the same for the majority of Cahors wines, but not all.

"In every restaurant there is always what we call *la cave à jour*," the everyday *cave*. He gestured at the cabinets all around him. "And you have to replace that daily stock, the champagne X that Monsieur drank last night, the two bottles of Château Y that Madame's party consumed, etc. It's a daily chore in every restaurant, and it takes time. If during service, I had to walk two hundred fifty feet, go down a staircase to fetch a bottle, and if I had to do that for every table, it would be a huge waste of time."

Vivian, Laurent's genial, burly young assistant, had shown me the big wine cellar on an earlier visit, two large rooms packed floor to ceiling with racks, the two oddities being a computer console and a telephone. The telephone was installed after Laurent didn't come home after the restaurant closed one night; his wife found him stretched out on the floor of the cellar, exhausted from banging on the door and shouting until three in the morning, after he had inadvertently locked himself in.

The computer uses a cellarman's program to track each bottle from loading dock to glass while also specifying the location of the wine in the cellar, a particularly helpful function given that Le Balandre stocks 20,000 bottles, restocking 6,000 or 7,000 every year. "There'll be more with the coming wine auctions," Laurent remarked, "but I think I have to stop at twenty or my accountant will not understand. We have put down something like $300,000 worth of wine. It is sleeping. And that's a lot for a restaurant with thirty-five seats! Too much, even. But it's what we choose to do. I buy today bottles that we'll be serving in fifteen years, and that's money that is sleeping. We don't have to do that. Pélissou at Le Gindreau [another one-star about twenty miles away], he gets by with five thousand bottles in his cellar."

Lunch service, a three-hour hustle, starts at twelve-thirty, the sommelier beginning with the serving of the first aperitifs, and continuing through the uncorking of many bottles, generally twenty-five to fifty depending on the size of the crowd—always at table-side so that the customer can observe and participate in the rituals of regarding the label, smelling the cork, and taking the first, confirming sip. The sommelier is constantly on the lookout for empty glasses in need of refilling and fetches new bottles of wine and all the other nonalcoholic drinks and mineral waters, finishing up with the coffee order, also part of his job. Afterward, he replenishes upstairs what was drunk in the afternoon, particularly if there was a large crowd. "And then we do the same thing at night. In the late afternoon, sometimes there's a wine tasting, and the sommelier hops in his car or on his scooter and goes off to a winemaker's to taste something."

It all sounded fairly routine, until Laurent began to talk about what happens during service, when his work is to give advice to customers, "for me the most interesting part of my *métier*," he told me. "It's the only job in the wine trade where you don't have to be patient. Take the barrel maker. You don't make a barrel in ten seconds. From the time he buys the wood to when the barrel is finished, ten years can pass!

"Imagine you're a good winemaker," he continued thoughtfully, "and you're thirty years old. You plant new vines on your thirtieth birthday. The moment of truth, when you know you can now make great wine from those vines, that will be your forty-fifth birthday, minimum. Oh, no! You screwed up! You put the chardonnay where it won't make anything but *merde*. You rip it out—because you're very rich." Replanting can cost tens of thousands of dollars an acre. "You replant with sauvignon blanc, and the day you know you made the right choice, you're ready to retire. Say you don't want to retire, you're very passionate, and the sauvignon was a mistake. You rip *it* out and replant. Not until you're seventy-five do you have the results. It's terrible! The winegrower, to confirm that he has indeed made the right decisions, he has at most only three chances in his lifetime!"

He went on, "In our work, I will recommend a wine to a client to have him taste something that will give him pleasure and that complements what he is eating. And I have the results in the next twenty or thirty minutes. If, after he has tasted the wine, it does not please him, either it's that I did my work badly, or his taste doesn't correspond at all to mine, or I analyzed his needs incorrectly. But in any case I have the result right then and there. It's good."

I have seen Laurent work at table, and his approach is very down-to-earth, very simple. When he brings the wine list to the table, the food order has already been taken, and the maître d'hôtel has already showed him the slip in the kitchen. Knowing that perhaps a majority will be having red meat or fish, Laurent is already thinking of the possibilities.

"Then, it depends on whether they are two, four, or six people, because there's always a question of quantity. If it is a couple, they're not going to take a full bottle of white and a bottle of red for their fish and meat. If they are four, however, that changes everything. They can have a white with the entrées and a red with the main course."

He always delivers a little joke, say, about how now it's time for you to do a bit of homework, as he hands over the thick, leather-bound *carte des vins*. "Generally, people look at it a bit, and then I come back because I've seen that they're a little lost (our wine list is rather impressive), or because they've chosen and they don't need any advice from me, which is sometimes the case.

"They might say, 'We're here on vacation, we don't know Cahors wines, and there are so many choices. We'd like to try one, and we put ourselves in your hands.'"

This is never a bad approach, and it is in fact often my approach, guaranteeing at least a minimum of exchange with the sommelier during which I always learn something and often end up trying something I wouldn't normally have considered, part of the pleasure of eating out in a restaurant where people know what they're doing.

"Or," Laurent continued, "they might say, 'I was thinking of ordering this wine; what do you think of it?' Or, 'I'm going to take that.' Those are the three reactions of the customers. The customer the least interesting to me is obviously Mr. I'll-Take-That, least interesting I mean in terms of having an exchange or a dialogue. Even if he chose something which I disagree with, even strongly, when the client has expressed his desire, I am obligated to say, 'Yes, sir.' It's like that."

There are sometimes, Laurent confessed with a touch of frustration, people who don't dare to ask advice of the sommelier. "If they don't know too much about wine, they can make a mistake. They'll choose, say, a Banyuls, a red dessert wine, thinking it's your classic dry red to drink with a meat dish." What do you do, I asked, when that happens, when they are about to make a real boneheaded decision that they won't be happy with once the bottle has been opened and the wine tasted?

"I may say, 'Pardon me, but did you know that is a sweet wine?'"

Sometimes, I might say, 'Hmmm. It's really not the time to drink that, as it is too young.' You can't say no, so you work around it: 'You know, Monsieur, that this vintage is a bit young yet, but if you would permit me to suggest an older one . . .' You suggest, but lightly, and you try to push them a tiny bit in the right direction. And you see immediately if it's going to be a 'no,' or if you can help them further. Often, such people have their particularities. Either they know the wine well or they just want what they want."

And then there's the problem of the price of the wine. By my Yankee logic, if I'm spending $75 a person for a meal, my natural instinct is to hold back on the wine, to choose perhaps a lower-priced bottle with the reasoning that a splurge on one thing means economy on the other. This kind of thinking is backward to the French, who do see the wine not as an extra, or something separate from, the meal, but as something worthy of being at its very heart. This conundrum is also one of the more difficult things about Laurent's job.

"The hardest problem for me," he told me, "for any sommelier when it comes time to order the wine, is to try to know the customer's budget. The ideal customer is the one who says, we're eating such and such, we want to really enjoy ourselves, and we have so much to spend on wine.

"There is no shame," he said forcefully, "all the more because you might end up with a better wine! Contrary to what one might think—and I don't know how Americans think about wine—but generally for our customers, well, you can really enjoy yourselves with a wine at $20, at $150, at $1,000 a bottle. The enjoyment of wine [in France] is not yet simply a question of money. One can find exceptional wines at $20 or $25 a bottle on a good restaurant wine list. The Vin de Lune, a dry white of Jean-Luc Baldès at Triguedina, I put on the wine list at $20 a bottle, and I think it is a truly enjoyable wine. . . .

"But you should never be ashamed to give your budget. It's true that in France money has always been a taboo subject, a lot more than in America, I think. But people don't dare [mention a budget]. Sometimes, our French clients will point to a wine on the list and say, 'We want something like that.' Well, the 'something like that' doesn't refer to the wine or the region or the grape but to the price beside it. It's a shame people don't just come out and say it. That's what I do when I go to a restaurant—I trust the sommelier—unless I've found a bottle that really interests me. I've traveled in Spain a few times with my wife, and that's what we do there. 'Listen, our wine budget is $80. Can you suggest something from the region that we would enjoy in that range?'"

When you do come right out and say, here's my budget, you give the sommelier the chance to strut his stuff, *and* you might end up happily surprised, whether you're shooting your wad or being more restrained. "The work of the sommelier, the responsibility of the sommelier, he should want to help you enjoy yourselves," Laurent insisted. "He knows exactly what he's got in his wine cellar, and he knows what might please you. If it doesn't, at least he knows he's responsible. It might not please you for other reasons, a wine not within your tastes, etc., but at least then he has all the criteria at hand."

But what about that other black hole—eliciting from the customers the sometimes amorphous information about what kind of wine they appreciate, that will please them? (One American restaurateur of my acquaintance calls this the "I don't know what I want but I know what I like" problem.)

"The best thing," Laurent advised, "is to tell the sommelier straight out. 'We like only red wine,' even if [you're] eating fish. And that does happen; it's not just an example. 'Our budget for the wine tonight, my wife and I, is $30.' So, then give me an idea of your budget and a little information about your likes and dislikes. I don't have to know everything. Take yourself. You might say, 'I know Cahors wine and I want to try something else, but let's stay in wines of the southwest, and maximum $30 a bottle.' That's great! I'm thinking, let's see, a Buzet, a Madiran, a Frontonnais, ah, but Madame is having fish, so we need something a little lighter. Something a little lighter, yes, a Gaillac because that will go well even if it is a red.

"But some customers don't want to go that far. They're not demanding. They don't want to have an exchange. For many reasons. Maybe wine isn't their thing, because they don't dare to ask, and we respect that, because they're on business and they're ordering a big wine, and a big wine is all that will do, period, end of sentence. They're there to talk business with their clients and not to talk with the sommelier. There are also people who don't like wine. They drink wine because they're eating out, but they don't love it. I respect that; it's not a problem."

At this point in our conversation, Laurent embarked on a long, lovely discursion on various fallacies about wine, about Frenchmen and their wine, and how various Europeans approach wine. He was so thoughtful and eloquent that I've let his words stand for themselves, without interruption.

> In France, there is a terrible thing, let me tell you. We think, because we're French, that we have been born with an innate knowledge of gastronomy and wine. And it is so bad that I think, today, we are of all the peoples of Europe—and I am a chauvinistic Frenchman!—the ones who know our wine the least well because we don't dare ask. The French confuse their own appellations. They don't know their varietals. But they may know the wine of their region, and they've been told so often [that they're superior] that they're convinced they know French wine. They make fun of the English as people who have no taste in food, as people who eat frozen dinners—you hear that sort of thing often from the mouths of Frenchmen—while it is the English who know wine the best of all the Europeans. They invented Bordeaux, and port, and they certainly participated in developing the wine of Cahors.
>
> It's terrible! You realize that there are French who will drink wine when they're out to eat without knowing anything about it, without asking anything about it, but drinking it because they're in a restaurant so they have to drink wine! If you want to drink water or orange juice, go ahead! Do what pleases you. That is the most important thing: you go out to eat in a nice restaurant to enjoy yourself. If you feel like you're forced to do something, well . . . Last night, I had a table of customers who drank nothing but Evian for the whole meal. Why should they order wine if they don't appreciate it?
>
> Each table is unique, and each customer has his own different reasons and is looking for a different kind of pleasure at the

table. You can see it with the Europeans. The French are the kings of gastronomy. They know a lot about food, and about good food. But they are nothing when it comes to wine.

It is totally pretentious, what I just said, but let's take, say, my father—whom I love a lot. Papa has eaten in all the Michelin-starred restaurants of France and northern Spain. He loves to do that! By the time I was fifteen years old, I had already "done" five or six three-star restaurants. It's fantastic to have a Dad like that. He would sell his soul to eat out in a fine restaurant, and to skip a meal, that's not something he ever does. [Laurent's voice dropped to a whisper and he looked away as if shamed at what was to come.] Papa knows nothing about wine! He drinks wine, he loves wine, he's a gourmet. But he knows nothing! Nothing at all! You say "Buzet" [a nearby appellation] to him, and he doesn't even know where it is.

He will give his money to the sommelier, the sommelier will find him a good wine, but Papa won't even know the grape. What he wants, and the only thing he wants, is the final result. When he buys wine, he's the kind of guy who buys from a wine club or gourmet society newsletter because the wines are preselected and he doesn't have to bother himself with the details and because in the end he just doesn't know how to do otherwise. But he will tell you if it is good wine, and if it pleases him or not.

If he goes to Bordeaux, he's lost. You say, "Cheval Blanc" [one of the very best Bordeaux reds] and that means something to him because he's heard of it, maybe, but La Gafellière, Pétrus, that means nothing to him. The wine grapes of Cahors, he probably knows because this is his region, but he couldn't tell you what grows in Bordeaux.

The English—and I generalize, and generalizations are always false—but nevertheless, a majority of English, they'll take the modest prix fixe, we have one at lunch for $35, but they'll order a $200 bottle of wine, all the while knowing the grapes it's made of, the appellation it comes from, the yield of the vines. They'll know everything. The English really know their wine; it's fabulous.

The Germans, they'll take the regular, five-course menu and order four bottles of wine for a table of four, but not necessarily four bottles of something grand that costs a lot. They are real trenchermen, the Germans. They eat. They drink. And they love eating and drinking, but perhaps without being very curious or knowledgeable about what it is they are consuming.

The elite are the Belgians. The Belgians are the most logical when they go out to eat. To me, being logical at the restaurant means that the wine is the third person at the table. That means that, if I am eating a menu at $50 with another person, that makes $100, and so I'll look for a bottle of wine at $50. And that's what I try to recommend to customers. I find it ridiculous to eat a $50 meal and order a $300 bottle of wine to go with it. Conversely, I find it equally ridiculous to eat a $100 meal with an $18 bottle of wine. It's as much a shame in the one case as the other. I think there are times when you have a budget of $50 per person for the food, and sometimes $20 a person. But it is logical for the quality of the menu to correspond to the quality of the wine that goes with it. Once I sold a 1982 Cheval Blanc—and I think the guy made a mistake in his choice—and he had ordered the mini lunch menu at $25 to go with a bottle at $300. I find it illogical, and a shame, to drink a grand wine with a quickie businessman's lunch. I say that everyone has his habits according to his culture. The Dutch don't eat out in [gastronomic] restaurants for whatever reason, or at least we don't see them here.

Americans are different, very different. We don't have many Americans, or at least, I think some Americans have avoided France in light of recent events. But Americans in general have a vastly superior buying power. I'm not joking. Often, they don't know their appellations much beyond Bordeaux, that's for sure. They're often very jovial, exuberant—I'm generalizing—ready to try everything. Either that or they will fall back on a surefire thing they know—a Bordeaux grand cru, period.

Last night we had two Americans at the restaurant, two bon vivants, very nice, who had never eaten here, didn't consult the sommelier, and ordered a Calon-Ségur 1990—a very good wine. I served the wine, we began to talk, to have an exchange about wine, and I had them taste a glass of Cahors. They're coming back to eat tonight. And tonight they'll entrust themselves to me. But generally, they go for the tried and true, take refuge in a wine they know. When they do venture afield, I find they have more to spend and less problem spending it.

Our American customers, either they're truly interested in the exchange we might have, or they're the ones who can't escape their habits: "I want chicken, a green salad, and a Coke." Period. Generally, when [that kind of client] comes to this restaurant, it's because [he has] made a mistake. It's not a criticism. But I know because, for this kind of person, spending even an hour at table is irritating. They want to fill up the tank as they would at home, eating what they would at home, and not get food poisoning in Old Europe. It's one way to travel, and I'm not sure if I were to go to the United States, I wouldn't seek out the familiar, too. It's intimately linked to culture, and that is linked to social class. You might love very good restaurants and grand wines, but it costs a lot of money. That's no secret. You can love beautiful cars, but you still have to write a big check to buy a Ferrari. If not, you can look at pretty pictures in the magazines.

For wine, it's not the same, not yet. In a gourmet restaurant, you can still find a bottle like that, a very good bottle, for ten bucks. But if you think you can go to a restaurant and find a great meal for $10, you're dreaming. It might be good, but it won't be memorable. And less and less today will it even be good.

Into the Mind of the Sommelier, or, How Do They Do That?

If you are like me, a good wine list can be every bit as compelling as a good book, particularly when you sit with a starched napkin in your lap, at the restaurant, your ears, eyes, mouth, and nose at the maximum of anticipation as you watch the plates of others move past your table. Or it can be as daunting as, say, chapter one, page one of Thomas Pynchon's *The Crying of Lot 49*. Looking from wine list to menu and back and soliciting the desires of the others in your party, you might find yourself a bit at sea as to how to reconcile the conflicts—or even where to begin. Often, you are alone in your quest. Except at the highest reaches of the American culinary experience, most restaurants do not have sommeliers; and the waiters, I find, when not pushing this week's wine specials (which they've badly overordered or bought in quantity on the cheap) generally don't have much of a clue after they've trotted out the canned patter they've been taught. This is a shame. Quite simply, you get what you pay for and you pay for what you get. In this case, that means genial but inept service and even worse wine service because most restaurateurs don't appear to give much time or energy to the training of their staff beyond "Hi, my name's Mary and I'll be your server tonight."

At the other end of this spectrum is the complaint often heard from those who do not drink alcohol at all. Restaurateurs take note. This is that, once the food is served, waiters often abandon such tables as they no longer hold further potential for upping the check.

I've watched Laurent teach a whole table at his restaurant how to begin to distinguish between wines from the three major regions of Bordeaux, a very difficult task, by focusing on the dominant landmarks of each grape (cabernet franc, cabernet sauvignon, or merlot); and I've spent hours eavesdropping as he guided the perplexed through the minefield of ordering the wine. In the hope of eliciting from him exactly what passes through his mind as he makes the calculations that lead to his recommendations, I asked him to take a sample menu, Le Balandre's "Flavors of the Market," a fall tasting menu, and to think aloud as he planned the wines around the various quite complicated dishes of the seven-course meal. Don't worry if you're not familiar with all the wines he mentions as possibilities; I certainly wasn't. Laurent naturally describes the characteristics of the particular kind of wine he is looking for, and, besides, we're here more for the general principles and ideas.

"Saveurs du Marché" Fall Tasting Menu

MISE EN BOUCHE

*Two or three bites or spoonfuls of something, usually salty,
to get the taste buds going*

LE FOIE GRAS DE CANARD ET CHUTNEY MAISON

Duck foie gras, preserved, not fresh, with house chutney

LES ESCALOPES DE RIS DE VEAU, LA PURÉE D'OLIVES VERTES ET NOIRES, LA VINAIGRETTE D'ÉCREVISSES

*Medallions of sweetbreads with a purée of green and
black olives and a crayfish vinaigrette sauce*

LES ÉMINCÉS DE SAINT PIERRE À LA CRÈME D'OSEILLE ET LE HOMARD AU BOUILLON DE CRUSTACÉS SAFRANÉ

*Thin slices of John Dory fish in sorrel cream with lobster
pieces in a saffron shellfish bouillon*

SUPRÊME DE PIGEON SEMI CONFIT, CUISSE RÔTIE AU LARD FERMIER, HARICOTS COCOS AU BOUILLON DE PIGEON ET HUILE DE NOIX

*Pigeon breast lightly braised in fat, the bacon-wrapped
thigh roasted, with white beans cooked in a pigeon stock
and finished with walnut oil*

PLATEAU DE FROMAGES

Usually your choice of two dozen kinds of cheeses

FANTAISIE GOURMANDE

A chocolate dessert usually with some kind of fruit coulis

This $70 tasting menu is a minefield for the sommelier, not only because it is so varied in raw material—foie gras, veal, fish and lobster, poultry, cheese, and chocolate—but also because various of the garnishing sauces and ingredients, particularly the sweet-sour chutney, the bitter sorrel, the rich crayfish vinaigrette, the exotic saffron, and the pungent walnut oil all have very marked, very individual flavors; and this is not to mention the sometimes overpowering intensity of an oozing triple-crème cheese like Epoisses or Vacherin. Keep in mind, too, that just as the chef has composed this meal to build from flavor to flavor in subtle stages, the sommelier should complement those dishes, accentuating them but keeping with the rest of the orchestra so as not to overwhelm any single course and interrupt the progression.

Back in the conference room, poring over the menu, Laurent began his discourse with a gentle admonition. "Often, Americans like to be French when they are here on vacation. So, they'll take a *pastis*, a Ricard [heavy, sweet, anise-flavored alcohols] for the apéritif. That's awful. You send your taste buds south for the whole meal. But it happens pretty frequently because for them, that's French. I do it too. If I go to Germany, I'll drink a beer, or in Belgium, the same. It's not bad, per se, but pastis is not a good idea before a very good, sophisticated restaurant meal like what we serve here.

"What we often do," Laurent told me, "is to propose wines by the glass for such a meal as this, and like that you can adapt the choice to each dish." I have noticed in my own travels that this is a fairly frequent practice, elaborate (and often expensive) tasting menus accompanied by equally elaborate (and expensive) by-the-glass selections paired to each dish.

"The problem," Laurent continued, "for example, is that this is a menu for which you could start with a red and then go to a white, but that is not done. White to red, fine; red to white, no. The adage says, *Rouge sur blanc, tu fous le camp! Blanc sur rouge, rien ne bouge.* 'From red wine to white? Get outta my sight! Red after white, it's a delight.'"

As this is one of the few orthodoxies I have ever heard from Laurent's lips, it is worth examining the reasoning behind it. White wines, particularly un-oaked or very lightly oaked French whites, are often fragile beings compared with their brawny New World, Australian, New Zealand, even South African cousins. All white wine lacks, by definition, the tannins of the reds; it is the skins, remember, that contribute much of the tannin, and in making white wine the juice is drawn off the skins before fermentation. The mouth, once exposed to those heavier red-wine tannins, is no longer, the French believe, receptive to any possible glory a white might offer. (They also tend to be more acidic.) The analogy one might draw is to drinking orange juice after brushing your teeth with a mint-flavored toothpaste.

"Foie gras," Laurent continued, pausing, then smiling. "If we're going to start with and stay with whites, I would propose a small glass of Jurançon *moelleux;* that would go well. It's a wine much less sweet than a Sauterne, but still it has some sweetness to it. It goes well with the foie gras without overwhelming it. With the medallions of sweetbreads there are two problems. First the crayfish vinaigrette, and second, we've just drunk a sweet white wine with the foie gras, which is also a substantial dish. There are two solutions. Either we'll have a huge white to dominate everything and break with what we just ate, which creates another problem—what the hell are you going to drink after that with the fish, a dish which has after all some noble ingredients?"

Two things of note here. First, from the very start Laurent is always scouting the territory ahead in order to avoid bringing in the cavalry—a heavier, richer wine—too quickly. He conceives of the experience of the meal as a progression and thus seeks to preserve the sense of crescendo, moving from lighter to heavier wines, all the while seeking to play off, and with, the flavors of each course. Also, he distinguishes here between "noble" and more everyday ingredients; John Dory is a "noble" fish while sardines are not. To the French, there are noble fishes, noble meats, noble seasonings (saffron versus thyme), and even noble grape varieties.

"[For the sweetbreads] I would choose a dry white *pas très gras.* Not a big one, not too rich, and without a long and strong presence on the palate. Something very fresh and with a sufficient tartness—a Sancerre [of sauvignon blanc grapes], a *vin de Lune,* there are hundreds of solutions. But especially not a chardonnay, because as a varietal, it's too rich, too concentrated, very perfumed. We just had a sweet wine with the foie gras, and a big wine, well . . . By the time you got to the third dish, you wouldn't have anything left! You would be saturated with strong flavors. So, you're going to accompany the crayfish aspect of the dish with the vivacity, the tartness of the wine, the vivacity giving a very fresh impression. Ah, we can breathe a bit! And the bit of fruit is what we finish on. That, that's good. We don't obliterate the first impressions of what we've just eaten and drunk, but *baaf*! We're going to do something radically different.

"We're coming from a wine that accompanies the foie gras, the Jurançon, which is very rich, very concentrated, very sweet, full of flavors and very obvious flavors because they are flavors of sweetness—apricot, vanilla, etc.—and we're going to a wine that will be on fruits like grapefruit. I often suggest a Gaillac Domaine d'Escausses made of 100 percent mauzac grapes; it has a good tartness—that grapefruit note, so it brings a bit of freshness to the second dish. The vinaigrette"—he paused, sighing deeply—"the vinaigrette is often a problem. What is a vinaigrette but vinegar? And what is vinegar but wine gone bad? It's like that; it fights with the wine in the mouth. But with the mauzac, you continue on your way, the wine dominating the crayfish vinaigrette. And with green and black olives, we're not eating something that uses a lot of noble ingredients. . . ." His implication here was that you don't need a wine of noble grapes like chardonnay or Riesling, but can fall back on a lesser variety like the mauzac.

"So, then." He ran a finger under the text of the menu, shaking his head and clucking. "*Bien*, the thin-sliced St. Pierre, a noble fish, rich, sorrel cream—let's skip right over that!—lobster, shellfish bouillon, saffron, wow! This is a very rich dish asking for a rich wine. Also, because we're coming from a lighter dish with a fresh wine that accompanied it, we're ready for a huge white wine. Our taste buds have forgotten the sweet aspect of the foie gras, and now we can go for a big wine—Tariquet Chardonnay Tête de Cuvée, say. Or, if you've got the means, a very big Tokay, a Chassagne-Montrachet, or a big Pouilly-Fumé? You need something rich and superlative. Superlative dish, superlative wine, absolutely."

Here Laurent closed his eyes, reeling off twenty or thirty wines half-aloud. Finally he looked up and raised a finger in the air. "A

Pouilly-Fumé? A velvety Trimbach Riesling? No! A rich wine, a fat wine, and given that we have a dish chock-full of noble ingredients, we need something noble in the wine. A big white Burgundy, why not? This is the moment. Not for the sweetbreads or the pigeon, but here. The Tariquet Tête de Cuvée Chardonnay is also good, rich enough, which will go with the sorrel. The sorrel is the problem in choosing a wine because it has a bitter side to it. You need a wine sufficiently rich to cover the bitterness, but [which will] not flatten the rest of the dish, the lobster, the St. Pierre, along with it.

"And so far," he pointed out, "we've been very logical in the progression of price, too, for a meal at $70. The sweet wine with the foie gras is at $5 a glass; the Gaillac with the sweetbreads at $6; and then for the fish, [with the choices I gave] we're between $6 and $15 a glass, the $15 if you go for the big white Burgundy. So if you consider that we're going to spend as much on the wine as the food, and we dropped $10 on the *apéro,* we've still got $20 left for the last courses. We can certainly find a great $10 glass of red for the pigeon, and then, if you want, a nice dessert wine for the last course."

Coming to the pigeon, Laurent perked up again. "Pigeon lightly cooked in fat—pretty delicate. The thighs roasted wrapped in farmer's bacon—that means salt, white beans. . . . It's an interesting dish!" he said, as if reading the description for the first time. "It uses some noble ingredients and others that are more everyday. We have many, many choices, and let's remember that it will be the only red of the meal. We could choose a good Cahors if we want something rich. Here, it depends on the customer's taste in red wine. Lighter would be a pinot noir. . . ."

And for the cheese, I asked, remembering another sommelier once stating baldly that *le fromage tue le vin.* Cheese kills the wine. The strong dairy nature of the former he had said is a natural enemy of the acids and tannins in the latter.

"It's true," Laurent began, doubt in his voice. "Often cheese kills red wines. The better way to think of it is: one cheese, one wine. A fresh Muenster demands a Riesling; a very ripe one a Gewürztraminer. It's often a regional marriage of local wine to local cheese, but it doesn't have to be.

It's true, though, that the only wine that truly complements a Roca-madour (a local specialty, a fresh goat cheese) is a good Cahors." Almost licking his lips, he continued his recitation. "Roquefort—a Jurançon white. Crottin de Chavignol [a small round goat's milk cheese from Sancerre]—Sancerre blanc. Camembert—a huge chardonnay. They all go together. Man, you take a sip of the chardonnay after a bite of the camembert, and you'll die. And then you'll reach for another bit of cheese just to have another sip of wine after it! So, here, for the cheese we'll stay with a red. Contrary to what we think in France, ninety percent of French cheeses go well with white wine. But it's what I was talking about before, the perpetuation of these old canards, especially in red wine regions like ours.

"So, 'Cheese kills wine.' True perhaps, but a little reductive. In this case," he said, pointing to the tasting menu in front of us, "foie gras with house chutney—chutney kills the wine. The calf sweetbreads with crayfish vinaigrette—the vinaigrette kills the wine. The St. Pierre with sorrel cream—the sorrel kills the wine. Pigeon breast, white beans in bouillon, and nut oil—the nut oil kills the wine. The gourmet fantasy dessert, I'm sure there's chocolate there, and that kills the wine, too. So we shouldn't drink any wine with this meal!"

As he put the menu aside, I remarked that I'd heard some pretty fanciful descriptions, often by sommeliers, of supposed flavors and aromas, so-called "notes" one could find in such and such a wine. After he'd stopped laughing and waving his arms as if to clear away the bad smell left behind by so much claptrap and folderol, he sat back and delivered a final few pieces of advice, which I've reproduced, again, almost verbatim here.

You can tell me that so-and-so's wine has notes of strawberry crushed by the hoof of a horse, et cetera, and I don't give a crap. Yes, but is it good? I can tell you that. Often, people tell me, when I bring the wine list, "We don't know anything about wine." Because they've seen me, the sommelier, who must know so much. . . . It's not true! It's a mistake! You know if it pleases you or not. You know it!

You can be a good wine taster only if you taste. You need to have tasted widely, and you have to develop a sense memory. That helps you to establish a reference point.

Take the taste of coffee; this you know because you drink it every day. You find it in wine, too, say, in an older Burgundy, a Côte de Nuits. *Fraîcheur*—coolness—if you want to know what it is, take an ice cube in your mouth! Our wine, here, the malbec, typically has very strong odors of black fruits like blackberry, currant, licorice. People say it [tasting] is in the genes. It is not in the genes. You can work as a sommelier for fifteen or twenty years, tasting wine regularly, and you might be the fourth best sommelier in the world—or the two hundredth. What makes that difference, that little bit, is in the genes.

Again, you can develop your gifts only by tasting wine, and tasting it in an informed and intelligent way. I'll give you an example. I used to be a whiz at mental math. Now, after six years of using computers here to do the bills, when I have to do it by hand, I make stupid mistakes. If you don't use your faculties, you lose them. Also, if you drink only bad wine, wine from a box, then bad wine becomes your reference. We all know what a *petit sablé* [shortbread cookie] is; at least we know what's in the LU or BN boxes [the Nabisco and General Mills of France]. But the real shortbread made by a Breton grandmother? The real thing is hard to find but worth the effort. And whether you make that effort is a question of culture, I think. Some people eat scallops in August, which, here, anyway, is not their season. They are of course better fresh, a different experience altogether if you eat them in the fall. That's a question of knowledge.

My advice to the curious is to go out and taste. Find a good winemaker—in a place where you can taste everything and everything is for sale!—and ask questions. Or find a good wineshop or go to good restaurants where you can talk to the sommelier. Buy a guide, any guide, and use it!

You have to stay simple with wine, and you should say what you think. Wine tasting is not an exact science, because there are things both very simple and incredibly complex. Everyone can come to know raspberry, blackberry, black currant in a wine. In Alsace, in some Rieslings, you have what they call a note of "hydrocarbon," which is nothing more than what you smell on your fingers after you've pumped gas into your car.

A certain kind of sommelier might say, "This wine has a note of a strawberry crushed by the foot of a horse." What the hell does that mean? Okay, strawberry, well, we know that certain wines have a jammy smell to them, but crushed by the foot of a horse?

Tell me "licorice" and I can find it. But others I can't find if I don't know them! You tell me, "exotic fruits"—litchi nuts, carambola, melon—but what if I've never tasted any of these because I don't live in a place where they grow? It's good to learn, but never lose sight of the pleasure, that wine is supposed to be enjoyed. Take those hydrocarbons. Sometimes it's a bad thing; the wine smells too much like diesel even if this is supposed to be a sign of quality! The fundamental thing of tasting wine is, once again, is it good? And for me, as a sommelier, how much does it cost? How much can I sell it for? Le Grand Cèdre from Château du Cèdre here, it's 75 euros a bottle! That's crazy. Perrin's Le Pigeonnier from his Château Lagrézette [Cahors's most expensive wine] is 80 euros a bottle [$96], of which 40 euros is marketing. It's worth only forty but it costs twice that. So much is image. Romanée-Conti, the most expensive wine in France—and a Burgundy, by the way, not a Bordeaux!—comes from the smallest appellation, 0.35 of a hectare [less than an acre]. It costs $7,000 a bottle! No wine is worth that; hell, no wine is worth $700 a bottle. So, it's marketing, to create a demand! Remember that.

12

Yves' Folly

Up on the Mountain at Clos St. Jean

One fine summer day I got out of my car at Clos de Gamot and went in search of Yves. We were going up to "the vineyard on the mountain" as he and his wife call it, which I had briefly visited some months earlier, when Yves had told me I must come back in high summer to get the full effect. I checked the vineyard offices, checked the packing room, and stuck my head into the big barn filled with empty stainless tanks, but he was not to be found. Finally, I saw that the door to the tasting room was ajar, and there he was, holding forth to two passing tasters across the wooden counter from him.

Although many Americans would be surprised to find the wine-maker himself in effect manning the store, and on a Sunday afternoon in summer at that, here in the Lot I had gotten used to it. The vine-yards are small, and it often falls to one of the family, sometimes the semiretired older generation, to greet visitors and present the various wines while pouring generous samples, even to pack up purchases and make change. As Yves talked, I half listened, observing out of the corner of my eye as he raised a glass to the light, pointing out the deep garnet hue typical of the malbec grape, then urged the visitors to inhale deeply, putting his own nose nearly into the wine at the bottom of his glass after swirling it to release its bouquet. His customers, two very tall, lanky Germans who had arrived on motorcycles, watched and imitated, even down to the way he held his glass, by gripping the foot between thumb and forefinger rather than by grasping the stem. It was a little comical, the spectacle of Yves, short, round, and balding, faced with a pair of wild-haired lads in leather jackets, the three bent over their glasses and sniffing daintily. Just then Martine walked in to relieve him, and he turned them over to her with wishes for a good tasting.

Five minutes later we were puttering along a side road in his old Citroën, across the broad plain of the Lot River east to Castelfranc from where we would head up into the hills to Clos St. Jean. This is the third and smallest vineyard of the Jouffreau-Hermann family, a little more than two acres of vines which have just begun to produce (with a further two to be planted soon), climbing a steep hillside just below the hamlet of Sals. It is Yves' attempt to re-create—and in thus doing to rediscover—a vineyard and, perhaps, a wine of the past.

Hardly out of the driveway, he was pulling over next to a particularly lush stretch of vines, pointing out the window. "Everything's been trimmed, the brush cut, and the grapes have just passed the *véraison*"—the point when individual grapes on the bunches first begin to turn from green to black—"which means that, here on out forty days, more or less, we'll see the harvest. Ah, the ripening vines!" he said with a contented sigh.

"And that's one reason you find me or my wife greeting customers on a Sunday, because we plan the vacations of the help around the harvest, before the harvest. Harvest is a time when you enter into a trance, when you are incapable of doing anything else but work the grapes. Before, all the help should take their rest, and us, too. Because a tiny error in harvesting leads to a mountain of problems later on. Remember, it's a whole year of work you can lose."

There is nothing more impressive than a healthy, well-pruned vineyard in full vigor, each *pied,* or woody rootstock, a few feet from the next, each a fat, deep-green column nearly as tall as a man, with six to eight bunches of grapes hanging down from the lower third. Their leaves are as big as your hand, fingers spread, and here, in the verdant valley, they were uniformly, almost unnaturally green, nearly the color of spinach. It being in the nature of the vines to perpetually extend themselves, they had all also had their feathery tops trimmed, much as you would trim the new growth of a hedge. Underfoot, there was sometimes low, pallid grass, or sometimes pebbles in a thin soil that had been turned at intervals to keep the weeds down. The vines had had their last treatment not long ago, and some still showed a sheen of verdigris, from the copper sulfate solution sprayed to combat various rots, mildews, and other plagues.

A few minutes later, we had crossed the vast garden of vines and begun to wend our way out of Castelfranc and up into the hills.

As we climbed, Yves gave me the capsule history of Clos St. Jean. "The Lot River leads to Bordeaux, and Castelfranc was a shipping point, a place of great commerce, as far back as the Middle Ages. All the hillsides were planted in vines, and the wine came down in barrels. And so it was natural to think about that history. We would be driving back from Cahors, and we'd always see those hillsides, this one particularly because of its exposure, with the sun shining on it in the late afternoon and the ruined stone walls. We knew it had been a vineyard, probably for a long, long time until phylloxera. My father-in-law, Jean, would say, 'So, if you could risk a big undertaking, really take a plunge, what would you do?' This was my answer, and this is what we did, starting nine years ago. He died before the first vintage, so he never had a chance to see it come to fruition."

Earlier, Martine had told me her own version of this story. "I remember, coming back from the city, from Cahors, with Papa. He pulled the car over and pointed up the hill. 'We're going to climb up there,' he told me. 'Come and see the place where Yves and I are going to plant some vines.' So we did, me in my city shoes, with heels, we crossed the stream and climbed up that steep hill and I thought, 'They've gone crazy!'"

Yves had turned off onto increasingly smaller, rougher roads, and still we were climbing as we chatted, eventually reaching the hamlet of Sals, a dozen restored houses, with neat gardens and cars with English license plates in the driveways. "Here we enter the British Kingdom," Yves remarked. "The land of country houses, each with a little swimming pool." He sighed. *"C'est la vie."* The road went from disintegrating tar to gravel, then, as we came over the crown, to rutted dirt, ending abruptly in a spectacular vista looking south from where we had come. All around was sere, burnt meadow, sad heaps of stone that had once been walls, and silence. "Only the crickets here," Yves said as we got out of the car, "only the crickets."

Bordering the back of the vineyard at the top of the hill were two stone walls on either side of what had evidently been an old road running straight down to Castelfranc and north to . . . to where, I wondered? "The Romans built their roads on the crest, like this one. It's a very old road, and it went from Castelfranc to Montgesty along the ridge," Yves told me. "It was used for hundreds of years, by wagons transporting wine down to the river port."

Yves turned back to the vineyard at our feet, looking expectantly from my face to the vines planted in rows marching straight down the hillside and back again. As I contemplated the sight before me, I began to understand why he had lingered so in the valley earlier. This vineyard, here, was one of the oddest things I have ever seen, a desert come to fragile life, a place of austere serenity and one in which it took no imagination at all to find oneself plunged back into the past. With a wind in our faces so arid it seemed to draw the moisture from our eyes, the endlessly repetitive sawing of the crickets, and the total absence of people who had left their mark in the stone ruins all around, it was desolate, even haunted.

It was almost as if Yves had planted a vineyard on the moon. There were some patches of ground so dry and bereft of soil that absolutely nothing could survive, others where a single stunted oak grew out of rocks without so much as a weed underneath it. Here and there a tree erupted among the vines. And though they were planted in rows, almost no row ran uninterrupted down to the bottom of the hill. The interruptions were many and various. Running like a thick diagonal scar nearly from the top to the bottom was a massive rock pile, twenty feet wide in some places and so tall you could not see over it. Walls of limestone weathered gray by the elements ran randomly in stretches short and long, and upwellings of naked stone burst through the sparse soil. In one corner a fallen-down *garriotte*, a conical shepherd's hut whose roof had been built painstakingly of layers of flat rock piled one on the other, was slowly surrendering to the call of gravity.

"'He is insane.' That's what they say," Yves remarked, seeing the look on my face. "And I couldn't care less. Of course, that doesn't stop other winemakers from coming up here and poking around when I'm not here, too."

The vineyard itself, as we walked into it, presented a fearsome aspect. I took several steps and began to slide down the hill on the loose stone underfoot, so steep was the slope. How could he work this land? I could only imagine the labor, even with just two acres of bearing vines—lurching down the hill with a forty-pound tank of spray on his back, then slogging up again. There was a tiny tractor off in one corner, with treads instead of wheels, but you couldn't spray from that, or prune, or harvest. He *was* crazy.

The vines, too, were a rude shock after the uniform fecundity of the valley. They were half-dead by comparison, stunted, barely coming to my chest, with slender canes and sparse foliage. Just to plant the roots, every hole, 8,000 of them, Yves had sunk by hand, using a heavy iron bar to break up the rocky subsoil. In an acknowledgment of the high winds and violent weather up here, each vine was staked to a length of iron reinforcing rod. On the vines, the leaves themselves were smaller, and, in even greater contrast to down below, every shade of green from chartreuse to lime to sickly yellow, some splotched with red and brown, or shrunken, twisted, folded onto themselves where disease or insects had ravaged them. There were so few of them that the meager bunches of grapes hanging down were completely visible. And the grapes! They were minuscule, like peas, so small in size and in number that each bunch looked as if someone had already plucked every other grape from it.

"There were forty or so acres of vines here as long ago as 1837, which is about as far back as we have been able to go. We planted the first vines in 1993, and it has taken us ten years just to begin to understand this vineyard. The huge problem is that, first, you plant in order to have a healthy vine, which won't die on you. And only then, maybe do you get grapes. The wine?" He shrugs and kicks at the pebbles at our feet. "I am all alone!" he says finally. "There is no one to explain to me what to do with these grapes, this wine. Will it age well? I don't know yet: 1997 was our first harvest, and it will take a whole generation to start to figure out these things."

We passed a section where the vines were even more raggedy and unhealthy, the leaves obviously stricken with some ailment. Yves fingered one. "These vines are sick. A kind of bug. I was tired, too much work, and I missed the boat. But all is not lost. There's good growth on top and the grapes are ripening. It's all part of the experience!" he finished with a grim smile.

We continued down through the vines, Yves pausing here and there to explain other anomalies of every sort. He pointed to a scraggly pine breaking up several rows of vines. "We leave some trees. Always. Trees in a vineyard bring animals, birds, other plants. It's ecology, seeking a balance. And besides, when you're hot and tired, you can't sit under the shade of a grapevine. You need a tree!"

I noticed that some sections of vines appeared much healthier than others and asked why that was so. "Ah," he said. "What we didn't know when we planted! Down at Château de Cayrou, we know what to do, when, how to do the work, what the vines need. Here, with just two acres of vines, it is a totally different affair, not the same at all. Here, yes, pruning is easy; a matter of days; the same with *rognage,* cutting the top leaves, which we do once a year. There is no bunch-thinning, because as you see there is no need, as each vine naturally produces very little. Harvest takes less than a day. Yet, every day I have to ask myself what I am doing, what I am going to do. Here, the *porte-greffe,*" the particular variant of rootstock onto which the malbec grapevine is grafted, "can change every hundred feet! And there are twelve different kinds of *porte-greffes* here, too, some of which haven't done so well and which we're still learning about."

At the bottom of the vineyard, we paused to catch our breath. "When we say we're going to work here, we say, 'I'm off to the mountain!'

From up top, visitors, they admire the view, how pretty it is, but once they're at the bottom looking up, they say, '*Merde,* you planted your vines on a mountainside!'

"There," he continued, pointing at a rough rectangle of vineyard at the bottom of the slope that was creased by a slash of yellowing, obviously unhealthy vines, "there I made a mistake. We thought that the richest soil would be at the bottom because organic matter flows downhill eventually and collects. But look at the slope. It undulates, and at the peak of each undulation you have *une balme*." This is a ridge of rock that pierces the surface and runs laterally across the hillside. The richer soil collects, he went on to explain, but in the shallow troughs. On either side of the trough, therefore, you have to plant a *porte-greffe* that tolerates poorer soil and less water. "Which we didn't do," he finished, "and now the vines are doing poorly. And look at those piles of stones on either side of the *balme*. Why are they there? Because the farmer who worked this land a hundred years ago or more, he *knew* that nothing would grow there and so piled his stones there. We should have known! Even the weeds are sparse." He shook his head.

"People sometimes ask me why I am doing this. And I don't even tell them how few grapes I get, enough for maybe fifteen hundred to two thousand bottles of wine from all this!" (And in 2003, none, as the wild boars, mad with thirst, devoured most of the grapes.) In the valley the yield would be three, perhaps four times as much. "I am not going to die stupid. As long as you're learning, you're alive. When learning ceases, you die. After all, with this, it's going to be my children who pass judgment. 'He did well,' or 'He screwed up,' they'll say."

Once again at the top of the hill, puffing and panting, I realized that there was *more* ground being cleared; tree roots were poking up here and there, rocks of all sizes were strewn about like confetti by the plow blade. Yves saw me looking at it and chuckled. "Yes. It's another two acres. My son says, 'Stop! Don't plant any more!' because he knows he'll have to take care of it. Over there, we planted in ground we didn't know. Here, I want to get to know the land first. Ten years of testing in the first vines has taught me a lot. So I plow, and I'll plow again and again. There were scrub trees everywhere, and you have to get the roots out. Then the larger rocks. It all has to be cleaned. So I plow, and I think about how I will plant it, and I plow some more. . . ."

Back at Clos de Gamot, Martine met us at the office door, a little more than curious to know what I had made of Clos St. Jean. Both she and her husband have a certain way of talking about the hillside vineyard, a certain way of watching you as they speak, watching to see that you understand. It reminded me almost of parents talking about a difficult but gifted child, hoping that you will see, as they do, past the troubled surface to the gifts within—and ready to protect their baby at all costs should you not.

Those few acres of vines obviously hold a deeper meaning for them, a significance that goes far beyond the vineyard as, for instance, a neat experiment in viniculture. The name, Clos St. Jean, is one clue, since Martine's father was also Jean and the vineyard represents in many ways the ultimate homage his daughter and son-in-law could make to his spirit. I also got the impression that it was a place they did not show to just anyone, and certainly not to other winemakers, who would never have asked anyway, as these folks are careful to maintain a surprising professional distance. It is certainly not that I was so special, I think, but rather that my interest was genuine (I had been asking them to spend some time with me up there for two years, by then), as was my desire to comprehend their passion. And passion it most definitely was, a passion whose ultimate expression, the wine yielded up so meagerly and after such travail, we were about to taste.

We went into the unadorned tasting room next to the office, and Martine and I sat at the large empty table. Behind us, Yves popped the corks of two bottles, each with a plain paper label bearing only the year, 1997 or 2000.

We all sat, and he poured a scant third of a glass. Now, I love to watch winemakers taste their wine, and not just because it is a naturally theatrical performance. There is much that is sensual in the act, and I have sometimes had the impression of being a voyeur, akin to catching someone bathing or dressing. Tasting wine also involves almost everything we are taught never to do at the table. First, you play with the wine, holding it up to the light, tilting the glass from side to side to observe the color and also to see how it sticks to the side. Then you swirl it rapidly before sticking your nose into the bell of the glass and inhaling deeply, eyes closed, sometimes moving your nose about as if to vacuum up every stray molecule of scent. Then you exhale and, in my case, search desperately for something intelligent to say. *This does not have the characteristic smell of a Cahors,* I thought. And that is what I said before taking a healthy sip, rolling the wine around in my mouth and, finally, swallowing, after which I couldn't help smacking my lips.

Instead of swallowing, you are supposed to aerate the liquid in your mouth. Yves was doing this now, pursing his lips and, with his chin slightly raised, sucking small amounts of air into his mouth while moving the wine back and forth over his palate. Yes, the sight and sound do resemble gargling, but the point is to distribute the wine around your taste buds, the air agitating the wine to bring out all its potential flavors and tastes.

"First of all," Yves said, "in the nose we are in the realm of the mineral world with hints of something hot, roasted. There is nothing of the fruits." (This is what I had picked up on, for most good Cahors does have some sweet fruit, generally red currants and blackberry, plum, or even raspberries.) "That roasted note lasts a long time in the mouth and accentuates itself over time. This we bottled three years ago, and it has evolved to this point. You feel the *matière,* and in the mouth . . . hmmm." He paused to sip and aerate. "It is the grape seed, not the juice, that you taste. And so this *matière* from the seed, while not being too strong, endures, persists in the mouth but without sharpness."

"You even have echoes of the wild plants and grasses," Martine added, her glass to her nose, "which you find up on the hill, the taste of a meadow."

"That is, of course, connected to the *terroir*," Yves continued, refer-ring to the magical ability of the wine to take on attributes and charac-teristics that reflect the land on which the grapes were grown, the weather, and a whole host of other related factors. "And these are young vines only four years in production. So this wine, as it ages, those flavors and aromas, they will become more concentrated. Even in the time it has been in the bottle, at first you have the individual notes, but they meld together with age, become concentrated."

"It doesn't even look like a Cahors," I remarked. "It doesn't have that garnet hue, or the viscosity. See, it doesn't stick to the sides of the glass."

"Yes, well," Yves ventured, correcting me gently. "Some of that is because 1997 was not a great year on the whole, not a year of strong, heavy wines. But for us, understand, this is the first modest harvest of young vines, a first experience of vinifying it, a point of reference, our first chance to understand this wine, these vines. It took ten years to get to this point." He finished, gesturing at the bottle.

"And it will take another ten," Martine observed, "before we come to truly understand how to work with the grapes to get the most from them. It takes a lifetime, really."

I wondered aloud in what ways its making was different from their other wines.

"That's a question for Madame," Yves said. "She is our *maître du chai*," he finished with a chuckle.

"This is not true!" she protested, but not too strongly and with a sparkle in her eye. I thought again of what a lovely, lively woman she was, short and sturdy like her husband, with long tresses of raven-black hair that set off her perfect white skin and eyes the color of a fall chestnut.

"I do everything but run a tractor," she was saying, "which, some-how, I just never learned to do. Anyway, first of all, to make this wine, it's a tiny tiny volume, fifteen hundred liters, an experience in minia-ture and so very different from how we usually do it. We use our small-est tank, a baby-sized tank, really. The times of pumping over, the fer-mentation times, the time it was oxygenated, everything was reduced, because with such a tiny volume, everything is concentrated. There is so little liquid from these grapes that, after the fermentation is finished during vinification, if you let the skins stay in contact with the juice too long, it gives the wine a bit of a rough edge, astringent, and you don't want that. So that means you pour off the wine earlier, too. The less the volume, the more you reduce the time the cap sits on the wine. With such a small volume, the balance is more fragile, the process more delicate."

"It is not disappointing, this wine," Yves said.

"You are always afraid, you know," Martine said matter-of-factly. "When you vinify, you really have no idea because you don't know what kind of reactions you're going to get and the climate is very different up there. It's very dry; it can be very hot."

"The grapes are smaller," Yves put in, "much smaller than down here in the valley."

"So you don't know what kind of reactions you'll get in the tank," Martine continued. "And the date of harvest is completely different, always the earliest. Not only because of the weather, but because we have to battle the animals—the boars, the birds, the deer—who come to eat the fruit. Sometimes it seems as though we split it, half for the animals, and half for us, a few grapes more for us if we're lucky."

"In 1998," Yves said, "it was bad, no rain in September, and the animals, the boars especially . . ."

"They were eating the grapes to satisfy their thirst!"

"It was easier than going all the way down to the river!" Yves joked.

"That's something else we don't have a problem with down in the valley. Sure, we have a few rabbits who come and nibble. And then up there," Martine added, "you also have to watch over the acidity levels in the fruit, because not enough acid leads to a wine that will not last in the bottle. Once it has attained a certain level, it can fall very quickly. These days it has become common—well, for some anyway—to harvest their grapes in an overripe state, that is, very very late in the season, which they can do because they spray them with a rot retardant. But they're harvested with a reduced acidity and so make a wine that maybe you can drink in two years, but in five you no longer have a wine. It's dead. So we need a delicate balance of acidity, tannin, and alcohol, and it begins with the harvested grapes. Down here, we know from what the weather does and from our long experience what the effect can be on the grapes. Up there, it's a little riskier and things can change very quickly. We test [the ripeness of the grapes] up there more frequently, just to be sure. You see, every year we learn something.

"That is its charm, too, Clos St. Jean."

By then, Yves had poured glasses of the still rough-edged 2000. "I don't know if you ever make black cherry jam," Martine continued, "but this wine has that aroma, of stewing black cherries." She laughed. "You know, even when it is fermenting, this wine, it perfumes the air of the barn with that smell, of black cherry jam. This wine just shares nothing in the nose with the other wines we make. I can recognize it in the barn, when it is fermenting, just by that smell alone."

Yves had been tasting, too, and then he picked up the bottle, tapping the "2000" scrawled on the plain label. "Ten years," he said, taking a contemplative sip. "Ten years to get to this glass of wine. What is it the Americans say, 'Time is money.' Where is the money? It's a good thing we don't ask ourselves that question too often!"

"But it's not for money that we do this!" Martine interrupted. "It's learning, it's passion, it's a sense of adventure."

"We go up to Clos St. Jean on Sunday evenings sometimes," Yves added, "just to gather ourselves in for the week, to feed ourselves on the spirit of the place."

"It is a vineyard of reflection," Martine said, looking at her husband. "Of meditation."

"Of reexamining what it is we're doing in the rest of our lives. Fundamentally." Martine added.

"Absolutely," Yves agreed. "We will get older and we will come to better understand it. Hopefully. Or we'll just be dead," he finished, laughing.

Martine said, "But it's also the desire to do other things. It's sad to always do the same thing over and over again. I don't mean it's not hard. It is. But in the doing you learn things, you discover things, you live other things. Sometimes it seems that we never get older, that we're still in a long apprenticeship where we are always learning," she continued passionately, echoing almost exactly her husband's words up on the mountain. "And that is something we've tried to pass on to our children. You can't take anything for granted. You have to earn it all over again with every harvest. You always have to fight."

She paused, her eyes resting on her husband's face across the table once more, pensive, then continued. "It is important to be a couple in this business because one completes the other. We have different sensibilities. Journalists come and they never want to see the two of us, always the one or the other but mostly him. Women have always worked beside their husbands in the vineyard, but people have trouble putting the two of us together with the wine. And that's something that no one ever emphasizes but that we do. We work as a couple, with no boss or leader. And that is a strength. I think of things he doesn't. He reminds me, too, and like that we're on top of things. In the heat of action, especially during the harvest and vinification, you can get so caught up that you miss what is really important. We can't imagine Franck coming to settle in here as a single person. Against nature, the daily struggle with all the other people you have to deal with, it would be too hard even after ten years. When he does take over, after a certain time, even though we'll still be here to help, it's not up to the parents. That is where it is so helpful to be a couple. Also, we have noticed that the loners, the young bachelors, they never last. It's too much work, too tiring, psychologically as well as physically, to do it alone."

We sat in silence for a minute or two, her words, touched with the concern that all parents have for their children's future, still thick in the air. Perhaps sensing that she had painted an overly bleak picture, she drew a breath and continued.

"When we get up in the morning, we're off to struggle with nature, with everything, and that's how we know we're alive, *because* we struggle. It's true, when we get up each day, we never know exactly what we're going to have to do. And it's a good thing, sometimes, let me tell you! People talk about age; well, at twenty you can be very old indeed. It's in the spirit. You arrive at the age of fifty with the desire to rediscover your youth, if perhaps with a little more moderation because the body is no longer what it was. But inside, we are always young, always learning. And if the concern for things financial holds you back from all this, from evolving, improving . . ." she stopped, seeming to consider her words carefully before finally shaking her head and taking a deep breath.

"Because the culture, the richness of France," she went on, "has always been evolution and innovation—in the vineyard, in haute cuisine, in the arts—to allow people to become true artists in their chosen *métiers*. And if we are going to come to the point where everything is homogenized, regularized, done according to strict norms . . ." Here she drew back and threw up her hands. "*Oui, oui!* It will certainly be more orderly. But people will stop innovating in their day-to-day lives and their professions, and we will wake up to find a great uniformity in what we make and consume. And that's terrible. Sad. Even with wine, now, they are introducing norms for this and that, and they want winemakers to make, here, in Cahors, wine which is more or less uniform, which has become a product, an enologically perfect product but one which is no longer our wine."

When I drove away that night, it was nearly ten o'clock. At the corner, where I turned to head out to the main road, I looked back, as I always did, to see Yves and Martine walking across the parking lot toward the house, heads bowed and in deep conversation. Lost in the large, open, dimly lit space, they looked small and tired. They had yet to eat dinner, and then they would be off to bed. The next day, a Monday, they would be back at work at eight.

As I drove through the forest of vines, I thought about what I had seen that day, about what the two had said. I remembered Yves, as we were leaving Clos St. Jean, looking back almost wistfully. "Up here," he had said, "it's the pure juice, you understand? From grapes at the limit of where vines will survive. . . ." I considered the whole of their endeavor, and not just the old-fashioned vineyard, for that to me seemed to be no more than the ultimate expression of everything else they did. Though they were not quick to criticize their neighbors, it wasn't hard to see that they disapproved of making up for a lack of complexity with new oak barrels, of harvesting late, fermenting fast, micro-oxygenating in the tank, and using other tricks to arrive at a wine to be drunk (and thus sold) young. That way, you didn't have to cellar vast numbers of bottles from older vintages for the customer who wanted a bottle to drink now. You did not have to, in effect, cellar his wine for him until he was ready to drink it, and all because *vin de Cahors,* real Cahors wine, is a wine which necessarily requires so many years in the bottle. This was because it was not a quaffable, fruity, effervescent spring wine. It never had been, until quite recently, until the market demanded it and the authorities sanctioned it.

At what point did all the various manipulations and shortcuts, the enological trickery and vinicultural sleight of hand combine to deform the wine to such a point that the intent of the appellation standard, the variety of grape aside, was turned on its head, becoming nothing more than a ridiculous conceit? When I thought of the Jouffreaus' quarter of a million bottles, the enormous demands of space alone that they must take up, capital sitting idle, probably uninsured, waiting on the pleasure of a discriminating customer, it was a positively nineteenth-century concept. I knew already that some in the small world of French wine see this family and others like them throughout the country as Don Quixotes, silly old fools spurning the modern out of respect for the past and relegating themselves to the sidelines as a result.

And the wine itself—their benchmark Clos de Gamot, for example— just to make this wine was a commitment: to long vinifications, to long aging and the additional labor it entails, to having the space for bottles and barrels, the space to store them and the money to buy them. How long could they go on? Although my heart was in vindication and triumph, the risk awaiting them at every turn of the season is plain to see. As winemakers, they live, like the vines of their beloved Clos St. Jean, at the limit of what the modern world will tolerate.

13

❧

WHERE TO TASTE IN CAHORS

Below you will find a list of three dozen vineyards in Cahors where you might enjoy stopping for a tasting. I have included some of Laurent Marre's favorites here, too, just to represent the point of view of a sommelier of the region. I urge you to sample more than just the reds, as at last count there were something like thirty-plus whites of chardonnay, sémillon, sauvignon blanc, and even viognier grapes; scores of summer rosés; and even a few sweet wines, of which Jean-Luc's Vin de Lune at Triguedina is widely seen as the best. Many of these will be perhaps better for drinking with a meal taken at a local restaurant or during your stay than for bringing home. All the whites and rosés are sold as *vin de pays,* by the way; these "wines of the region" may not legally be sold with "Appellation d'Origine Contrôlée Cahors" on the label because here that designation of highest quality applies only to red wine of malbec, tannat, and merlot grapes. Within the reds, there also is incredible variety in what you can find, and I have tried to choose with an eye to helping you experience that.

The vast majority of these wines can be bought for under $20, many at half that price. All these vineyards, however, will have some more expensive bottles: *grande cuvées,* special vintages, old vine and single parcel offerings, and more rarely older vintages, sometimes even going back fifteen or twenty years. The exceptional years of the last fifteen are generally acknowledged to be 1990, 1995, and 2000, with 1996 and 2001 merely very good. The years 1991 through 1994 were weak at best. In the 1994 vintage, Laurent Marre points out that "Lagrézette, Les Bouysses, Lamartine, and Clos de Gamot at least are welcome surprises." Finally, 1997, 2002, and 2003 are all, again according to Laurent, vintages heavy with fruit and thus to drink young.

Before we begin, a few notes. When you go to a wine tasting, *une dégustation,* the winemaker is inviting you into at least his place of business and sometimes his home. Do call ahead and, just as at a restaurant, make a reservation. If your group is large, that is only polite; also, you can ask for an English-speaker to be on hand. While it is possible, especially in the summer, to drive around and stop in spontaneously, it is best to have a plan. Bring plenty of mineral water, eat first if at all possible, and have a designated driver. Tasting at three vineyards in an afternoon will probably mean sampling at least a dozen different wines, and the permitted blood alcohol level for drivers is lower in France than in much of the United States. Remember that.

There is an etiquette to wine tasting, too. I don't mean by this that you have to speak a special language and arrive knowing varietals and *terroirs* and such. I mean that you should bring a certain respect to the occasion. This is not, for example, a wonderful adventure for young children, who might find it less than exciting to be still for so long. It helps to taste with few distractions, in a quiet place, where you can really pay attention to what you're drinking and what you're learning—and you'll learn lots. If you are interested, ask if you might see everything before the tasting. These winemakers, or often some member of the family, are usually quite willing to show off their entire operation, from a stroll through the vines through the *chais,* the barns where the wine is fermented, and the cave where it is aged. If you avoid their busy times—the October harvest and winemaking being the worst time to go—and if you've always phone ahead for an appointment, you can generally be assured of a long, educational, and winy visit. I can guarantee that you will never be charged a dime for a tasting. The welcome is warm, and your visit sincerely appreciated. Do reciprocate that generosity with the purchase of a bottle or two. The winemaker will pack wine for travel, and some vineyards will even, given sufficient quantity, ship or arrange shipping for you.

Finally, in my experience, lively interest and good questions, in whatever language, enrich the experience for everyone. Don't be shy about your own opinions and reactions to what is in the glass! And don't be shy about spitting, either. Your host will pour a quarter to a third of a glass of each wine—any less and you wouldn't be able to smell it fully—but no one expects you to drink it all. After smelling it and taking it into your mouth, you can swallow or spit into the receptacle (*le crachoir*), generally a barrel set discreetly to one side, always on hand for that purpose. Never spit on the floor, even if it is gravel and you see other tasters doing it! The barrel is also where the dregs of your glass go before you try the next wine. After swirling the wine in the glass to help it release its aromas, I will sniff deeply, then take one sip into my mouth, swish it about over the tongue and into my cheeks, and swallow it. I may take one or two more sips as the winemaker talks about specific things I might find in that particular wine, but then avail myself of the barrel so that I don't get too addled. If all this sounds rather elaborate and fussy, well, that's why it is called a wine tasting and not a wine drinking.

When you arrive, your host or hostess will generally show you what the vineyard has to offer and ask you what you'd like to taste, always the most recent vintages. In 2005, for example, you'll most likely be offered 2001–2003. Don't expect that a winemaker will open a 1995 or an old vines vintage for you; and sometimes, because the white wines are made in such small quantities, they will not be available. If it interests you, ask what is for sale that is not on the "official" list. You might take home a very special older bottle. Here is a fundamental guideline: the longer you stay, the more interest you show, and the more questions you ask, the deeper your experience will be. When a good winemaker has in front of him an enthusiastic audience, it often prompts him to pull out all the stops, or a few of them. You may even end up tasting directly from the oak aging barrels, which is an experience in itself.

This brings me to my last point, that *vins de Cahors* need some aging before they reach their full potential. You can drink them young, some vintages particularly; but then you must open them a few hours before the meal and carafe them, the exposure to the air allowing them to "open up," to release the maximum of their potential in the nose and in the mouth. While some of those who export to the United States are finally realizing that it is better to sell only wines ready to drink, this is definitely one area where the good wineshop owner can earn his keep by educating the customer.

A good place to begin a tasting adventure would be with the three winemakers who are the focus of this book—but not all in one day! All of them either speak English or have staff members who do. Yves, Martine, and Marise do tastings at Clos de Gamot, and there is a full-time tasting room, too, at the grander Château de Cayrou—an authentic château with lovely grounds and an ever-changing exhibition of the work of local artists. Clos de Gamot is near Prayssac, and Château de Cayrou is not far from Puy l'Evêque; telephone, 05.65.22.40.26. Gamot's Old Vines vintage is probably the most authentic malbec in the whole valley, and the wine of Cayrou makes a very pleasing contrast. You can buy very old wines here, and this can be interesting if you want to see how these wines evolve over time. As Yves and Martine do not use new barrels for aging, this provides a good contrast for later comparison at Triguedina and Clos la Coutale.

At Clos la Coutale, Philippe Bernède's vineyard outside Vire-sur-Lot—telephone, 05.65.36.51.47—Philippe or his mother leads the tastings. You'll know that Philippe is around if you see Pétrus, his enormous gentle Dalmatian, who follows him everywhere. The wine of Coutale is softer and does not require great age to be appreciated. His *grande cuvée*, Le Grand Coutale, is a good example of sophisticated Cahors winemaking in an almost international style: a big, rich, oaky wine that you might want to serve on its own, the better to appreciate it.

Clos Triguedina, also near Puy l'Evêque—telephone, 05.65.21.30.81—has a very special tasting room, with stained-glass windows, a miniature museum of old-fashioned winemaking equipment, and a whole array of very different wines to be tasted. Prince Probus, its top-of-the-line offering, is consistently one of the best Cahors has to offer; and Clos Triguedina is a sophisticated wine worthy in its own right. Aside from his red wines, Jean-Luc Baldès makes a special sweet wine of chenin blanc grapes and also a dry white of note. Triguedina is also a good place to taste quite simply because of the range of things you can find there and the variety of vintages available, particularly in magnum sizes.

There are many other Cahors vineyards whose winemakers make and sell outstanding wine. Below are thirty or so of my personal favorites in no particular order and with the occasional side note, but this does not mean that you won't make your own discoveries if you choose to wander the appellation, glass in hand.

Château du Cèdre, Verhaeghe and son, Vire-sur-Lot, 05.65.36.53.87. These wines are more international in style—the reds heavier, fruitier, and marked by the wood, and they also offer an excellent white of viognier grapes. Olivier Tesseire, the winemaker, has shown himself willing to try different things, to our great good luck.

Château Les Laquets, Cosse Mathieu, Carnac-Rouffiac. One of Laurent Marre's consistent favorites.

Château de Chambert, Marc and Joel Delgoulet, Floressas, 05.65.31.95.75.

Château Paillas, Germain Lescombes, Floressas, 05.65.36.58.28.

Château Pineraie, Jean-Luc Burc, Puy l'Evêque, 05.65.30.82.07.

Château de Haute-Serre, Cahors, Vigouroux family, 05.65.20.80.80. Vigouroux is one of the largest wholesale bottlers as well as the owner of this vineyard and Château de Mercuès, just behind the hotel on the heights dominating the north of Cahors. Haute-Serre is a plateau vineyard, and its wines are very different from those in the valley.

Château Saint-Didier Parnac, Franck and Jacques Rigal, Parnac, 05.65.30.70.10.

Château les Bouysses, Les Côtes d'Olt, 46090 Mercuès, 05.65.30.71.86.

Les Producteurs des Côtes d'Olt, 46140 Parnac, 05.65.30.071.86. This is the Cahors cooperative, and worth a visit just to appreciate the vast range of wines it makes and the scale of its operation.

Château de Caïx: S.A.R. le Prince Consort du Danemark, 46140 Caïx; Luzech, 05.65.20.13.22. A setting and a wine befitting the royal owner.

Château la Caminade, Resses et Fils, 46140 Parnac, 05.65.30.73.05.

Château de Camp del Saltre, Delbru et fils, Route du Collège, 46220 Prayssac, 05.65.22.42.40.

Château Croze de Pys, Roche et Fils, 46700 Vire-Lot, 05.65.21.30.13. One of my recent favorites, especially the 2000.

Château Eugénie, Jean et Claude Couture, Rivière Haute, 46140 Albas, 05.65.30.73.51.

Château la Coustarelle, Michel et Nadine Cassot, Les Caris, 46220 Prayssac, 05.65.22.40.10. Of note, L'Eclat, their *grande cuvée*.

Château de Gaudou, Durou et Fils, Gaudou, 46700 Vire-Lot, 05.65.36.52.93.

Château Gautoul, formerly owned by Alain Senderens (yes, the famous chef), Meaux, 46700 Puy l'Evêque, 05.65.30.84.17.

Château les Grauzils, Francis et Philippe Pontié, Gamot, 46220 Prayssac, 05.65.30.62.44.

Château Lagrézette, Alain-Dominique Perrin, 46140 Caillac, 05.65.20.07.42. With the help of a noted Bordeaux enologist, Perrin's team makes Bordeaux-style Cahors. It is the most expensive Cahors you will find, but his underground operation is quite impressive.

Château Lamartine, Gayraud et Fils, 46700 Soturac, 05.65.36.54.14.

Château Leret-Monpezat, Jean-Baptiste De Monpezat, Leret, 46140 Albas, 05.65.36.26.34.

Château Nozières, GAEC Maradenne-Guitard, 46700 Vire-Lot, 05.65.36.52.73.

Château Quattre, 46800 Bagar en Quercy, 05.65.36.91.04.

Croix du Mayne, François Pélissié, Anglars, 46140 Anglars-Juillac, 05.65.21.41.08.

Domaine du Garinet, Michael and Susan Spring, 46800 Le Boulvé, 05.65.31.96.43. Notable for its sauvignon blanc and often cited as proof that Cahors can produce outstanding whites.

Domaine Pineraie, Burc et Fils SCEA, Leygues, 46700 Puy l'Evêque, 05.65.30.82.07.

Domaine des Savarines, Biesbrouk et Borde, 46090 Trespoux-Rassiels, 05.65.22.33.67.

Château Paillas Germain, Lescombes, 46700 Floressas, 05.65.36.58.28.

Château les Rigalets, Bouloumé et Fils, 46220 Prayssac, 05.65.30.61.69. Of note, their special vintage La Quintessence.

OTHER INFORMATION

One of the best (and least touristy) wine-related events is a festival called *Le Bon Air Est dans les Caves*—The Good Air Is in the Wine Cellars—in Albas in May (town hall, telephone 05.65.20.12.21, for dates). This village climbs a hill on the banks of the Lot, and it was formerly a major wine shipping and storage center. During the festival, many of the wine cellars built into the bottom floors of the houses are open, each one featuring the wine of one vineyard and the music of one group, everything from jazz to a cappella ballads in patois to Gypsy music to rock 'n' roll. You can subscribe to the modest but filling dinner held down below or pick up foie gras or goat cheese sandwiches as you stroll. The entrance fee is $9 or

$10, for which you get a petite tasting glass which serves as your entrée to each cave. Things get progressively wilder as the evening wears on, so you might want to wear your dancing shoes and leave the kids at home. Other summer festivals of wine are in Cahors at the beginning of August, and in Puy l'Evêque in July.

A list of all the vineyards of Cahors is available by mail from: La Maison du Vin de Cahors, 430, avenue Jean-Jaurès, bp 61, 46002 Cahors cedex, telephone 05.65.23.22.24. On the web, you can learn more about Cahors and its wines and gastronomy at: www.quercyen-france.com/decouv-gastro.php, www.lot-tourisme.com/sectionterroir.html, and www.quercy.net/gastronomie/index.html.

To help you plan your visit, there are also regional tourism offices throughout the valley: Cahors: Place F. Mitterrand 46004 Cahors, 05.65.53.20.65. Duravel: Le Bourg, 46700 Duravel, 05.65.24.65.50. Luzech: Maison des Consuls, 46140 Luzech, 05.65.20.17.27. Mauroux: Mairie, 46700 Mauroux, 05.65.30.66.70. Prayssac: Place d'Istrie, 46220 Prayssac, 05.65.22.40.57. Puy l'Evêque: Place du Rampeau, 46700 Puy l'Evêque , 05.65.21.37.63. Sauzet: Mairie, 46140 Sauzet, 05.65.24.22.24. These offices have information about local B&B's, festivals, markets, and seasonal celebrations.

Interested in planning a stay in the Cahors region? Following are several organizations that have rental listings located all over the Lot, with more complete information and prices.

French Affair, www.frenchaffair.com, an English booking service with a very complete website with pictures of assorted properties and online booking, payment, and reservation from moderately expensive to expensive cottages to villas. Its standards and level of service are very high, it has English area representatives, and the prices reflect this.

Gites de France, ADTRL, address: Maison du Tourisme, Place F. Mitterrand, 46000 Cahors, France. Telephone 05.65.53.20.75, E-mail: gites.de.france.lot@wanadoo.fr. There are 750 listings throughout the department, and you can book through this organization. English spoken. Catalog available.

Clévacances-Lot, address: Maison du Tourisme, Place F. Mitterrand, 46000 Cahors, France. Telephone 05.65.53.01.02. E-mail: 46@clevacances.com. Approximately 300 listings. English spoken. Catalog available at nominal cost.

Hotels are thin on the ground in this part of France, but one of the best, with a fantastic restaurant—with Gilles and Laurent Marre presiding—is L'Hôtel Terminus and Le Restaurant Le Balandre in Cahors: terminus.balandre@wanadoo.fr.

The nearest luxury hotel is Le Château Mercuès fifteen minutes away, a restored castle perched on a hill above Cahors. Telephone 05.65.20.00.01. E-mail: mercues@relaischateau.com.

Questions and comments? E-mail me at michaelssanders.com, where you can also read about local appearances and travel opportunities; order personalized, signed copies of my books; and find an annotated list of references used in the preparation of this book.

About the author

About the book

Insights,
Interviews
& More . . .

Read on

Meet Michael S. Sanders

© 2005 Pierre-Jérôme Atger

MICHAEL S. SANDERS worked for many years as an editor—at Poseidon Press, Simon & Schuster, and Pocket Books—prior to becoming a full-time writer. He thereafter earned his living with a combination of what he calls "utility outfield writing" for industry publications and the occasional magazine, and importing rugs from Russia and Ukraine. After writing several novels based on his business experiences in those countries and his knowledge of the Russian community in Brooklyn, he moved to Maine. He worked as a bookseller for the years it took to write his first book, *The Yard: Building a Destroyer at the Bath Iron Works* (2001), and maintains a profound respect for anyone in retail. His second book, *From Here, You Can't See Paris: Seasons of a French Village and Its Restaurant* (2003), took its inspiration from a year spent in a tiny French village with his family. His next nonfiction book will likely involve yet another far-off adventure with his wife, daughter, and black Lab.

Visit the author online at www.michaelssanders.com. ◆

2

Invitation to a Wine Tasting

MANY OF US are familiar with the Friday night wine tasting scene at the local wine shop, or, if we've ventured to vineyards in wine country here or abroad, with the basic tasting room set-up, with its bar, bottles, glasses, and the bucket or barrel tucked discreetly into the corner for spitting. In France, however, there is a kind of tasting that the public never sees—official tastings which take place some months to some years after the harvest and whose purpose is to ensure that what is in the bottle lives up to the label. French wines are divided into four classifications which are in descending order of quality and, most often, price: AOC *(appellation d'origine controllée);* VDQS (wines denominated of superior quality); VDP (wines of a distinct region); and VDT (table wines). Each classification has separate and different rules that dictate, among other things, the way vines in a given parcel are trained, how many vines are planted per hectare, the actual grape varieties and their proportion in the final blend, the maximum allowed yield, whether or not irrigation is permitted, and the quality and location of the vines themselves.

Michael S. Sanders

Philippe Bernede in his tasting room at Clos la Coutale

Yves Jouffreau-Hermann of Clos de Gamot, one of the winemakers I had been ▶

3

Invitation to a Wine Tasting *(continued)*

> 66 In France there is a kind of tasting that the public never sees—official tastings which take place some months to some years after the harvest. 99

> 66 The *Maison de Vin* is one of those unfortunate blocky, stucco-covered 1970s abominations, all concrete and steel, with all the charm of a hospital. 99

writing about for the previous two years, invited me one late winter day to go along with him to the *Maison de Vin*, the regional administrative offices of the appellation of Cahors, to attend one such tasting. He invited me because he thought it would interest me and because he had taken it upon himself to ensure that my education in the French ways of wine was as complete and varied as possible, particularly if I were going to write a book about it. The jury is generally made up of winemakers, wine wholesalers, an enologist or two, and a few of the local officials; today's group was going to taste five rosés, two dry whites, and one sweet white, all of whose makers hoped to be able to put "Vin de Pays du Lot" on their labels. By 10 A.M. most of the members were milling about outside the tasting room, gossiping and trading news about the previous harvest and how the new wine was coming along. Here, by the way, if you're picturing some quaint eighteenth-century stone building with old wooden floors and smoke-blackened beams, you can give it up right now. The *Maison de Vin* is one of those unfortunate blocky, stucco-covered 1970s abominations, all concrete and steel, with all the charm of a hospital, an antiseptic place where, glancing about into offices and rooms, my first impressions were that I might as well have been in a state welfare office or tax department, so little was wine in any form in evidence.

Monsieur X, who was the ringmaster of the day's ceremonies, finally arrived with the key and let us in to one of the oddest spaces I have ever seen. The room was sixty feet on a side, entirely open, with a modest platform at one end. The rest of the room was taken up by what looked like library carrels in rows— basically wooden desks with walls on the left and right but, in front, not a wall but a wide railing whose purpose was a mystery to me. Monsieur X invoked the gravity of the day's events, handed out scoring sheets, and all fifteen jurors seated themselves in the carrels, as did I.

Earlier, on the drive in, Yves had explained that he and his wife, Martine, volunteered every year to participate because they thought it was important—important to stay in touch with their fellow winemakers and what they were doing, and important to maintain the quality of the wines of their appellation. Even so, it was burdensome. The jury didn't just gather, taste, grade, and leave. No, before the first sip was gargled and spat, the two had gone through six half-day workshops that began with an examination of the physiological and behavioral bases of wine tasting, its techniques and methodology, and ended with test tastings at which ▶

Michael S. Sanders

Family Harvest: Sabine and Jean-Luc Baldes with their daughter, Juliette

❝ It was burdensome. The jury didn't just gather, taste, grade, and leave. ❞

5

Invitation to a Wine Tasting *(continued)*

benchmarks for the various criteria had been set.

Test tastings? Benchmarks? "Well, take acidity, especially in a white wine," Yves said. "When is a white wine flabby, lacking acid? And when is it sour, with too much acid?" Essentially (and here I am simplifying to an extraordinary degree what is a subtle and complex process) they had tasted together samples of wine manipulated in various ways to sketch out rough benchmarks for the various descriptors of how the wine looked (*la vue*—its appearance), smelled (*le nez*—the nose), and tasted (*la bouche*—in the mouth). For acidity, a sample might have either naturally lacked acid (confirmed by testing) to fix the low end, or been doctored with increasing amounts of citric acid to establish the upper end. The descriptors within each category can describe things quite obvious—the color of a rosé, for instance, should not be orange but some shade of pink, and definitely not red. They can also be maddeningly opaque—the four descriptors for a rosé under *"Nez"* are intensity, cleanness, finesse, and complexity, and rosés are the least complex wines to judge!

Each of our carrels was outfitted with, to the left, a miniature stainless steel sink whose faucet was controlled with a foot pedal, and, to the right, a translucent light panel whose illumination helped us judge the color of a wine. Corks began to pop, and, from my place in the back row, I then heard the first notes of what became a chorus of clinks, the gentle

> ❝ Each of our carrels was outfitted with, to the left, a miniature stainless steel sink whose faucet was controlled with a foot pedal, and, to the right, a translucent light panel whose illumination helped us judge the color of a wine. ❞

scrape of wineglasses being swirled on the stainless steel of the tabletop, the distinctive whooshes, gargles, and spitting as the room began to taste en masse, the whole place punctuated with the periodic susurrus of various sinks going off and on, throats being cleared, and the muted words of tasters talking to themselves.

I was just wondering if I should stand up and ask for some wine when a disembodied hand appeared at the front of my carrel and slid a bottle labeled only with a numbered tag along the front rail. I poured a sample,

Michael S. Sanders

Yves Jouffreau out in the vines, August 2003, testing for ripeness

then slid the bottle to the right, where another disembodied hand reached for it. We were tasting the rosés first. I looked at my tasting form, my *fiche technique,* which asked me to rate first the appearance of the wine on a scale of 0 to 5 in two subcategories of intensity and orange-ness. Intensity. Hmmm. The wine was very pale pink, so I gave it a 2, acceptable. Orange-ness? Yves had told me that an orange tinge in a rosé is a sign that it is already beginning to oxidize; the constituents that give it its color already coming apart and falling out of the wine. In other words, the ▶

orange is a sign of a poorly made wine. This rosé had no hint of orange about it, so I gave it a 4. And then the next bottle appeared. I glanced down at my *fiche,* noting that I had four more evaluations to make under *Nez,* and a further seven under *Bouche.* I skipped to the next sample, quickly pouring, swirling, and then sniffing.

Intensity, cleanness, finesse, and complexity. I could handle that. I stuck my nose in the glass and inhaled. Yaggh! Now, here's a thing about tasting new, five-month-old wine. It stinks. Literally. Many of the leftover chemical constituents of fermentation do not have a pleasant odor. Given sufficient time, they disappear altogether, and the ordinary consumer has no idea the lovely buttery-vanilla notes of their chard were once masked by the unforgettable pong of a teenage boy's gym socks. Yves again: "You have to taste past the stink, Michael. The odor of fermentation sits on top of the wine, but you can still perceive what else the wine has to offer." He was right, of course, and when I went on to taste this sample, it confirmed what my nose had been telling me. This wine had a fault, a rankness in the nose and mouth that signaled something had gone wrong during its making. I failed it down the line.

By this time, I had passed on two more bottles without even trying to taste them, deciding to concentrate on the *Bouche* descriptors in the next sample, a white. Intensity, acidity, fruit/floral, bitterness, richness, persistence of the alcohol, and

> **❝ I stuck my nose in the glass and inhaled. Yaggh! Now, here's a thing about tasting new, five-month-old wine. It stinks. Literally. ❞**

something called *franchise*, which I never did figure out. I swirled and smelled, took a sip, spat, sipped and swallowed, passed on the next two bottles untasted, and set to work. Okay, right off, this was a very light wine, both in color and body and richness. After an initial burst of fruit in the mouth, it just sat there. Not enough acidity. It had a sugary quality rather than a sweetness I could tie to any flavor (vanilla has sweetness, for example, as do all the jam fruits), and, being so light and flaccid, there was no persistence of taste, or alcohol, on the back end. Failed.

I had just begun to take up the last sample when, as if on cue, everyone else rose and handed in their sheets, then gathered in small groups to discuss their scores. Of the eight wines we had tasted, four failed. Bummer. That meant their makers would have to sell them, probably in bulk, as *vin de table,* for pennies a liter. They were not worth the cost of the label, bottle, and cork.

I related my amazement at the speed with which the others had tasted, the whole event having taken less than fifteen minutes from start to finish. "It is a thing of first impressions, Michael," Martine advised. "You shouldn't think about it too much, just react to what is in the glass." She is right, I'm sure, but I'm still thinking about it. ❧

> " Of the eight wines we had tasted, four failed. Bummer. That meant their makers would have to sell them, probably in bulk, as *vin de table,* for pennies a liter. "

The War on Wine

I MUST HAVE SOME LUDDITE BLOOD. I don't own a Blackberry or a mobile phone or a digital TV, don't possess a single video game, and prefer my clothes of wool or cotton. I like to split firewood and forage for wild mushrooms, will never own a car that doesn't have a stick shift, and prefer to know something about the food and drink I put in my mouth, preferably the person who produced it. As well, I've never met a foie gras I didn't like, couldn't live without my Macintosh, and have just spent far too much money on a five-burner, dual-fuel, stainless steel stove for my kitchen. So much for consistency, but that is who I am.

The subjects that have drawn me in as a writer—so far, shipbuilding on the Maine coast, the life of a rural French restaurant and its village, and the winemaking families of this book—are all bound up in tradition and authenticity. My experiences have led me to conclude, in broad strokes, that our customs and traditions don't just have a value, they have a price when they are lost, and it is never a bad thing to examine them in detail, to deeply consider the implications of that loss, the price we pay when a world open to us is closed to our children and their children after them. Within each book, I have shared my observations, in particular looking at those rare phenomena of the modern world in which the old ways stubbornly cling to life, enduring and

> " I like to split firewood and forage for wild mushrooms, will never own a car that doesn't have a stick shift, and prefer to know something about the food and drink I put in my mouth, preferably the person who produced it. "

adapting. Some kinds of history, it turns out, are pretty hard to kill.

Today, in every winemaking country, there is an epic battle raging which has everything to do with these notions. The press identifies the combatants variously as the New World vs. the Old World, technological winemakers vs. traditional winemakers, corporate agribusiness vs. the small winemaker, or "international" style, varietal-based wines vs. appellation wines. Simply put, it is far easier for a corporation to sell a standardized, branded product line with its predictable price points, production costs, and return, than to bring to market something like wine, which, by its very nature, tends to vary every single year. What the ordinary consumer does not realize is that the outcome of the first skirmishes of this battle is already determining what is in their glass and what they can buy at the market. More nefariously, what they also don't realize is that, thanks to the wonders of modern technology, it is now possible to manipulate wines in a thousand ways—with rot retardants to yield riper grapes, with laboratory yeasts known to produce certain flavors, with reverse osmosis machines to remove water or alcohol, with oak chips or tannin powders added to the fermenting tank—to create wines that have trademark tastes and smells; wines that have been, in effect, standardized too.

Traditional winemaking is built on the idea of appellation, that the actual place from which a wine comes—its landscape, geology, and climate, the way the vines are tended, the centuries of savoir-faire that the family ▶

66 Within each book, I have shared my observations, in particular looking at those rare phenomena of the modern world in which the old ways stubbornly cling to life, enduring and adapting. 99

The War on Wine *(continued)*

winemaker brings to his craft—all of these are more important than the kind of grape he is growing. Many Americans, however, tend to associate their tastes with a particular kind of grape, and our winemakers (and more and more foreign ones, too) are happy to cater to our desire to see zin, or chard, or merlot, or cab painted boldly on the front label, and, once the bottle is opened, even more boldly on the palate. Beyond uselessly broad geographic areas, we do not have appellations here, and besides, the whole idea of appellation is one which arises out of hundreds of years of winemaking experience and history, neither of which we yet possess.

We are a notoriously impatient people, and, in a rush to establish our own identity in wine—trampling the traditions of other cultures in our haste—I believe we are making a mistake. We need to learn to walk before entering the sprinter's blocks, to listen and take what is good from others instead of defensively running them down as old-fashioned or behind the times. The world is a large enough place for the expressions of thousands of winemakers, but that huge variety, that lovely chaotic landscape of wines as various and distinct as the landscapes they come from, that is under threat.

As a consumer, your choices determine the future. The supermarket wines will always be there—unchanging, branded monoliths. Go to your local wine shop. Avoid any place where every shelf is stuck with tags enumerating which wine guru gave what pointless grade to the wines. Do you let the waiter order your dinner at the restaurant? The furniture salesman choose your living room sofas? Ask. Taste. Learn. Above all, enjoy. Wine is supposed to be about pleasure, not an onerous burden fraught with risk. Remember that. ❧

66 American winemakers are happy to cater to our desire to see zin, or chard, or merlot, or cab painted boldly on the front label, and, once the bottle is opened, even more boldly on the palate. 99

Have You Read?

FROM HERE, YOU CAN'T SEE PARIS: SEASONS OF A FRENCH VILLAGE AND ITS RESTAURANT

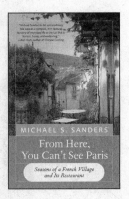

From Here, You Can't See Paris is a sweet, leisurely exploration of the life of Les Arques (population: 159), a hilltop village in a remote corner of France untouched by the modern era. It is a story of a dying village's struggle to survive, of a dead artist whose legacy began its rebirth, and of chef Jacques Ratier and his wife, Noëlle, whose bustling restaurant—the village's sole business—has helped ensure its future.

Sanders set out to explore the inner workings of a French restaurant kitchen but ended up stumbling into a much richer world. Through the eyes of his family, one discovers the vibrant traditions of food, cooking, and rural living, and comes to know the village's history. Whether uncovering the darker secrets of making foie gras, hearing a chef confess his doubts about the Michelin star system, or absorbing the lore of the land around a farmhouse kitchen table after a boar hunt, their life in Les Arques turns out to be anything but sleepy.

"In one of his first nights observing the restaurant's busy kitchen, Sanders watched hungrily as Jacques Ratier, the chef, whipped up a little ragout of liver, vegetables, and bread. As Sanders pondered the culinary secrets about to be unearthed, Ratier 'threw it into a heavy-based but shallow bowl that looked very familiar, looked in fact like my dog's food dish' and whistled for Nougat, his yellow Labrador retriever. Moments like this, described in Sanders's gracious prose, distinguish the book from patronizing books on rural Europe."

—*New York Times*

THE YARD: BUILDING A DESTROYER AT THE BATH IRON WORKS

For a century, the Bath Iron Works has been building some of the finest, deadliest ships in the U.S. Navy. But now the Maine shipyard is facing mounting competition and a pressing need to modernize, especially in the way it launches ships. No more will the great gray leviathans roar down the "ways"— the traditional inclined ramp—into the Kennebec River; this ancient technology will give way to the modern dry dock.

The Yard captures this moment of change and the end of an era, as old ways give way to new, through the eyes of the workers as they build and launch a U.S. Navy destroyer. From the first cutting of steel to the destroyer's triumphant commissioning, Michael S. Sanders chronicles the complex evolution of a ship coming into being—and the incredible world in which it happens. It is a world rich in danger, humor, and lore, one filled with uncertainty, hope, and not a little fear of change as this venerable company fights against steep odds to find its place in a new world.

Have You Read? *(continued)*

"Sanders is not only observant, but possessed of an ability to translate detailed observation into meaningful description."

—*Boston Globe*

"Sanders does an admirable job of conveying the life history of a destroyer. He is a superb expository writer."

—*New York Times Book Review*

Don't miss the next book by your favorite author. Sign up now for AuthorTracker by visiting www.AuthorTracker.com.